FROM SIBELIUS
TO SALLINEN

FROM SIBELIUS TO SALLINEN

*Finnish Nationalism
and the Music of Finland*

Lisa de Gorog
with the collaboration of Ralph de Gorog

Contributions to the Study of Music and Dance, Number 16

GREENWOOD PRESS
New York • Westport, Connecticut • London

Library of Congress Cataloging-in-Publication Data

De Gorog, Lisa S.
   From Sibelius to Sallinen : Finnish nationalism and the music of
Finland / Lisa de Gorog ; with the collaboration of Ralph de Gorog.
    p.   cm. — (Contributions to the study of music and dance,
ISSN 0193-9041 ; no. 16)
  Discography: p.
  Bibliography: p.
  Includes index.
  ISBN 0-313-26740-5 (lib. bdg. : alk. paper)
   1. Music—Finland—20th century—History and criticism.
2. Nationalism in music. 3. Sibelius, Jean, 1865-1957. I. De
Gorog, Ralph Paul, 1922- . II. Title. III. Series.
ML269.5.D4   1989
780′.94897′0904—dc20   89-11733

British Library Cataloguing in Publication Data is available.

Library of Congress Catalog Card Number: 89-11733
ISBN: 0-313-26740-5
ISSN: 0193-9041

First published in 1989

Greenwood Press, Inc.
88 Post Road West, Westport, Connecticut 06881

Printed in the United States of America

The paper used in this book complies with the
Permanent Paper Standard issued by the National
Information Standards Organization (Z39.48-1984).

10 9 8 7 6 5 4 3 2 1

Copyright Acknowledgment

Grateful acknowledgment is given to use excerpts
from the following:

Concerto in D Minor, Op. 47
By Jean Sibelius
Used by permission of International Music Co.

CONTENTS

MUSIC EXAMPLES

ACKNOWLEDGMENTS

The authors gratefully acknowledge the kind permission granted by the following music publishers to cite excerpts of musical works for which they hold the copyright: Breitkopf & Haertel, Wiesbaden; Robert Lienau, Berlin; Wilhelm Hansen, Copenhagen; Fazer Music Inc., Helsinki; Novello and Company Limited, Seven Oaks, England; and the International Music Company, New York. To Suomalaisen Kirjallisuuden Seura, Helsinki we give our thanks for their permission to quote musical and literery excerpts from their publications.

We also wish to express our appreciation to the Department of Romance Languages of the University of Georgia for the use of their laser printer and other facilities. We acknowledge the valuable help given by William F. Coscarelli, music bibliographer of the University of Georgia Library. We wish to thank Helena Valeur-Jensen of Copenhagen and Paula Soini of Helsinki for their help in finding materials for us in their respective countries. Finally we wish to thank Karen Coker for her patience in typing the entire manuscript and for producing a camera-ready copy of the book for publication.

FROM SIBELIUS
TO SALLINEN

INTRODUCTION

The prevalent view from outside Scandinavia has been that twentieth-century composers of the region have been struggling to escape from the shadows of Jean Sibelius and Carl Nielsen. However, the recent spread of other recorded music has somewhat improved the position of young Scandinavian composers in the international arena. Consequently, Finnish music, a concept previously synonymous with Sibelius, has enjoyed a veritable upsurge of new international interest. This is particularly true of opera, the genre Sibelius was never able to master.

Aulis Sallinen, the best known of Finland's present-day opera composers, is one of many who have had to cope with the disadvantage of Sibelius's imposing reputation. The more well known Sallinen's works have become outside his native land, the more burdensome that reputation has become to him. In an interview connected with a performance of one of his operas, Sallinen admitted that a mention of Finnish music always leads to a discussion of Sibelius, but neither he nor his Finnish contemporaries feel they are overshadowed by Sibelius: "You can't deny your roots, of course, but Sibelius is already past history."[1]

The Finns have been partly responsible for the emphasis on Sibelius. After gaining their independence from Russia in 1917, they realized that "independent" was only a meaningless word in a document unless the nation proved itself worthy of that status on the international scene. They realized that public relations were important, and in the publicity game the names of Jean Sibelius and sports figure Paavo Nurmi were trump cards. Whether the Finnish government's willingness to grant Sibelius a stipend at the time of his First Symphony was dictated as much for patriotic as for practical reasons can only be guessed at today.

The Finns' attitude towards the marketing of their heroes has been ambivalent, as the following story, which appeared in the *New York Times* on February 2, 1979 attests:

> At the opening of the 1952 Olympics in Helsinki, he [Paavo Nurmi] carried the torch into the stadium. He was 55 years old, with knobbly knees and a gleaming skull, but he went once round the track and then to the topmost rim of the stadium with the torch held high. "That man was thrown out as a professional," an English journalist protested to the head of the Finnish organizing committee, "How could you let him carry the Olympic torch?" "Because Sibelius is too old," the official said.

The Finns have taken a slightly cynical view of this state of affairs, yet they cannot refrain from such hero worship. Their adoration has even gone to such lengths as naming individual Finn Air planes for Paavo Nurmi, Jean Sibelius, J. K. Paasikivi, and the like.

It is due to the Finnish tendency towards hero worship that the myth of Sibelius was blown out of proportion. To this end they had the willing cooperation of the composer himself, who enjoyed being regarded as an enigmatic Olympian. Even today the essence of Sibelius remains elusive despite numerous books and articles published about the composer and his output. While the Finns have been solicitiously marketing the cosmopolitan Sibelius, fairly little is known outside of Finland of those aspects of his oeuvre relating to Finnish nationalism, either in inspiration or in musical expression. The fact that nationalism played an important role in firing Sibelius's imagination is seen in the large number of compositions he based on the national Finnish epic, the *Kalevala*, but too often his interest in nationalism has been equated with patriotism. That these manifestations of nationalism can be unrelated and find expression in varied ways is shown by Sibelius's most overtly patriotic piece, *Finlandia*, one of his least typically Finnish works. The following discussion will seek to clarify these aspects of Sibelius's oeuvre as well as their impact, or lack of it, on post-Sibelian music in Finland.

Finlandia is known to many American church-choir singers because of its hymn, and the "Alla marcia" movement of *Karelia* has made Sibelius a showman. However, the average concert-goer knows Sibelius as the romantic composer of the Violin Concerto and the Second Symphony. Is he, then, a romantic composer, a representative of the trend in composition generally recognized by that name? Yes, he is a European romantic, but he is also the first truly Finnish composer. In order to understand the significance of this paradox and its impact on Finnish music after him, we have to throw some light on the duality of Finland's culture, the cause of the dichotomy in Sibelius's music as well as of the music of Finland in general.

Although the role of cultural conditioning in our sense of music, both on the creative and the receptive level, has been recognized, its weight in a given case is difficult to estimate by a person unfamiliar with that cultural sphere. In discussing the "Western" idea of funereal music with slow tempi and a low range, Leonard B. Meyer pointed out how, in contrast, in many cultures loud moaning and wailing with a monotonous melodic line of high pitch and fast tempo is considered an appropriate expression of grief. These are also prominent characteristics of the *itkuvirret*, the "weeping songs" of the ancient Finns.

Due to the commonly sketchy knowledge of Scandinavian cultural variety, most music lovers have considered Sibelius a typical representative of that region, and yet Scandinavia is not a cultural unit despite some unifying factors.[2] Finland, with its Finnish, Swedish, and Lappish elements, displays greater variety within the country than the other Nordic lands. For example, the *sauna*, an almost sacred institution for the Finns, where they like to philosophize, as did Sibelius with his house-boy Heikki, has only recently spread to Swedish speakers in Finland. On the other hand, the cultural picture of Finland has also been complicated by the fact that its elite members tended to adopt the views and interests of the other Baltic countries, especially before the era of National Romanticism. Thus, when Sibelius emerged in the early 1890s as the leading composer of the country, the small educated class was so attuned to the German-Scandinavian school of music that many of his countrymen considered his music too innovative when he started to introduce specifically Finnish elements into it, something which caught many an audience by surprise.

It stands to reason that the works by Sibelius that are the most intimate expressions of the unique features of Finnish culture and of the Finnish mind have remained most enigmatic to foreigners. Ernest Newman tells a story of a rehearsal of Sibelius's Fourth Symphony in London, on which occasion he was approached by a fellow who asked to look over the score. Newman, an ardent proponent of Sibelius's music, was happy to comply with the man's wishes. After a few minutes of the rehearsal the fellow said to him: "Queer stoof, eh?" To this Newman replied that it was not the kind of music that was easy to take in at a first hearing since "it came from a different civilization from ours and

... without a little imaginative insight into the history and the mental and physical environment of a nation it was hardly possible to understand all that a typical representative of that nation was driving at in his art."[3] Even today, interest in Sibelius's music is limited chiefly to listeners in the cold and temperate climes.

In his late years especially, Sibelius was often distressed at the lack of understanding of his works, mainly on the part of young conductors. Sometimes when he heard a performance of one of his works on the radio he would complain about it for days. Once he wrote to the Finnish conductor Georg Schneevoigt: "It is inconceivable how unfamiliar my works continually are to the present-day conductors."[4] He complained in particular about the tempi, which were sometimes twice as slow as they should have been or, most often, too fast. Sometimes he wondered whether he should put in metronome markings for the benefit of conductors, but then he rejected the idea and concluded that "one can't put everything into notes. A great conductor gets inside the work and feels the innermost endeavours of the composer. He must be able to read between the notes. If anyone doesn't understand that, metronome marks won't help him much."[5] Sibelius felt that the score should gradually penetrate the conductor's mind "by means of a patient psychological experience."[6] Yet he often wondered how a conductor or a biographer with a different cultural background could interpret the mind of a Finnish composer: "People who write about me have no sense of historical perspective. If they had, and if they knew what Loviisa looked like when I was a child, they would understand me in an entirely different way."[7]

Newman was aware of the strong association of Sibelius's mind and music with his environment when he said of the composer: "He seems to have inhabited a mental world entirely his own. To what extent that world can be regarded basically as a Finnish world only a Finn can say."[8]

Although much has been written about the birth of genuine Russian music from the pens of the "Mighty Five," a parallel phenomenon in Finland has been largely ignored. What the Five accomplished in Russia, Sibelius did all alone in Finland. At the time Sibelius began his career, the dichotomy that characterized the situation in Russia between a small continental-trained musical elite and the large peasant population with its tradition of folk and church music was also true of Finland. In order to understand the forces that shaped both Sibelius's inspiration and his musical expression, as well as their ramifications for post-Sibelian music, we have to look at the historical events that shaped the country's culture.

THE HISTORICAL PERSPECTIVE

Sibelius was keenly aware of the significance of environmental factors and he considered them more crucial on the unusually sensitive mind of the artist than hereditary factors. Regarding Edvard Grieg, he wrote: "as far as inspiration is concerned, I think that nature and landscape play a greater part than national origins. Let us take the case of Grieg [a Norwegian of Scottish ancestry], whose music it is impossible to conceive in any other than a Norwegian landscape."[1]

In order to understand the values that influenced Sibelius —who grew up in the small provincial town of Hämeenlinna (the Castle of Häme, in Swedish Tavastehus, the House of Tavast, a medieval bishop of Finland)— some knowledge of the physical environment is important, as are a few facts about the historical, linguistic, and religious aspects that shaped the life of a middle-class boy in that town in the 1860s and '70s.

Finland's northerly location is one important factor: about one-third of the country is north of the Arctic Circle. The country's isolation from the cultural mainstream of Europe was instrumental in shaping the minds of its inhabitants who, as far as is known, were originally Lappish until the time when the Finns arrived there from south of the Gulf of Finland, probably about the beginning of the Christian era. The migration of the Finns took them from their ancestral home near the Ural mountains to a region near the Volga River just like their relatives, the Hungarians, but the Finns continued to push further north to an area south-east of the Baltic Sea, where they came into contact with the Goths. The Finns arrived in Finland partly across the

Gulf of Finland and partly further east over the Karelian Isthmus. Even today there is a small Ingrian population, close relatives of the Finns, in the Soviet Union south of Leningrad, and south of the Gulf of Finland live the Estonians, another related group.

The second largest ethnic and linguistic group in Finland is Swedish. How far back this population group dates has been a matter of considerable dispute. Some say that it is very old, even older than the Finnish population, while others claim that it goes only as far back as the period when the Swedes made several excursions to Finland to bring Christianity to the pagan Finns. The fact that there is no occurrence of Scandinavian runic inscriptions in Finland may give weight to the evidence supporting later Swedish settlement. The period of the Swedish crusades to Finland extended from about 1155 to 1500[2], and each major excursion meant the building of a large castle at the new outpost, starting with the Castle of Turku (Åbo) and followed by the castles of Hämeenlinna, Viipuri (Viborg), and Olavinlina (the Castle of St. Olav at Savonlinna).[3] An English monk, Henry, who had become bishop of Uppsala, led the first Swedish crusade to Finland. There is a legend that Henry was killed by a Finnish peasant on a frozen lake. He was later canonized and became the patron saint of Catholic Finland; the fall fair of Turku, *Heikin messu*, was named in his honor.

Naturally, as a result of these crusades Finland became a Catholic country, and several of the medieval churches are still there with their wooden statues made in the style of the North German school of sculpture. The oldest cathedral, Turun Tuomio-kirkko, is 750 years old. In the sixteenth century Finland was converted to the Lutheran faith by one of Luther's Finnish students, Mikael Agricola, and the Lutheran church became the state church of Finland, to which more than 92 percent of the population belong.

For over six centuries Finland was part of the Swedish kingdom, and most commercial and cultural exchanges were with Sweden and the Hanseatic cities of North Germany. The dichotomy of the cultural and socio-economic structure of the country dates from that period.

In contrast to the peasants of the continent, the farmers of Sweden-Finland were freemen, but they had very little influence in the country's political and cultural life, which was controlled by a few noblemen, most of them of Swedish, Danish, or German origin. They were men who had received large landed estates from Swedish kings as a token of gratitude for heroism during various wars. The few native Finnish noblemen were members of the lower nobility who were appointed to lesser posts as bailiffs or magistrates or military officers because of their command of the vernacular.

Closely connected with the country's political and religious situations was the language issue. It has traditionally been the lot of the inhabitants of small countries like Holland, Sweden, and Finland to have to devote time and energy to foreign language study, since the countries' cultural and economic welfare has depended largely on exchange with foreign countries.   The language issue played an important part in the life and works of Sibelius.

After the Finns left their ancestral home near the Volga River, they came into contact with the Goths south of the Baltic. The contact between the Finns speaking a Finno-Ugric language and the Goths speaking a Germanic language led to the introduction of Gothic loan words into Finnish, which has, to the delight of students of Germanic linguistics, preserved them in a form closer to the original than any other language: Gothic *kuningaz*, Finnish *kuningas*, German *König*, Swedish *kung* (older: *konung*), English *king*.   By moving further north, the Finns came into contact with the Baltic languages, from which they also preserved a few loan-words.   When they pushed still further north, they left behind the Ingrians, whose language is practically the same as the Karelian dialect of Finnish, and the Estonians, whose language has many features in common with Southwest-Finnish dialects.

Because Finland remained in close contact with Sweden for centuries, it is natural that the transfer of customs and governmental institutions introduced a large number of Swedish loan-words into Finnish in the fields of religion and education: Finnish *kirkko*, Swedish *kyrka* (church); Finnish *pastori*, Swedish *pastor* (pastor, minister); Finnish *lukkari*, Swedish *klockare* (sexton); Finnish *koulu*, Swedish *skola* (school), just to give a few examples of how Finnish treated these loan-words.   A number of them are from the field of government: Finnish *lääni*, Swedish *län* (province); Finnish *kaupunki*, Swedish *köping* (marketplace, town), derived from the Gothic verb *kaupjan* (to buy, trade). Finnish purists have tried to fight this trend of taking over a Swedish loan-word, even if in a Fennicized form, together with the institution.   In some cases this fight has been successful, as in the case of Finnish *telefooni*, which has been replaced by Finnish *puhelin*, based on the *puhu-* "to speak" root.   In other cases the purists' suggestions did not meet with the approval of the people, as in the case of *radio* for which the language board tried unsuccessfully to push *sinko*, based on the *sinko-* "to throw" root.

The position of the Swedish language in Finland was strengthened by the cultural influence of Sweden and by the fact that the learned men of the land were either Swedish speakers or bilinguals of Finnish peasant origin, who received their education in Swedish and were trained to express themselves in writing in Swedish, German, and Latin, but not in Finnish.   Thus the situation was completely artificial in the sense that the majority of the population spoke Finnish and yet the written language of the country was Swedish. If a Finnish peasant had to resort to a court of law, he had to find an attorney who could supply his documentation in Swedish and argue his case in that language. The only place where the peasants could hear Finnish outside their homes and villages was the church when the Reformation started to emphasize the sermon in the vernacular. Trained as they were in Swedish, German, and Latin, however, the ministers' Finnish often deteriorated to unintelligible gibberish.

Finland as a Finnish country seemed to be doomed to oblivion because of the superimposed Swedish culture. Although Tacitus referred to the "Fenni," mentions of Finland in the annals of European history are scarce. Some Renaissance scholars, like the Swedish bishop Olaus Magnus, provided some information about Finland in their Latin texts, but the facts included in those works were not necessarily of a reliable nature.

One of the earliest sources of information about Finland available to a larger public was Voltaire's preface to *Charles XII*. After indicating Finland's geographic location, Voltaire described the climate as harsh with hardly any spring and fall; winter reigned nine months and then the heat of summer followed hard upon the excessive cold. After describing the northern lights and the clear air of the region, Voltaire said that the people were well developed and healthy due to the purity of the air and the harshness of the climate, which hardened them, and they lived to a good old age as long as they did not undermine their constitutions by the abuse of strong drink.[4]

While Swedish remained the language of government and largely of the church —the parish registers of even purely Finnish-speaking congregations were kept in Swedish— the Finnish peasants lived isolated in their small rural communities. Occasionally a farmer would send his son *papin kouluun*, to study for the ministry, and the son would end up joining the bilingual middle class, often even adopting a Swedish or a pseudo-Latin name, such as Tammelinus, Helsingius, and so on. Thus the descendants of the owner of the Sibbe farm took the name Sibelius.

Under the circumstances, there was no great need for books in Finnish. Although Mikael Agricola published a Finnish *ABC-kiria* (ABC book) in 1540, books printed in Finnish were slow to appear after Agricola's translation of the New Testament into Finnish in 1548. It took another generation for a Finnish hymn book to appear in print and in 1642, almost a hundred years after Agricola's translation of the New Testament, a complete Finnish translation of the Bible appeared.

Agricola's spelling, vocabulary, and even his sentence structure show strong Swedish, German, and Latin influence, which is natural since he had no written tradition of Finnish to base his work on. However, Agricola never forgot his native Finnish, and he included in the introduction to his prayer book some Finnish proverbs, the oldest printed samples of Finnish folklore. An even more curious publication by Agricola was the introduction to his translation of the Psalms into Finnish, in which he included a list of ancient Finnish "gods." Among them he mentioned Ainemöinen who "forged runos."[5] Agricola's list included also Ilmarinen, Tapio, and Ahti, the latter another name for Lemminkäinen.

In a way Agricola was the first champion of the Finnish language long before the language struggle in Finland really began. When he published his first books in Finnish, printed in Germany, some Swedes protested stating that there was no need for books in Finnish since nobody understood that language anyway. To this Agricola replied, "The Finnish language is understood by Him who understands the mind of every man."

The position of Swedish in Finland was naturally strengthened by Swedish governments, which were anxious to suppress Finnish as much as possible. However, there were two notable exceptions: Duke John of Finland, brother of Erik XIV, and Per Brahe. Duke John's father Gustavus Vasa gave him the most densely populated part of Southwest Finland as a duchy and made him governor of the rest of the country in 1556.[6] John was married to a Polish princess, Katarina Jagellonica, and he wanted to establish an independent Finnish-Polish kingdom. To further his political ideas, he learned Finnish and even addressed his noblemen in that language. It is not surprising that Duke John at Turku Castle later found his way into Sibelius's *Scènes historiques* in "Festivo."

Count Per Brahe was sent over to Finland by Queen Christina's chancellor Axel Oxenstierna to be Governor-General. Brahe became a representative of Finnish nationalism long before the movement in its modern form started and he, too, insisted that Swedish noblemen should study Finnish.

However, there were many Swedish government officials who felt that Swedish should become the universal language of the land gradually replacing Finnish. Among them was Israel Nesselius, a Swedish-born professor at Turku University. He advocated that Finnish should be preserved "only in a couple of backwoods districts as a kind of relic of ancient times."[7] In order to establish uniform customs, he even wanted to ban the *sauna*, since that institution was not known in Sweden.

The fact that Sweden sent numerous government officials to Finland fostered a situation in which the two linguistic groups represented two social classes, with a sharp boundary between the educated class and the common people. This was reflected even in their way of dressing: Swedish-speaking men wore "gentlemen's clothing," while the farmers dressed in simple suits made by the village tailor of coarse, often home-woven wool, and heavy boots. A lady belonging to the gentry was expected to wear a hat, whereas a peasant woman was considered either pretentious or frivolous if she dared to wear a bonnet instead of a kerchief.

The social distinction between the Finnish and Swedish populations was maintained because of the limited educational opportunities offered in Finnish. The church was the only institution to do pioneering work in spreading the knowledge of reading and writing in Finnish among the peasants. The minister and the cantor taught the children of the parish to read. The minister's right to refuse a person the publishing of nuptial banns unless he passed his Catechism test made even the less bright avid pupils, according to Aleksis Kivi in his work *Seitsemän veljestä* (Seven brothers).

With the awakening feeling of nationalism around the world during the eighteenth century, some educated men in Finland started a movement aimed at raising Finnish "to the rank of the civilized tongues of the world." Among them was Henrik Gabriel Porthan, "father of Finnish history," and professor of Latin and elocution at Turku University. He was among the first to study Finnish dialects.

The nineteenth century was an important period in Finnish history. If the country were to assume any role of importance on the world scene, the political, cultural, and linguistic conflicts had to be brought to a harmonious solution. Fortunately Finland had leaders like Juhana Vilhelm Snellman who, inspired by the spirit of Baltic romanticism, were able to guide the intellectual trends in the country.

Snellman, a philosopher and statesman, was among the first to push for Finnish as the first language of the country. His basic philosophy, expressed in his famous statement "Swedes we are not,

Russians we can never be, let us therefore remain Finns," was embraced eagerly by the Finnish-speaking population. However, his appeals met with considerable hostility among the Swedish speakers and even the educated bilinguals, who considered Swedish culturally superior to Finnish. Snellman lived to see the birth of the Finnish-language secondary school system that he fought for. The system grew rapidly and by 1889 the enrollment in Finnish-language secondary schools was equal to that of Swedish-language schools.

After fire destroyed most of the city of Turku, the university was moved to Helsinki in 1828, and the first Finnish-language chair was established about that time. From 1851 the professor of Finnish was M. A. Castrén, who did pioneering work in Finno-Ugric studies. It was ironical that after Castrén's work on his arduous trips in Siberia, some representatives of the pro-Swedish movement used his work to try to prove that the Finns were ethnically and linguistically barbarians: "Without the benefit of Swedish culture the Finns ... would be on the same level as their relatives in Siberia."[8]

Despite considerable interest in Finnish studies, the language made slow progress as a written language. Snellman himself wrote only in Swedish and even the records of the Finnish Literary Society were kept in that language. It was only in the 1850s that Finnish became really established as a printed language after Elias Lönnroth's publication of the first edition of the collection of epic folk poetry, the *Kalevala*, in 1835.

Today Finland is one of the truly bilingual countries of Europe. The distribution of the two linguistic groups is partly geographical, with the largest part of the country being Finnish-speaking and the western and southern coastal areas Swedish-speaking. In North Finland there are a few thousand Lapps, who speak Lappish. In addition, there is a large number of bilingual communities, due partly to the fact that every high school student is required to study "the other native language." This bilingual status was the result of a long and arduous struggle on the part of the Fennophiles.

The first language legislation in Finland was issued in 1858. It stated that the minutes of municipal meetings in communities where church services were conducted in Finnish should be written in that language. In 1863, Czar Alexander II, the Grand Duke of Finland, issued an order whereby Swedish was to remain the first language of the country, but Finnish was to be made "equal to it in matters relating to the Finnish-speaking population." An imperial order issued in 1886 allowed the use of Finnish as an official language in internal matters. Only the language legislations of 1919 and 1922 established the country as a bilingual country where Finnish and Swedish are the official languages: a community is considered bilingual if at least 10 percent of its population speaks the minority language, in which case educational and government services have to be provided in both languages.

When radio broadcasts were started in Finland, they were conducted in a truly bilingual manner with news, weather reports, and so on, read in both languages. Today most radio stations broadcast in either one language or the other and the listeners' chances for bilingual exposure are thus diminished.

The geographical location of Finland and its political position between East and West have influenced various aspects of life in the country. Similarly, the strong link between religion and education in the Baltic region and the bilingualism of the country must be taken into consideration in order to understand the impact of the environmental factors on Sibelius, and it is against this background that we must view his works.

As far as is known, Sibelius's forefathers had been farmers in South-Central Finland at least since the sixteenth century. They were most likely Finnish speaking because the parish of Artjärvi (Artsjö), where the Sibbe farm was located, was and is mostly Finnish speaking. However, this cannot be stated with certainty since the parish registers were kept only in Swedish.

What is certain, nevertheless, is the fact that with the composer's grandfather's move from Artjärvi to the coastal town of Loviisa in 1801 the family became Swedish speaking. The move also meant that grandfather Johan preferred to disregard his peasant origins and join the middle class. Johan was only sixteen when he moved to Loviisa and it would have seemed logical for him to want to go to school there. Obviously the family did not have the necessary funds for that. Instead, Johan became an assistant to a shopkeeper and later, a bookkeeper. His status was obviously enhanced by his marriage to Katarina Fredrika Åkerberg, his employer's niece and a daughter of a doctor born in Sweden. Thus Johan Sibelius, a Finnish peasant, became a *herre*, a Swedish-speaking gentlemen.

With the next generation the transition of a branch of the Sibelius family from the peasant class to the bourgeoisie was completed when Johan's and Katarina's son Christian Gustaf was sent to secondary school to the near-by town of Porvoo (Borgå), where his Latin teacher was the poet Johan Ludvig Runeberg.

After a period of medical studies, in which Christian Gustaf was constantly distracted by his interest in the Academic Choir and playing the guitar, he served as a naval doctor during the Crimean War and, in the early 1860s, he became the military doctor for a battalion stationed at Hämeenlinna, as well as the town doctor.   In 1862 he married Maria Charlotta Borg, a minister's daughter, eighteen years his junior, who bore him three children, the second of whom was born in 1865 and baptized Johan Julius Christian Sibelius.

In trying to determine the decisive hereditary factors in the future composer's psyche, the strongest basic similarities seem to exist between him and his grandfather and namesake Johan. Although the composer's grandfather had joined the bourgeois class, his love for the countryside and the gloomy forests of Artjärvi stayed with him all his life.   During the holidays he liked to return to his native village for wolf hunting.   The other side of Johan's personality reveals a man fond of reading, and his library included works by Cicero and books on such varied topics as geography and logic.   A love of nature and a love of reading were also characteristic of the composer and, like his grandfather, the only form of sport he was actively interested in was hunting.

The composer's father Christian Gustaf, on the other hand, had nothing of the peasant in him.   He belonged to the small but increasingly influential bourgeois class of Finland, whose interests and tastes were determined by the trends in Sweden and Germany. Although the bourgeoisie of Finland tended to have feelings of inferiority towards their Baltic neighbors, being in most cases less wealthy and the last to receive new cultural influences due to slow communications, they were, nevertheless, part of the Baltic community.

At the time Sibelius began his career, the traditional Kantian thinking of the Baltic community was being challenged by Darwinism on the one hand and by Johan Gottfried Herder's emphasis on native cultures on the other.   Thus Sibelius's generation of young intellectuals was exposed to a world of conflict between traditional values and new ideas.

PRE-SIBELIAN MUSIC OF FINLAND

The characteristic dichotomy of Finnish history that exists between native trends and outside influences is reflected in the country's culture, including its music.

Most Sibelius biographers have portrayed the composer as coming from a country with no musical tradition to speak of. This view is erroneous, as it takes into consideration only the scanty art music tradition of Finland, ignoring the fact that by the beginning of Sibelius's career there was a growing awareness of the country's native cultural resources. This awareness was a result of the spread of nationalistic ideas in the Baltic region.

While it is true that, due to Finland's geographic isolation from the cultural centers of Europe, the country's art music tradition is a recent development, a rich tradition of music has been preserved orally from one generation to another in remote villages. It is due to the isolation of the Karelian villages that the early folk song tradition was preserved there until the latter part of the nineteenth century.

In what sense does the early Finnish tradition of folk music differ from the songs still sung around the country today and considered folk songs? The essential feature of early Finnish folk music, the so-called runos (chants), was its close relatedness to the spoken word, which distinguishes it from the later folk song with often only scanty regard for the lyrics.

The runos were usually recited by two people, most often sitting at opposite ends of a bench facing each other, joining their hands and locking their fingers, all the while moving their bodies back and forth in the rhythm of the recitation, taking turns reciting, which took place either unaccompanied or accompanied by the kantele, a harp-like five-stringed instrument. The runo-singers, both men and women, were illiterate, but their good memories guaranteed them the esteem of their neighbors. Larin Paraske, for whom a statue was raised in the Esplanaadi Park in the center of Helsinki, was able to supply Lönnroth with dozens of runos.

A close union between word and music is also characteristic of the folk tradition of the other Finno-Ugric peoples, as pointed out by Robert Austerlitz (regarding Mansi[1] or Vogul) and by Béla Bartók. When the latter started to collect Hungarian folk songs, he realized that they were bound to the words to the extent that "words and melody ... were indivisible."[2]

Finnish is a language in which the accent is always on the first syllable of the word and in which the accent is quantitative rather than qualitative. This gave early Finnish music some of its most important characteristics: spondaic, dactylic, and trochaic rhythms. The way the suffixes are added to the roots of the words offers a clear parallel to trochaic, spondaic, and dactylic patterns: in *kaa-taa*, (cuts down, pours), the long vowel being indicated in the orthography. A long vowel in both syllables creates a spondaic rhythm, since the first syllable stress is quantitative.

On the other hand, with a one-syllable root with a long vowel like *maa* (land), the addition of a case ending leads to a trochaic rhythm *maas-sa* (in the land) (with the Finnish division into syllables), and the addition of an enclitic possessive pronoun *maas-sa-ni* (in my land) results in a dactylic rhythm. Naturally, the same changes of rhythm can be observed with longer roots:

> a two-syllable root: saa-ri (island), saa-rel-la (on the island), saa-rel-lam-me (on our island);
>
> a three-syllable root: kuo-le-ma (death), kuo-le-mas-sa (in death), kuo-le-mas-sa-ni (in my death);
>
> a four-syllable root: naa-pu-ris-to (neighborhood), naa-pu-ris-tos-sa (in the neighborhood), naa-pu-ris-tos-sam-me (in our neighborhood).

On the basis of these examples it is easy to see why descending cadences and spondaic, trochaic, and dactylic rhythms of 2/2, 3/2, 5/4, 7/8, and so on, often in an alternating pattern, occur in Finnish folk song in conformity with the language.

An indication of the importance of cadence in the folk song of the Finno-Ugric peoples lies in the fact that Ilmari Krohn based his classification of Finnish folk songs on the final cadence. This method was adopted at first by Bartók and Zoltán Kodály in their classification of Hungarian folk songs. They abandoned this criterion in favor of another based on rhythmic characteristics, only to modify that system after realizing that the intervals between the notes and in particular between phrases were of decisive importance as well. Even with this revised classification, they ended up putting undue emphasis on the descending cadences and had to add a group of rising melodic lines, which they found to be quite common.[3]

Since all Finno-Ugric languages have the accent on the first syllable of the word, although it is more quantitative than qualitative, it would be logical to assume that an upbeat would be rare in their music. This was confirmed by A. O. Väisänen regarding the folk music of the speakers of Ob-Ugric languages.[4]

An example of the incompatibility of an upbeat with Finnish prosody could be offered in the form of the Finnish national anthem, based on a poem by the Swedish-language poet Johan Ludvig Runeberg. Fredrik Pacius, a transplanted German, learned Swedish, but his upbeat to the music of the opening line "Vårt 'land, vårt 'land ..." (Our 'land, our 'land ...) with three upbeat notes is not in harmony with the demands of Swedish. When the lyrics were translated into Finnish, the upbeat was even more impossible from the point of view of the language, which would have required "'Maam-me,'maam-me...", since the possessive pronoun is enclitic in Finnish. Therefore the translator had to resort to the unstressed interjection "Oi" (Oh) in "Oi, maam-me 'Suo-mi ..." to make the lyrics fit the tune somewhat better.

Even if the flexible rhythms of the Finnish language suggest free-flowing rhythms for the runo-songs, they did, in fact, rely often on rigidly set rhythms, obviously as a memory aid in an oral tradition. Most commonly the rhythm of a typical runo melody is dictated by an eight-syllable line containing four beats:

'Va-ka   'van-ha   'Väi-nä- 'möi-nen

Rhythmically the runo melodies fall basically into two categories: (1) those with prolonged final beat and (2) those without prolongation.[5]

5/4 ♪♪ | ♪♪ | ♪♪ | ♩ | ♩

Example 1

4/4 ♪♪ | ♪♪ | ♪♪ | ♪♪

Example 2

The pattern of four beats to a bar in the Finnish folk song was more common in the southern runo areas and the pattern of five beats to a bar in the northern regions. This fact led two Finnish runo specialists, Kaarle Krohn and Armas Launis, to suggest that since the four-beat pattern seems to have occurred only in the West-Slavic and Finnish-Estonian area, in addition to isolated samples from the Mordvinian and Cheremissian regions, it is likely that the type was known to these ethnic groups at the time they lived in the area south of the present Finnish-Estonian region. This would seem to make contact between the Fennic groups and the West-Slavic groups likely. Can the occurrence of four beats to a bar in Finnish-Estonian music be traced back to this period and the contact with Russian music? Ilmari Krohn has expressed doubts on the grounds that the pattern is also common in Faroese and French music and thus by no means limited to the area in question.

Launis suggests that the five-beat bar, rare in Estonia but common in eastern Finland, could have developed under Scandinavian influence and then spread eastward from western Finland, which would represent a parallel course of the runos from west to east. To support his theory, the Finnish folklore specialist Otto Andersson points out that the most common rhythmic pattern of Edda songs, the *fornyrdislag*, represents a pattern of five-beat bars:[6]

$$5/4 \quad \text{♩♩} \mid \text{♩♩♩} \mid \text{♩♩} \mid \text{♩} \mid \text{♩} \quad \text{etc.}$$

However, this theory is undermined by serious doubt that the Edda songs were ever sung like the runos of the *Kalevala*. A few Edda songs are still sung in the Faroe Islands and Iceland, but in the opinion of most specialists, these melodies were invented later to fit the lyrics.

With the contrast between the fluid rhythms of the Finnish language and the rigid rhythms of the folk songs which act as a memory aid, it is easy to see why the performers prefer the latter.[7] These rigidly set rhythms are implanted in the child's mind literally in the cradle: the lullaby is one of the most common types of Finnish folk song. This writer observed an old country woman in the Finnish-speaking coastal area near Loviisa rocking her grandchild while making up her own lyrics to a monotonous 4/4-5/4 tune. The singer interrupted her singing to attend to her guests, only to pick it up as if there had been no interruption.

A typical runo-song is monotonous both rhythmically and melodically, and it is inherently open-ended. A song can go on in a repetitious fashion indefinitely. A collector of folk tunes observed an eleven-year-old girl in a Karelian village singing continuously for an hour and a half, making up her own lyrics to a tune, and repeating a short rhythmic and melodic phrase with only minor variations.

Two basic types of melody are important in the older Finnish folk song: one built on the tendency of repeated notes, the other on a stepwise progression. The former is often combined with a descending melodic line at the end of a phrase, in keeping with the falling intonation of the language. If we take a folk song like "Soi, soi, sorapilli" (Ring, ring, bad reed), we can see the two basic melodic types combined:

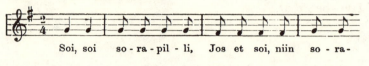

Soi, soi   so - ra - pil - li,   Jos et soi, niin   so - ra-

ja.   Vis-kaan vet-teen, tuik-kaan tul-leen   Ki - ven   al - le

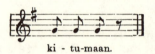

ki - tu-maan.

Example 3 Courtesy of Suomalaisen Kirjallisuuden Seura.

A spondaic or trochaic repetition at the end of a phrase or a phrase ending in a prolonged note, allowing the other runo-singer to pick up the recitation, are also common features of the early Finnish folk song.

In examining the example cited, we can detect another important characteristic: the tendency of the melody to wind around the leading note and to stay within the range of a fourth or fifth. This trend was also observed by Bartók in both Hungarian and Slovak folk melodies.[8] This leads to speculation as to whether this melodic trend is connected with the fact that all these languages stress the first syllable of the word. The theory is particularly tempting since Russian folk music is also prone to fourth and fifth intervals but with the distinction that it avoids the emphasis on the leading note. According to Väisänen's findings, the most common interval in the Ob-Ugric folk song is the melodic fifth, followed by the fourth, diatonic more often than pentatonic, the sixth, the seventh, and the octave, in descending order.[9] A few words of caution, however, are in order. It is, of course, difficult to ascertain the intervals of folk songs, particularly in cases like those of Finnish runo songs transcribed only recently with accuracy, since folk singing in general does not adhere to any degree of precision. We should also emphasize that in general the Finnish folk song is monophonic and, therefore, involves only melodic intervals.

Tonality is the aspect of music least connected with properties of the spoken work, as indicated by the earliest type of musical notation in which the length of notes was tied with the length of syllables and the pitch was indicated as up or down (‿ ⌣). Therefore, it stands to reason that tonality would be difficult to determine on the basis of an oral tradition. The impression one gets of Finnish runo songs, as presented by singers like Larin Paraske, is that they were often of wavering tonality and that the attempt to force them into a modern system of notation is in many cases only an approximation of the original. The slight attention paid to the tonalities of runo songs is confirmed by the fact that collectors of these songs rarely referred to the tonal accuracy of the presentation. Thus the information we have of the tonalities of the runo melodies is rather conflicting. Joseph Acerbi, an Italian explorer who extended his trips to Finland at the turn of the nineteenth century, maintained that the primitive five-stringed kantele was tuned to a, b, c, d, e[10], while Ernst Tanzberger claimed that it was tuned to g, a, b, c, d.[11] Leea Virtanen defines a typical runo melody as a five-beat tune in a minor key. Väisänen confirms that the diatonic scales are by far the most common in the Ob-Ugric folk song. He transcribed his Karelian basic kantele themes in "G major or G minor for the sake of convenience," but claimed that D major or D minor would really have been more appropriate.[12]

In his pioneering study, *An Introduction to the Study of National Music* (1866), Carl Engel concluded that the tuning intervals of certain stringed instruments were derived from those of songs, and he cited as an example the tuning of the "five-stringed kantele as g, a, b-flat, c, d." He concluded, "the intervals from which the Finnish songs are principally constructed are exactly the same; indeed, in many of the airs the compass does not extend above the dominant, and the number of intervals is therefore limited to those five of the kantele."[13] However, he felt that there was nothing peculiar in the construction of the instrument to lead to the adoption of just that order of intervals: "Indeed, it appears highly probable that the five strings were originally tuned in accordance with the five intervals of the pentatonic scale, because the kantele resembles certain instruments of Asiatic nations which have this scale; and because the intervals of the *gousli*, a five-stringed instrument of the Russian peasantry, greatly resembling the kantele . . . constitute nearly the same scale; with *c* as the tonic, the order of them being a, c, e, g, a."

The wavering tonality of the Ob-Ugric folk melodies was confirmed by Väisänen,[14] who stated that they did not make any clear distinction between the diatonic and chromatic scales, whereas the difference between the diatonic and the pentatonic was more clearly defined.[15] The pentatonic scale occurs in 31 percent of the Mansi (Vogul) samples that Väisänen collected, but it is rare in the Ostjak samples.

Recent studies of the Finnish folk song have concluded nearly unanimously that the pentatonic scales are almost absent in them, except for occasional occurrences in Russian Karelia. They also occur in the *juoigos* of the Lapps. The fact that melisma occurs more often in the pentatonic than in the diatonic scale made Väisänen conclude that, as far as the Ob-Ugric folk melodies are concerned, the diatonic scales are the more original and the pentatonic, more recent. However, after his trip in 1905 to collect Hungarian folk songs Bartók wrote: "I had the feeling that these wonderful, pentatonic melodies came from a forgotten age. They were several centuries old."[16]

Another piece of evidence for the scant influence of neighboring lands on early Finnish music is the fact that the oldest instrument in Scandinavia, the *lur*, was unknown in Finland. A type of harp was known in Scandinavia and the British Isles, as was the *goosli* in Russia. In Norse literature, however, harp-playing (*harpaslåtter*) is nearly always a separate art from singing or chanting, for which the usual word is *kveda*.[17] We learn from the fourteenth-century sagas, that harp-playing came into its own quite early as an art form, while the Finnish kantele's status as an instrument in its own right is fairly recent and coincides with the expansion of the original five-stringed instrument. Originally, there was also an instrument stringed with horsehair, the *jouhikko*, but that was supplanted by the metal-stringed kantele.

The main purpose of a runo melody was the presentation of a verbal story in a simple, mainly syllabic fashion relying heavily on parallel repetition and outright reiteration. Rarely did a runo singer use "wonderful, sonorous decorations,"[18] and it is believed that some singers added those to a simple tune in order to enhance their own reputation. Both group-type and melismatic tunes became more common only with the later folk song, a crucial distinction between the earlier and later types of folk songs.

In contrast, recitation became popular in the other Scandinavian countries only in the Middle Ages with the chanting of ballads, probably under French influence. The ballad was usually composed of four-line stanzas, often made up of four and three stresses alternating, with an invariable refrain, *omkvaed*. This tradition later influenced Finnish folk music.

When we consider the medieval period, the influence of church music becomes an important factor. Much of the older alliterative Edda verse goes back to the pre-Christian era (before 1000 A.D.) and displays metric and other poetic features in common with *Beowulf*.[19] Skaldic poetry, however, the poetry of the *skalds* (court poets), becomes enmeshed with influences of church music, as evidenced by the hymn *Nobilis, humilis,* dedicated to the memory of St. Magnus, Earl of Orkney, who died in 1115. The hymn was probably written in the thirteenth century in Latin, but it suggests the influence of some skaldic meters. What is striking from a purely musical point of view is the harmonization, chiefly in thirds. *Organum*-style singing in parallel fifths was established by the beginning of the fourteenth century in Iceland as a result of the efforts of a French monk at the beginning of the twelfth century. These are early indications of the success of missionaries whose work was directed at teaching Gregorian plainsong in Scandinavia.

After the conversion of Finland to Christianity, begun in the mid-twelfth century, the church music of Finland naturally came under the influence of German plainsong, as did the music of other Nordic countries. However, the picture of the influence of church music in Finland is complicated by the fact that Finland, in the fourteenth century, came into contact with the Parisian Dominican missions and thus under the influence of Romanic-type church music. Although St. Birgitta (1303-73), founder of the Vadstena Order, encouraged the composition of hymns, she forbade the use of polyphony at Vadstena, contrary to the practice of *organum* singing established in Uppsala Cathedral before her time. It is likely that the Birgittan convent established at Naantali (Nådendal), north of Turku, likewise observed the ban on the use of polyphony. However, it probably did not have any practical significance, since the monastic schools founded in the thirteenth century in Turku, Viipuri, Rauma (Raumå), and Kökar observed the rules established by the Uppsala Diocese.

Despite the influence of church music, the tradition of oral music survived for centuries. An interesting piece of evidence attesting to the strength of this tradition is the fact that the first Finnish version of the lyrics of *Piae Cantiones ecclesiasticae et scholasticae* was printed in 1616 without the musical notation of the original, published in 1582 for use in Sweden and believed to be the earliest Swedish musical work printed in mensural notation. (The first Scandinavian musical notation of a ballad in *Codex runicus* [ca. 1300] was non-mensural).

The original collection of *Piae Cantiones* contained fifty-two songs, although later editions contained more. The texts are chiefly in Latin with a few alternate Swedish versions. Most settings are monodic; about a dozen are polyphonic. The majority of tunes are based on German or French sources, while some are of Swedish or Finnish origin, according to Veikko Helasvuo.[20] Paavo Helistö, however, claims "apparently about half of the 74 songs in the first edition were of Finnish origin."[21]

Thus we have clear evidence of influence of foreign music in Finland by the sixteenth century, but we have to remember that there was not yet any tradition of printed music in the country and, consequently, the oral tradition was still dominant. However, some foreign influence can be detected in the later type of folk song.

The purpose of the early Finnish folk song was the recitation of the runos. Both the lyrics and the music depended on the accentuation of the Finnish language with the main stress on the first syllable of the word. German and the Scandinavian languages, on the other hand, as Indo-European languages, have accent meters similar to English. Therefore, when the later type of Finnish folk song came under the influence of church music and the music of neighboring lands, there was a conflict between the quantitative meter of Finnish and the accent meter, as pointed out in the case of the Finnish national anthem. Thus, the later Finnish folk song often mutilated the lyrics, as melody starts to take on an increasingly important role. Similar differences were observed by Bartók, who called the genuine Hungarian folk song "Bauernlied" and the citified folk tune "volkstümliches Kunstlied".[22]

Despite foreign influences in the later-type Finnish folk song, features of it set it apart from the folk songs of the other Scandinavian countries. Whereas in the recitation of the early Finnish folk song, the runo-song, the rhythms of language and music are interdependent, the later folk song is based most often on 2/2 or 2/4 rhythms and constructed of short, four-line stanzas, typically with either the rhyme scheme of a b a b or a b c b. The melodic line usually progresses in small ascending or descending steps, with the second and fourth lines ending commonly in a repeated tone.

Although the mood of the later-type Finnish folk song is frequently nostalgic, as in the Scandinavian folk song in general, there are differences as well. Due to the influence of the languages in question, Finnish songs rely often on duple time, while in the Scandinavian folk song triple time is more common, as in the well-known "Näckens polska" (Neckan's Polka) from Sweden. The melodic line of the song is characterized by greater rhythmic fluidity and a wider melodic range than that of typical Finnish folk melodies.

Just as there are chanted riddles and even dance-like tunes among earlier Finnish folk songs, there are also gay and playful songs among the later-type folk songs, and dance-like rhythms have their definite place in them as well. The evocation of dance movement of "Linjaalirattaat" (The Buggy) is definitely Finnish in character with the duple rhythm and the tendency of lines ending in a repeated tone:

Example 4 Courtesy of Suomalaisen Kirjallisuuden Seura.

However, a word of caution seems appropriate regarding the classification of folk songs into "earlier" and "later" ones. Naturally the "age" of a folk song is impossible to determine, especially in a case like that of the Finnish folk song, in view of the country's short tradition of written records, and thus we are only concerned with certain characteristic features of the earlier and the later folk songs.

Although there was a rich oral tradition of music in Finland, the art music scene was more bleak. With few noblemen to sponsor the arts, except for Duke John's court at Turku, the Finnish middle class had to assume an active role. When the bourgeois class of Finland grew in number, they continued the tradition established by Duke John. The city of Turku has had its own orchestra since 1790, and many young men were trained to become church musicians at Turun Urkurikoulu (the Turku Organ School). The Turku Musical Society organized concerts and recitals, and according to Otto Andersson, music by Mozart was performed in Finland for the first time in 1796. He mentions also that the Finnish composer Erik Tulindberg owned the scores of six quartets by Haydn as early as 1781, which was the year Haydn's name occurred for the first time in a concert program in Stockholm.[23]

The appearance of the first composer of art music in Finland coincides with the establishment of a twenty-piece orchestra in Turku, which was comprised of University of Turku teachers and students. Erik Tulindberg (d. 1814), who did graduate work under the direction of Porthan, composed a violin concerto and six quartets. In spite of his activity in composing and arranging concerts, Tulindberg had to earn his living as a civil servant, at first in Oulu (Uleåborg) and later in Turku. His work in the field of music was recognized, however, and he was the first Finn to be appointed a member of the Royal Swedish Music Academy.

While Tulindberg was a civil servant in Oulu, he met Joseph Acerbi, and Tulindberg's posthumous papers included a handwritten clarinet piece above which "Qvartetto 3. per Acerbi" was written, probably in Acerbi's own writing. The Andante movement of this piece, called "Runa Finnoise," is based on a Finnish runo melody, and it is thus the first known attempt at adapting a runo melody to art music. The English explorer E. D. Clarke, who traveled in Finland and was interested in runos, maintained that Acerbi had also made a piano arrangement of the work.

This type of interest in Finnish runo songs, however, did not as yet have any practical consequences. The art music of Finland continued to be dominated by composers with international training and interests. Thomas Byström's Three Sonatas "pour le Clavecin ou Piano-Forte avec accompagnement d'un violin obligé" were printed by Breitkopf & Haertel in 1801. His *Air russe variée*, a piano work, has recently been recorded by Eero Heinonen.

Active on the Turku music scene around 1800 were Fredrik Lithander and his brother Carl Ludvig Lithander, two of eleven children born on the Estonian island of Dagö of Finnish parents. After the parents' premature death, the family moved to Turku. Carl Ludvig, in particular, is still remembered as a composer, and his Piano Sonata in C Major, dedicated to Muzio Clementi, and his Haydn variations have been recorded by Eero Heinonen. The former work, which adheres to the standard style of the writing of the period, surprisingly employs a Swedish folk song in the last movement.

A prominent name of the period is that of Bernhard Henrik Crusell (d. 1838), a bookbinder's son from Uusikaupunki (Nystad). He was an instrumentalist in a military band and attracted Abbé Vogler's attention by his clarinet solo at a recital in Stockholm and was asked by Abbé Vogler, who was court music director in Stockholm at that time, to join the court orchestra.[24] In 1801 Crusell was appointed a member of the Royal Swedish Academy of Music. His wide travels included a trip to Paris, where he studied with François Gossec. Crusell's compositions, few of which have been preserved, include chamber music and songs as well as incidental music for an operatic performance in Stockholm.

Crusell had a sentimental attachment to his native land. During his last year he composed three songs to words by Runeberg, which included "Svanen" (The Swan), one of the most popular songs in Finland. He sent the songs to the poet along with a letter echoing Runeberg's belief that religion, love, poetry, and music originate from the same divine source. Crusell's songs had considerable influence on later composers of songs in Finland, including Sibelius.

The Scandinavian vocal tradition was represented in Finland in the next generation by Karl Collan (1828-71), who composed numerous songs in the standard romantic liederstyle with the influence of Scandinavian folk song. For many of these settings, often nostalgic moods of nature, he used poems by Topelius and Runeberg. A number of them are so popular that they have often been erroneously considered folk songs.

This Scandinavian variety of the romantic lied received an official seal of approval with the hiring of Fredrik Pacius as the University music teacher in Helsinki in 1835. Although he was a Hamburg-born pupil of Ludwig Spohr's, he soon became an "honorary Finnish-Swede" and set a number of patriotic Swedish-language poems to music, including "Vårt land" by Runeberg, which soon achieved the status of a national anthem. Runeberg himself composed a melody for "Vårt land," as did the Finnish composer F. Ehrström, but Pacius's tune became the official one. Thus the Finnish national anthem was composed by a German to a poem written originally in Swedish by a Finn.[25] In 1852 Pacius composed an opera, *King Charles's Hunt*, to a libretto by Topelius. The chorus at the première included Christian Gustaf Sibelius. The opera was significant in the sense that it was one of the early popular successes of art music in Finland, and it inspired artists in other fields as well. After Pacius's death Jean Sibelius was annoyed at the florid obituaries and said in a written statement: "With respect, I fail to discern anything other in Pacius's music than reminiscences of Italian and German opera."[26]

Despite the fact that Lönnroth published his first edition of the *Kalevala* in 1835 and inspired musicians and folklorists to collect folk melodies, the art music scene in Finland was still in the hands of Germans, including Pacius's successor at the university, Richard Faltin.

However, about this time, in the middle of the nineteenth century, the first faint signs of Finnish influence on art music started to appear. The first symphony in Finland was composed by Axel Gabriel Ingelius (d. 1868); the Scherzo finnico movement of this work used the 5/4 rhythm of Finnish runo melodies.[27] Filip von Schantz, who died at the age of thirty the same year

Sibelius was born, was a promising conductor and composer, whose *Kullervo* overture was performed at the dedication of a new theater in Helsinki in 1860. This was the first large-scale work based on the *Kalevala* and on the same cycle of poems that inspired Sibelius some thirty years later. Both Ingelius and von Schantz were pioneers in the sense that they were able to see the possibilities of the *Kalevala* and of Finnish folk music in the service of art music.

Although we can talk about the beginning of an art music tradition in Finland during the nineteenth century, very little of it filtered down to the public. This was due not so much to a lack of interest as to the lack of opportunity. There were no permanent orchestras in the country, and the activity of the small orchestra connected with Turku University was disrupted by a fire that destroyed most of the city in 1827, by the moving of the capital, and by the establishing of a new university in Helsinki. There was also a shortage of competent musicians. Except for the Organ School in Turku, opportunites for musical training were almost nonexistent. Martin Wegelius realized this, and, thanks to his tenacity the Helsinki Music Institute opened its doors in 1882. Wegelius was admirable in his efforts to recruit competent teachers abroad and writing music textbooks. In 1939 Wegelius's Institute was renamed Sibelius Academy in honor of its most famous pupil.

The same year that the Helsinki Institute of Music was established, 1882, Robert Kajanus started a symphony orchestra, believed to be the first permanent orchestra in Scandinavia. Originally, the orchestra had about thirty German members and only a few Finnish musicians. Since 1914 it has been known as the Helsinki City Orchestra, and Kajanus was its conductor for half a century. Although Ferruccio Busoni referred to Kajanus rather condescendingly as a musician "with some talent,"[28] Kajanus's contribution to the music scene of Finland should not be underestimated. He established the tradition of Friday evening symphony concerts, which for years were held at the University of Helsinki Festival Hall.

Both Kajanus and Wegelius had received their training in Germany, and Kajanus's compositions, such as *The Death of Kullervo* and the *Aino* symphony, show his indebtedness to Wagner despite their *Kalevala* inspiration, as does his *Finnish Rhapsody*, based on Finnish folk melodies.

In spite of some early signs of Finnish folk tunes in art music by Ingelius, von Schantz, and a little later by Kajanus, the art music tradition of Finland continued to develop under German-

Scandinavian influences. This trend received a strong boost when Wegelius hired Busoni as a teacher in his Music Institute.

Busoni did not know how isolated Helsinki still was at that time, and the internationally known pianist was shocked to discover that most of his piano students were young ladies whose level of training had not yet reached beyond Cramer and Clementi. There was no student orchestra, and there were no classes in wind instruments. "There was a violin master, a Hungarian ... who played in the Viennese manner taking no interval without a pronounced slide, and a violoncello master who three years before had been a commercial traveller."[29] Busoni was horrified and wrote to a friend that he felt like "a clown in a circus with a troop of performing geese."

No matter what Busoni's personal feelings were, credit must be given to his arduous efforts and dedication to improving the musical life of Helsinki. A few weeks after his arrival he gave a recital and included several Beethoven piano sonatas. This was followed by several more recitals with programs ranging form Bach, Mozart, Scarlatti, and Handel to Brahms, Liszt, and Chopin. He also performed the Schumann quintet with the Institute's quartet, in which Sibelius played second violin. Busoni, however, was determined to make his stay in Helsinki as short as possible. He suffered from loneliness, augmented by the fact that he did not know either of the country's two languages, and he suffered even more from the fear that his own talent would deteriorate in the backwoods atmosphere of Helsinki. Even the applause of the concert audiences in Helsinki made him doubt his own value: "it was a certain sign of his own mediocrity, he felt, if he pleased an audience of mediocre minds."[30]

Sibelius could understand Busoni's feelings very well. He too was aware, time and again, of the backwardness of Finland when it came to performing and appreciating art music. Later when Martti Similä told Sibelius that he had to finance his debut as a composer himself and suffer a considerable financial loss, Sibelius remarked to him, "In the old days, I used to count about 177 individuals in Helsinki who really understood music — now there are perhaps not quite so many."[31] He understood all too well what a composer or a performer faced in Finland. He once traveled some six hundred miles to Oulu to conduct his works only to discover that the orchestra there included only one cellist, who did not attend the rehearsal.

If Busoni's stay in Helsinki and the German training of the Finnish composers of the period established firmly the German-Scandinavian art music orientation in Finland, the same trend was discernible with the spreading of citified tastes in popular music.

Before the era of the radio and the phonograph, "home-made" music was important. While the peasant population sang folk songs or hymns at their gatherings, the middle-class often enjoyed home performances of easy piano pieces by the *Mamsell*, (governess), or by a small family ensemble. The Sibelius family ensemble featured Janne playing the violin, his brother Christian the cello, and his sister Linda the piano. Their repertory adhered to the continental and Scandinavian tradition, with Haydn, Mozart, Beethoven, Mendelssohn, Schumann, and Grieg predominating.

In general there was a lively interest in the bourgeois homes of Finland in musical soirées. As an indication of musical interests, the collection of musical instruments at one nineteenth-century country manor in the Swedish coastal area included a piano, a violin, and a guitar. A list of the sheet music in the same house mentions rondos by Haydn and Pleyel, a Mozart sonata (No. 1 in D Major), opera music including Verdi's *Trovatore*, Wagner's *Lohengrin*, Beethoven's *Fidelio*, and Naumann's *Gustaf Vasa*, as well as music to Bellman's *Fredmans epistlar*, and twelve songs by Crusell.[32] Many families kept their own song book, which they eagerly tried to keep up to date.

Traditionally, the relatively large bilingual population of Finland has sung Swedish songs at Finnish gatherings and vice versa. Even in the purely Swedish-speaking coastal area, the sheet music collection of the home mentioned above included Finnish Christmas carols. A song popular in one group often gained popularity very quickly in the other. The only exceptions were the songs of Bellman and Wennerberg, which remained relatively unknown to Finnish speakers.

Why were Swedish speakers attracted to the music of Bellman and Wennerberg? The interest can be attributed to their close contact with Sweden, where the songsters reigned in the field of entertainment.

Carl Michael Bellman was a colorful figure of late eighteenth-century Stockholm. He wrote incidental poems for special events at the court of Gustav III (later on of Scribe-Verdi *Masked Ball* fame) and he composed and wrote the lyrics for numerous drinking and satirical songs. Many of them were Bible parodies, as the title of his best known collection, *Fredmans epistlar* (Fredman's Epistles), suggests. Many songs, such as "Gubben Noak" (Old Man Noah), became immensely popular. The opening of the oldest epistle, "Käre bröder, så låtom oss supa i frid" (Dear brothers, let us drink in peace), is an exhortation to the brothers of "the Order ofBacchus" for a gay evening. A boisterous night at the café is usually followed by a humorous song of repentance. A number of Wennerberg's *Gluntarna* are also drinking songs or songs about student life in Uppsala. They are strongly influenced by Bellman, but by Wennerberg's time (the early nineteenth century), their spirit turned more romantic. One of Sibelius's first assignments as Wegelius's student in Helsinki was to compose the watersprite's song for Wennerberg's play *The Watersprite*.

Although Bellman is considered important in Swedish letters as the first poet to sing of the beauty of city life, his later songs are pastoral scenes reminiscent of the paintings of the rococo period. However, these songs are not as neatly organized as the rococo paintings, and often they convey audio-visual impressions and sensations of odors mixed in an illogical fashion, which is at the same time both romantic and realistic.

In both Bellman's and Wennerberg's observations of nature, there is a strong link with the poets' education. In Bellman's fantasy world especially, Bacchus, Venus, Jupiter, Neptune, Amor, and Pan mingle freely with the world of reality, and logic often has to yield to imagination.

As music, the songs of Bellman and Wennerberg have no great value. Bellman found his melodies in folk songs and popular tunes, often with only minor revisions. Wennerberg's songs are not musically significant either, but the catchy tunes to half-serious, half-humorous lyrics made them immensely popular.

What is interesting about Bellman's songs is the fact that they had snob appeal, as pointed out by James Rhea Massengale in a recent study: "The great majority of Bellman's melodies is comprised of popular French *chansons*, many of them 'Schlager' tunes in Paris or Stockholm just at the time Bellman reworked them."[33] Even the fact that the *Epistlar* which portray dances use the minuet or the contredanse shows that they were designed to appeal to the middle and upper classes. The polka and the mazurka, on the other hand, were considered peasant dances; in the *Epistlar* there is no mazurka and only one polka.[34]

Although Swedish popular songs by composers like Bellman and Wennerberg did not have much of an impact on the popular music of Finland outside of Swedish circles, Sweden's influence was still considerable even in this area. For example, the polka spread to Finland through Sweden and became an immensely popular dance among the Finnish-speaking population during the eighteenth century. The gradual growth of the urban population introduced a dance called *purppuri* among the peasant population. In performances of both the polka and the *purppuri*, the fiddle became an important instrument as early as the seventeenth century, replacing to a large extent the kantele, only to be replaced in turn in the 1880s by the accordion. All these developments can be ascribed to the influence of Swedish popular music in Finland.   It was only as a result of the Finnish nationalistic movement that the kantele was reintroduced to West Finland, especially for folk song accompaniment.

The foreign influence on dance music and popular songs was so strong that people became just as familiar with German-Scandinavian style music as with their native tunes, especially when the popularity of the music was enhanced by lieder by composers like Oskar Merikanto and Erkki Melartin.

As the art music and the popular music tradition of Finland became gradually more and more foreign-influenced, the demise of the native tradition would have been inevitable without the impact of the Finnish nationalistic movement.   Inspired by this spirit, Sibelius showed the Finnish people the value of their national heritage in their folk poetry and folk song as did the "Russian Five" in their land.   The value of their tradition of folk music became a way of revitalizing art music in the manner of Mussorgsky in Russia and Bartók in Hungary.

SIBELIUS AND FINNISH NATIONALISM

To understand the enormous impact Finnish folk poetry and folk song had on Sibelius's music in terms of inspiration and expression, we have to trace the cultural and political evolution of Finnish nationalism.

One of the most crucial moments of Sibelius's career came during his student year in Vienna, while he was rereading the *Kalevala.* He realized that the best way to find his own musical identity was through national Finnish music. This intuitive resolution was a bold one given his early background and the scant regard leaders of Finnish music at that time had for anything but the continental music tradition. What were the reasons for Sibelius's declaration of independence?

Some of the reasons probably derive from his childhood at Hämeenlinna. He grew up fatherless — his father having died in a typhoid epidemic when the boy was only two and a half years old — and poor, although not starved, in a society that expected a comfortable, if not luxurious, standard of living for its middle-class members. These circumstances were to affect him deeply both in childhood and in his adult life. Christian Gustaf Sibelius's widow and three children had to share lodgings with her mother and unmarried sister, whose well-meaning but at times oppressive care resulted in rebellious moods in the teenaged Janne, as the family called him.

If the impact of the extended family circle was at times confining, the small Finnish-speaking town of Hämeenlinna could hardly be characterized as anything but provincial, cut off as it was from the main stream of cultural activity. This sense of isolation led the small Swedish-speaking community of Hämeenlinna to look for diversion in close circles of friends and thus musically gifted amateurs like Christian Gustaf Sibelius used to entertain many a social gathering with songs, often by Bellman and Wennerberg, to guitar accompaniment.

One of the rare cosmopolitan contacts that the townspeople had was with the Russian garrison. At the time of Sibelius's childhood, the relationship between the Finns and the Russians was spared the animosity that the Russification of Finland and the First World War were to bring about. There was even social contact between the natives and the Russians. The children of the Russian garrison's staff attended local schools and learned Finnish and Swedish. The local children learned a few words of Russian, such as *maroshi*, which they used in imitation of the Russian ice cream vendors.

The sense of isolation was to be a blessing for the development of Sibelius's creative mind. It nurtured the introverted side of his psyche and made him unusually sensitive to the moods of nature. It was, perhaps, a sign of the boy's tendency to react to environmental impulses in music when the little lad, obviously quite instinctively, started to sing "Run, my little reindeer," a children's song well-known in Finland, when his father's coffin was being carried out of the house. The importance of nature as musical inspiration is seen in the eight-year old boy's first "composition," a short piano piece which he called "Vattendroppar" (Drops of water).

However, Sibelius's childhood can by no means be characterized as Dickensian. There was a sense of security and bright childhood memories supplied by two grandmothers and numerous aunts and uncles. There were the joyous summers at the grandmother's in Loviisa, when Janne's favorite aunt, Evelina, took the children out on a row-boat and let them launch little home-made bark boats. The harbor was a most exciting place and the arrival of the Sibelius family's ship from Spain with its exotic cargo of spices and oranges was naturally a big event. Things like an occasional cruising of a deluxe yacht, perhaps even that of the Russian Imperial family, on the near-by waters and the German-style *Badeanstalt*, which attracted a host of summer guests, gave Janne a foretaste of something more grand and exciting than the monotonous sameness of the schoolboy's life at Hämeenlinna. If Loviisa appealed to Sibelius's extroverted side, Hämeenlinna with its sense of isolation nurtured the introvert in Sibelius, and the realist in him knew that he had to go to school, whether he liked it or not.

After one year of Swedish-language elementary school, Janne, a poor student, was transferred to a Finnish-language elementary school, the first public elementary school in the country to use Finnish as the language of instruction.[1]   There the boy's performance improved, and he was able to write one year to his *farmor*, his grandmother, that he was the ninth in his class.

In 1876 Janne was enrolled at Hämeenlinnan Normaalilyseo, a Finnish-language secondary school, which gave him a solid education in the sciences and humanities, as well as in foreign languages. In Sibelius's time Latin and Greek were an essential part of the curriculum, a fact emphasized by the numerous quotations in these languages that the composer used in his correspondence and in his sketch-book. Since the children of Finland are exposed to foreign language studies at the age of eleven, or even earlier, it was possible for Sibelius later to study music in Berlin and Vienna without any major language problems.

The *Kalevala*, which Sibelius knew earlier from Collan's Swedish translation, was studied in the Finnish courses, contrary to the assertion of many Sibelius biographers who have stated that the composer studied the work in Finnish only during his post-student days with the aid of his fiancée. Sibelius spent countless hours analyzing poems and memorizing passages of them while he was a student at Hämeenlinnan Normaalilyseo. However, the same was true of Sibelius's *Kalevala* studies as has been true of many generations of English-speaking pupils' Shakespeare studies: the student remained indifferent and unimpressed, only to discover the beauty of the work after his school years, except for the story of Kullervo, which fascinated the young Sibelius.

All along his school performance suffered from lack of interest and concentration, although he admitted later to Karl Ekman that there were periods in history that fascinated him, as did literature and natural science, and his collections of pressed plants, insects, and butterflies were outstanding. Occasionally mathematics could arouse his interest as well.

The fact that Sibelius was capable of performing well in school if he was interested in the subject can be seen from his matriculation essay in Finnish. From the choice of topics Sibelius picked out "Gustav II Adolf, founder of Protestantism." Judging from the emphasis of the title, Sibelius could have been influenced in his choice by the view of history, prevalent at the time, which overestimated the religious motives behind the actions of Gustavus Adolphus in his fight against Catholicism and almost made him a martyr. On the other hand, Sibelius's interest in the Thirty Years' War could have been motivated by a naïve fascination with the unconventional fighting methods of the eight thousand Finns in

Gustavus Adolphus's army who were nicknamed *hakkapelis* from the Finnish battle cry "Hakkaa päälle!" (Chop down the enemy!) Anyway, Sibelius must have felt inspired because he managed to write an essay that was above his usual level of achievement. His interest in this period of history was to surface again in *Scènes historiques.*

During his school years Sibelius became absorbed in his music studies to the extent that he neglected his other studies and had to repeat his fifth year of secondary school. At the age of fourteen he began violin lessons with Gustaf Levander, the military band master at Hämeenlinna, but it is not certain whether the music program in school had any impact on him at that time.

Music has traditionally played an important role in Finnish schools. Since the Lutheran Church is the state church, it has been easy for music teachers to include church music in their instruction,[2] and the school day has started customarily with a hymn and a prayer. Thus a lad like Janne, who only went to church at Christmas, was exposed, nevertheless, to church music daily. Many music teachers have been competent musicians, as was Sibelius's teacher Emil Genetz.

Although the education Sibelius received at Hämeenlinna was too strictly programmed to appeal to his impulsive mind, it did implant in him a healthy respect for Prussian discipline, a valuable lesson for his later years. From the point of view of Sibelius's career, it is significant that the dichotomy between his Swedish and Finnish backgrounds widened during his years at Hämeenlinna. He spoke Swedish at home and with most of his friends, and yet the majority of the few thousand inhabitants of the town were Finnish speakers. After his first year of school Sibelius received his entire education at Hämeenlinna in Finnish. Thus he learned to appreciate the world of Runeberg and of Swedish-language literature in general at home and at his grandmother's at Loviisa, while the Finnish-language town of Hämeenlinna and his education there opened the young composer to the influences of Finnish nationalism and of Finnish folk song and poetry.

The deeper implications of the world of Runeberg on the one hand and of the *Kalevala* on the other go far beyond the society in which Sibelius grew up. They were manifestations of the conflict between the Baltic world as influenced by the Enlightenment and the Kantian philosophy of reason, which was incompatible with Christianity, and the idiosyncratic folk cultures, whose role was enhanced by romanticism.

The ideas of the Enlightenment were by their very nature accepted eagerly by the people of the Baltic region, whose own innate inclinations were compatible with its emphasis on the rational and on a universal human truth. Because, in Kant's view, the basic elements of that truth are inherent in every rational man, the ideas of the French Revolution about equal rights for all rational men were easily accepted in that region. Yet the ideas of the Enlightenment were in many respects incompatible with religion and, therefore, people like Kant formulated their own brand of the Enlightenment by adhering to at least some of the traditional values of religion if not to many of its basic tenets. Thus there is a curious mixing of eagerness for new ideas and of clinging to old ones in the thinking of the people of the region, a feature which the rest of the world has found somewhat baffling.

When Hegel's ideas became the cornerstone of Baltic romanticism, it had begun to be emphasized that a religion of humanity without special ethnic and cultural features was not in keeping with reality, and the soil was well tilled for the acceptance of folk cultures. Thus Baltic Romanticism, more clearly than Continental High Romanticism, grew out of the Enlightenment rather than as a reaction against it.

These Baltic trends are reflected faithfully in the thinking of Finland's intellectuals. Porthan's Aurora Society, which discussed literature in the spirit of the Enlightenment, included members like Franz Mikael Franzén, whose wide interests ranged from reading Shakespeare, Milton, and Klopstock to writing historical novels and poetry. Several rococo-style poems by Franzén inspired Sibelius to write solo voice settings.

Without the influence of the romantic movement and its emphasis on folk cultures Runeberg would have remained a typical Swedish Finn and rather ignorant of anything Finnish. Without Hegel's influence Runeberg would have clung to his youthful enthusiasm for Swedish culture, and without Herder's emphasis on the value of national characteristics, as they are reflected in the poetry and songs of a nation, Runeberg would not have become interested in the dual culture of Finland. He had been familiar with the Swedish-language folk songs of coastal Finland since his childhood, and on his travels to the Finnish-speaking areas of Central Finland he became acquainted with Finnish folk poetry. Thus his Swedish-language poetry reflects the influence of Finnish folk poetry.

Sibelius was familiar with Runeberg's poetry ever since his childhood, and it is easy to understand why his first published compositions were songs to lyrics by that poet. However, there was also a practical reason for Sibelius's Runebergian inspiration: there was not much Finnish-language literature in existence beyond folk poetry and religious literature at that time. Although

Lönnroth and many of his followers had collected tens of thousands of folk poems by the beginning of Sibelius's career, this era also marks the birth of Finnish-language art literature.

The best known work of the first prominent Finnish-language writer Aleksis Kivi, his *Seitsemän veljestä* (Seven Brothers), was published in 1870. August Ahlqvist, a contemporary and bitter enemy of Kivi, was a professor of Finno-Ugric languages who published creative works under the pseudonym A. Oksanen and is often called "the father of Finnish lyric poetry." J. H. Erkko, who was to have collaborated with Sibelius on his projected opera *The Building of the Boat*, based on the *Kalevala*, and Paavo Cajander, on whose poem "Vapautettu kuningatar" (The Liberated Queen) Sibelius based a cantata, were among the prominent writers of the period. The first Finnish-language poet to turn out really meritorious lyric poetry was Eino Leino, who was thirteen years younger than Sibelius. Under the circumstances, it is not surprising that the composer turned most often to Finnish-Swedish or Swedish writers of Sweden for inspiration.

The songs by Sibelius that adhere to the standards of Nordic song repertories found immediate acceptance.[3] They include such typical specimens as "Kyssens hopp" (The Wish for a kiss), which Sibelius composed, appropriately, on his honeymoon, and "Våren flyktar hastigt" (Spring is flying), both Runeberg settings. Among the more dramatic songs received well by Scandinavian audiences we could mention "Den första kyssen" (The first kiss) and "Flickan kom ifrån sin älsklings möte," generally known in English as "The Tryst," both Runeberg settings. An indication of the fact that this type of song had common Scandinavian appeal is the solo voice setting of the latter poem by Wilhelm Stenhammar, the composer and conductor. Opus 35 by Sibelius (1907) contains two dramatic songs: "Jubal" and "Teodora," the former a Josephson and the latter a Gripenberg setting, both Swedish-Finnish poets. Cecil Gray thought highly of the latter setting and wondered whether Sibelius would have made, after all, a good opera composer.

Sibelius's first international successes were with his solo songs. When Ida Morduch-Ekman, the mother of Sibelius's biographer Karl Ekman, sang a Runeberg setting, "Se'n har jag ej frågat mera" (Since then I have questioned no further), for Brahms, with Hanslick accompanying, Brahms liked the song and asked Miss Morduch to repeat it. Another dramatic song, "Svarta rosor" (Black roses) was well received at the Paris Exhibition of 1900.

An early work by Sibelius, *The Rapids-Shooter's Brides*,[4] a ballad for either baritone or mezzo-soprano with orchestral accompaniment, is to mediocre lyrics by A. Oksanen. Sibelius's score is in the traditional German-Scandinavian style of writing, except for the hero's recitative, which shows Sibelius's sensitivity to the demands of the text. Because of the fact that Sibelius was reading Heine at the time and planning on a tone poem based on his works, he was attracted to Oksanen's poem about Vellamo, a water-sprite of Finnish folklore, falling in love with a rapids-shooter and destroying him and his fiancée Anna out of jealousy. The parallels between the story of Vellamo and Heine's "Lorelei" are obvious. Although the Sibelius work does not represent the composer at his best, it was well received in Helsinki, and even some critics welcomed the idea of Sibelius staying away from his more innovative tendencies.

Young Sibelius found it easy to identify with Runeberg's idealistic views and his genuine admiration for, if not adherence to, the Lutheran church of Finland. However, the young composer's worries about a rapidly growing family and the failure of his plans for an opera based on the *Kalevala* made it easy for him to identify with the Swedish writer Viktor Rydberg. Rydberg's thinking is characterized by the conflict between idealism and the realities of daily living. Obviously his symbolic poem of "Skogsrået" (The wood-nymph), representing the temptations of life as a threat to duty, reflected Sibelius's feelings as a head of a household, a role he was entirely unsuited for. Sibelius made the Rydberg poem into a melodrama for voice, piano, two horns, and strings in 1894.

Whatever doubts Sibelius might have had about Runeberg's view of life in high school after reading August Strindberg's *Giftas*, a collection of short stories on married life, and *Röda rummet* (The red room), identifying with the artist-hero of the novel, Strindberg's influence on the school-boy seems to have been prompted more by fantasy than as an expression of true feelings, since the early compositions reflect a genuine Runebergian spirit. However, in 1902, when Sibelius joined a new circle of friends, the Euterpists, Strindberg's ideas started to compete more strongly than before with Runeberg's views.

The Euterpists' circle derived its name from the musical journal *Euterpe*, founded in Helsinki in 1901. The group consisted of Swedish speakers, among whom were architects, a drama critic, and so on. With the new circle Sibelius's thinking turned somewhat away from Finnish national romanticism and the earlier group of friends called Symposium, due to new ideals and influences the Euterpists received form Sweden known there as *åttiotalet*[5] (the 1880s). The beginning of the new movement is usually counted from the publication of Strindberg's *Röda rummet* in 1879.

With Strindberg's influence the Scandinavian intellectuals started to embrace Schopenhauer's pessimism and Eduard von Hartmann's view, according to which the world process was a struggle between blind impulse and Kantian reason. Although prompted by Darwin to take a new look at man and his environment, Strindberg could not maintain his mental balance basing his views on Darwin's law of competition and natural selection, and he had to turn to Kierkegaard's preoccupation with the meaning of true Christianity.

Both Strindberg and Sibelius were inspired by Swedish mystics like Erik Johan Stagnelius, and as early as 1887 Sibelius composed a suite called *Trånaden* (Longing), which was intended as an accompaniment to Stagnelius's poem "Suckarnas mystär" (The mystery of sighs). Sibelius's attraction to Stagnelius can be easily understood. The Swedish poet expressed many of the same ideas as Runeberg, and one of the leading themes in both poets' works is nature as a symbol of man's yearning for heaven. Each poet wrote a poem called "Flyttfåglarna" (Migratory birds), using the symbolism of bird migrations for man's transitory soul. In "Suckarnas mystär" man and the entire creation are doomed, and only after being purified can man attain the freedom he sighs for. Stagnelius was strongly influenced by Jakob Böhme's and Swedenborg's mystic beliefs.

The Christian-based mysticism of Runeberg and Stagnelius influenced many of Sibelius's solo songs, the bulk of which are concerned with Nordic moods of nature. In a song like "På verandan vid havet" (On a balcony by the sea), a Rydberg setting from the early years of this century, we are dealing with more than moods of nature: nature is a manifestation of eternity. The poet asks the reader whether he remembers the silence when everything — the shores, the sky, and the sea — seemed to be sunk in yearning for eternity. The key phrase of the poem with its reference to nature exuding a sense of foreknowledge of God points to Christian-based mysticism, which was a strong force in the thinking of the Scandinavians, including Kierkegaard.

On the other hand Strindberg, who also had a strong streak of the mystic in him, had considerable influence on Sibelius during the Euterpist period, but Sibelius never accepted Strindberg's approval of Georg Brandes's attacks on the status quo in social and literary matters. Although many Scandinavian intellectuals were enthusiastic about Brandes, Sibelius characterized him as "too cold and clear."[6]   Therefore, Sibelius's output leans clearly towards traditional Baltic bourgeois thinking rather than the more extremist view of the Euterpists in their admiration for Brandes.

During all of Sibelius's career there is in evidence a grip that the spirit of the Baltic community had on him. Whenever he was not involved in a major composition — sometimes even while working on one — he would return to the safe world of Runeberg and set one of his poems to music or compose a solo instrument piece, many of which are called "humoresques" or "romances" in the style of his fellow Scandinavian composers. They are expressions of a world based on idealism, even to the point of naïveté, interpreted in a style that is a curious mixture of romantic lyricism and touches of realism in true Runebergian spirit. The fact that this part of Sibelius's output shows the least amount of development in the man and the composer justifies the belief that without the influence of Hämeenlinna and the Finnish nationalistic movement, Sibelius might never have been able to rise to the front rank of composers.

As for many of Sibelius's countrymen, Finnish folk poetry was to become one of his chief inspirational sources. In order to understand the causes of this state of affairs, we have to take a look at the developments that led to the prominence of Finnish folk poetry and of folk song in the country's cultural life.

While much of the Finnish nationalistic movement, as well as of the Finnish-Swedish nationalistic spirit, can be accredited to the spreading in Scandinavia of Herder's ideas and his emphasis on the importance of a nation's own identity, including its language, there was a growing interest in Finnish folklore both in Finland and even abroad ever since the days of Agricola. The publisher of the oldest dictionary containing Finnish words was a Swede, Ericus Schroderus (d. 1639), who included in his *Lexicon Latino-Scondicum* some words pertaining to Finnish folklore.[7] The first Finnish grammar, published in Turku in 1649 by the Swedish-born professor and later bishop Eskil Petraeus, included Finnish riddles as examples of Finnish prosody.

Much of the early collecting of folk poetry was carried on by ministers and physicians, who were in close contact with the peasant population. By far the most ambitious work by a non-specialist was done by Zacharias Topelius, Sr. (d. 1831), a medical doctor who wrote down Finnish folk poetry while traveling among the peasants to vaccinate them against smallpox. Topelius published altogether eighty-three runos and magic sayings and twenty-eight folk poems of the more recent type.[8] His work was important also in pointing out Karelia as the region where the runos were best preserved.

Inspired by Herder's ideas and by Thomas Percy and James MacPherson, whose *Ossian's Songs* were originally considered genuine folk songs, Porthan published his *Dissertatio de Poesi*

Fennica in the latter part of the eighteenth century and laid the groundwork for systematic study of Finnish folk poetry.   He called attention to the existence of different versions of the runos and discussed their meter and other characteristics.

In the early nineteenth century, there were several Finnish scholars in Uppsala who were interested in Finnish folk poetry. They came into contact with a young German scholar, Hans Rudolph von Schröter, who was in Uppsala for the purpose of publishing Swedish folk poetry in German, and with the aid of the Finns he put together *Finnische Runen* without knowing a word of Finnish.   It was published in 1819 and contained thirty-four poems and magic sayings in Finnish together with a German translation.

The famous Danish philologist and folklore specialist Rasmus Rask visited Turku in 1818, and his trip inspired several Finnish scholars to engage in studies of Finnish folklore and folk poetry. One of these was Reinhold von Becker, a professor at Turku University, who gave Lönnroth, a medical student and son of a poor village tailor, some runos dealing with Väinämöinen.   On the basis of these and some additonal runos published in a Turku weekly, Lönnroth finished his master's thesis entitled *De Väinämöine priscorum Fennorum numine* in 1827.[9]   The following year he made his first trip to Karelia to collect folk poetry in the field.   As the result of this trip and subsequent trips he published in 1835 his *Kalevala taikka vanhoja Karjalan Runoja Suomen kansan muinoisista ajoista* (Kalevala, or Old Karelian runos from the ancient times of the Finnish people).   In 1849 Lönnroth published his complete edition of the *Kalevala* and in 1840 a collection of lyric poems, which he called *Kanteletar*.   Soon the *Kalevala* was referred to as the national epic of Finland.

The term "national epic" brings to mind works like *Beowulf*, or the *Nibelungenlied* or the *Iliad* and *Odyssey*, with a more or less continuous plot relating stories of heroes who were brave, intelligent, and superhuman.   How does the *Kalevala* compare with these works?   The main difference lies in the fact that the heroes of the *Kalevala* are more human than superhuman and, therefore, the work is more democratic in spirit than the more chivalrous character of the other epics.

The runos of the *Kalevala* are probably from the late Viking Age (about 800-1300 A.D.), and they include long cycles on three heroes, Väinämöinen, an old seer, Ilmarinen, a mastersmith, and Lemminkäinen, often characterized as the Finnish Don Juan and thus the only romantic hero of the work, a fact indicated even by his epithets *kaunis Kaukomieli* "the beautiful one who longs to get far away" and *lieto Lemminkäinen* "reckless Lemminkäinen."

There are also individual runos that are either loosely or not at all connected with the main cycles. Since Lönnroth compiled the material gathered from different locales and from dozens of runo-singers, there is no real unity of style in the work. It is generally accepted that Lönnroth himself composed lines 1-110 of runo I, lines 513-620 of runo L, and some connecting lines.

As to the impact of the *Kalevala*, it is fair to say that without it Finnish-language culture might never have acquired the dominance it has today in Finland. The publication of old Finnish runos prompted works inspired by the spirit of nationalism in the fields of art, music, literature, and architecture. The Finnish Pavilion of the Paris Exhibition of 1900 was an expression of this spirit, as were Kajanus's *Aino* Symphony and Armas Järnefelt's *Korsholma*, which derived its inspiration from a medieval castle of the same name outside the Ostrobothnian city of Vaasa. On the heels of Sibelius's *Kullervo* there was a number of works inspired by the spirit of the nationalistic movement. Akseli Gallén-Kallela based a number of canvases on the *Kalevala*, and Juhani Aho published his novel *Panu* about the dawn of the Christian era in Finland and inspired Sibelius to consider a tone poem based on the work, although this was one of numerous plans by Sibelius that never materialized. Eino Leino published his poems *Helkavirsiä* (Whitsuntide songs) based on old poetry still found in western Finland not far from Hämeenlinna. Despite the title of the songs, the theory is accepted by many scholars that they originate in a pagan tradition of a spring festival that later coincided with Whitsuntide, just as Christmas with a pagan mid-winter feast of the Germanic peoples and with the Roman Saturnalia.

Had Sibelius not been brought up in the Finnish-speaking town of Hämeenlinna and not read the *Kalevala* in school in the original Finnish, most likely he would not have joined the Finnish nationalist movement. He would have remained as Baltic in his outlook as the Järnefelts who, despite their interest in the Finnish language and in Finland's struggle for its independence, were basically cosmopolites. The head of the family, Lieutenant-General Alexander Järnefelt, although one of the early champions of the Finnish language, was above all a conservative, upper-class Baltic. His wife Elizabeth, who came from a Baltic noble family, and in particular their son Arvid, the writer, liked to pose as Tolstoyans, upper-class idealists dressed like peasants. Sibelius, who liked to dress like a gentleman, disapproved of this posing. During his years at Hämeenlinna he had acquired a more genuine understanding of and feeling for things Finnish than the Järnefelts in their literary salon, which attracted liberal Finnish speakers only, because Mrs. Järnefelt had refused to study Swedish.

Among frequent guests at the salon was the writer Juhani Aho, who fell hopelessly in love with the Järnefelts' youngest daughter Aino, who, however, accepted Sibelius's proposal for marriage in 1890, shortly before his year of study in Vienna.

Sibelius's stay in Vienna was not musically productive and his attempt at putting into practice the conviction that the only way for him to find his own musical identity was through reliance on Finland's untapped musical resources proved to be difficult indeed. He kept tearing up numerous musical sketches based on the story of Kullervo. He showed Fuchs some of them, only to have his teacher call them "crude and barbaric." He suddenly gave up work on his composition and wrote what were to have been the first two movements, calling them *Overture* and *Ballet Scene*, and sent them to Kajanus. A few days later he wired Kajanus not to perform them, but Kajanus ignored the cable and conducted the *Overture* on April 23, 1891, which was Sibelius's debut as an orchestral composer.

The interesting feature of the *Overture* and the *Ballet Scene* is the manifestation of the duality of the composer's inspiration, a characteristic that was to surface time and again in various forms during his career. The *Overture* was the first large-scale work to point to the Finnish-influenced, runo-inspired style, as can be seen from a statement by Karl Flodin, the leading music critic in Helsinki: "Sibelius is now definitely going his own way; whether he does so consciously is an open question. However . . . undeterred by traditional rules, he hearkens solely to the inspiration of his own genius [which is] so incontestably original and individualistic."[10] The *Ballet Scene*, on the other hand, originated in Sibelius's cosmopolitan side and revealed his enthusiasm for the Viennese waltz, although Sibelius's spirit is closer to that of Ravel's *La Valse* and lacks the typically Viennese gaiety. It is worth noting that Sibelius's piece dates from 1891 and Ravel's, from 1919.

However, Sibelius was not ready to abandon work on *Kullervo*. Why did the topic haunt him? The cycle of poems had attracted others before Sibelius. Aleksis Kivi, the first noteworthy Finnish-language writer, wrote a tragedy called *Kullervo* in 1864. There were precedents also in music: Filip von Schantz had composed an overture to *Kullervo* and had planned an entire opera based on the story, but his plans were thwarted by his early death, and Kajanus had written an orchestral piece, *The Death of Kullervo*.

Even before these works there had been academic interest in the runo on Kullervo. In 1853 Fredrik Cygnaeus, a literary critic, published a study entitled "Det tragiska elementet i Kalevala," in which he emphasized the tragic element in the story of Kullervo.[11] He interpreted the protagonist as a man destined to be a hero, born with the power of a giant and a burning desire to use it. But when he became a slave, his ambition turned into hatred. At the end he is destroyed, not by outside forces but by the conflicts within himself.

In his mid-twenties Sibelius felt that despite his talent he was a failure with no major work to his credit, a realization that was all the more poignant because of his desire to marry Aino Järnefelt. Thus he was driven partly for personal reasons to the story of Kullervo, but why did he choose the symphonic form with vocal parts? He obviously considered the symphony the most appropriate form to bring out the dramatic conflict inherent in the topic, and the inclusion of vocal parts may be connected with the runo inspiration as well as with Kajanus's *Aino* Symphony, which has a choral finale. Sibelius had heard the work performed in Berlin during his student year. A powerful performance of Beethoven's Ninth Symphony during that year may also have influenced Sibelius.

The first musical sketches for *Kullervo* were based on an actual Finnish folk tune according to a letter Sibelius sent to his fiancée from Vienna. Although, to this writer's knowledge, the final version of *Kullervo* does not quote any Finnish folk tunes, there are themes in it that *could* be folk tunes. This made the Finns realize that they were dealing with a work of art which, for the first time in Finnish music, expressed something of the essence of folk music. The Finns were keenly aware of the cultural significance of *Kullervo*, and at the end of the première Sibelius received a laurel wreath with the inscription "Siitäpä latu menevi, ura uusi urkenevi" (The course will lead this way, the path lies newly opened) on the ribbon.[12] The symbolism of the event was all the more poignant because of the fact that the quote is from a runo and that the wreath was handed to Sibelius by Kajanus, up to then Finland's leading composer. Although the première was musically only a qualified success — the orchestra almost drowned out the soloists, probably because of the poor acoustics of the University Festival Hall — it broke the Järnefelts' resistance to Aino's marriage to Sibelius, which took place in 1892.

Sibelius took a considerable step away from continental music with his *Kullervo*, but he could not forget his admiration for Wagner during his student years. After his return to Finland he felt that if German mythology could provide Wagner's inspiration, so could Finnish runos serve as a starting-point for a Finnish opera, a logical notion since opera is a product of social culture to a greater extent than any other form of serious music.

The first concrete idea for an opera probably came from Adolf Paul, a friend of Sibelius's in Helsinki, where they had been Busoni's students. Although Paul afterwards lived mostly in Germany and Sweden, he visited Helsinki quite often and used to join Kajanus, Gallén-Kallela, and Sibelius at meetings in Helsinki restaurants. It was at one of these "Symposium" sessions that Paul suggested to Sibelius that the two of them should work on an opera, because "that's what we still badly need in Finland. Besides both of us need money."[13] However, Sibelius did not have much faith in Paul as a librettist and he asked J. H. Erkko for his cooperation on a libretto based on the *Kalevala* episode of Väinämöinen building a boat. Erkko did not turn out to be of great help and Sibelius tried to work on the libretto himself. When he showed it to Kaarlo Bergbom, the director of the Finnish Theater and founder of the Finnish Opera, Bergbom felt that the libretto lacked dramatic tension and conflict.

Basically Sibelius felt that Bergbom was right, but he could not give up his idea for an opera. He studied the scores of *Tannhäuser* and *Lohengrin*, and some influence of the latter can still be detected in "The Swan of Tuonela," which was to be the overture to *The Building of the Boat*. He was so overwhelmed by *Parsifal* at Bayreuth that his "innermost heartstrings throbbed."[14] Then he saw *Lohengrin* and his enthusiasm for Wagner started to fade in the highly commercial atmosphere of Bayreuth. After seeing performances of *Tristan* and *Götterdämmerung* in Munich, Sibelius decided that his was not an operatic talent but rather that of a "tone painter and poet" in the style of Liszt. He studied the scores of some of Liszt's tone poems and the *Faust* Symphony, and the tragic hero of the latter work may have been instrumental in changing Sibelius's "steadfast old Väinämöinen" into "reckless Lemminkäinen."

An important event was Sibelius's visit to an exhibit of Arnold Böcklin's paintings. He was intrigued in particular by "Gefilde der Seligen," a symbolistic painting of swans gliding on a black body of water, which obviously in his mind became associated with the swan of "Death's dark river" in the *Kalevala*. As a result, Sibelius's sketches for *The Building of the Boat* started to crystallize into *Four Legends*, the original title of *Lemminkäinen*, which premiered in April 1896 with the composer conducting. Afterwards Sibelius revised "The Swan of Tuonela" and "Lemminkäinen's Homecoming," and they appeared in print in 1900. The other two legends, "Lemminkäinen and the Maidens of Saari" and "Lemminkäinen in Tuonela," were not performed again until the centenary celebration of the *Kalevala* in 1935. It is commonly believed that the scores for the latter two legends were found among Kajanus's papers, although Harold Johnson claims that Sibelius had them all along until he donated them to the Kalevala Society in 1921.

"The Swan of Tuonela" was based on an initial sketch Sibelius made while visiting Erkko in Kuopio, where they were supposed to be working on the libretto of *The Building of the Boat*, and "Lemminkäinen in Tuonela" was probably based on the original idea for the opera of Väinämöinen in Tuonela.[15]   The title of the first legend, "Lemminkäinen and the Island Maidens," as it was first called in English, has caused considerable controversy. It was believed to have been based on runo XXIX of the *Kalevala* until some experts started to say that the correct title should be "Lemminkäinen and the Maidens of Saari," because the episode most likly refers to runo XI.

A number of scholars have argued about the name Saari (island) and most agree that it does indeed refer to a specific island, most likely either to Hiidenmaa or Saarenmaa off the coast of Estonia or else to Ahvenanmaa (Åland) between Finland and Sweden. Kaarle Krohn and some others believe that Saari refers to Ahvenanmaa,[16] but, in this writer's view, the references in the Lemminkäinen cycle to Kyllikki's suitors coming from Estonia or Ingermanland, as will be pointed out in connection with Sibelius's *Kyllikki*, make Saarenmaa the more likely answer and, therefore, "Lemminkäinen and the Maidens of Saari" the more appropriate title. When Nils-Erik Ringbom asked Sibelius about his view, the composer answered: "[It is] correct to view the island episode as the background of the work," and he added, "I merely wanted to depict the wanton life of the hero and not any specific action in detail."[17] This statement confirms that Sibelius wanted to treat the topic symbolically, and thus the title of one legend is not all that significant. From the textual point of view, there are passages in the two runos, XI and XXIX, that are almost identical, especially in the verses that describe Lemminkäinen's wantonness, the aspect of the hero that the composer was most interested in.

In psychological terms, "Lemminkäinen and the Maidens of Saari" could reflect Sibelius's feeling of inferiority towards the Järnefelts, as expressed in Lemminkäinen's mother's warning to her son (runo XI):[18]

> My son, do not curry favor with those above you,
> You may not be welcome among the mighty of Saari.

Sibelius, nevertheless, had a healthy dose of pride in his talent, as stated by Lemminkäinen (runo XI):

> I may not be high-born and my house elegant,
> But I have a flashing sword, a brilliant blade . . .
> It was sharpened by the Demon, polished by gods.

"The Swan of Tuonela" and "Lemminkäinen in Tuonela" are based on the part of the cycle of poems where the hero, after abducting Kyllikki and getting angry at her for breaking her promise of never going to young people's dances, goes to Pohjola to look for a new wife. The Mistress of Pohjola promises her daughter to him, if he manages to accomplish three deeds: to shoot a deer, to bridle a gelding, and to shoot the swan on Death's dark river. Lemminkäinen goes to the river where Soppy Hat, a herdsman, is waiting for him. The herdsman kills Lemminkäinen and throws the body into the river. The blood-stained son of Death completes the task by cutting the body into pieces.

When Lemminkäinen's mother sees blood oozing from a broom in the house, she recognizes that as a bad omen and sets out to Tuonela with a rake in her hand. After a great deal of misinformation about her son's whereabouts, she finally finds pieces of her son's body in the river and starts to rake the waters in order to harvest all the parts, which she puts together with infinite patience, fitting bones to bones and veins to veins. She calls him to life with the help of ointments and charms and by finally evoking God.

When Lemminkäinen wants to make another attempt to gain the hand of Pohjola's daughter, his mother gets angry and tells him to leave the wretched swans alone. However, in "Lemminkäinen's Homecoming" the hero is seized by wanderlust once again, when he hears his boat lament that he has not been to war for a long time (runo XXX). Despite his mother's pleading, Lemminkäinen sets out to Pohjola once more with his old companion-in-arms Tiera (Snowfoot). This time the Mistress of Pohjola conjures a terrible frost in order to destroy Lemminkäinen and his men, but the hero manages to save himself and his crew by using charms. After wandering in the woods, they return home.

While in Sibelius's *Kullervo* the protagonist, in true romantic spirit, represents the composer, Lemminkäinen is the symbol for only one facet of him, his wanderlust. This has induced some observers to claim that the *Lemminkäinen* suite really is a symphony. We might recall that in his later years Sibelius liked to refer to the suite as a symphony. Others, meanwhile, have argued that the suite could not be considered a symphony because of the programmatic use of a leitmotif. Sibelius himself denied this by stating that, despite a certain similarity between given motifs, the parallels were not intentional. In his view, there was something "too calculatingly purposive" about the use of a leitmotif.[19]

Some analysts feel that Sibelius was trying to deny Wagner's influence on him, but there is, indeed, good reason to believe that Sibelius's use of a given motif in various contexts could reflect a practice known to him since his youthful years from Bellman's music. Massengale refers to the Swedish song-writer's use of "signature" melodies, for example a march-like tune to represent Corporal Mollberg in *Fredmans epistlar*.[20] We should also remember that Sibelius saw a performance of *Der Freischütz* while he was a student in Helsinki and of *Lélio* in Berlin and that already Weber used some recurring themes as representations of a person or an idea, as did Hector Berlioz in *Lélio* and the *Symphonie fantastique*, although Sibelius evidently became acquainted with the last-mentioned work a few years later, in 1898.

On the other hand, Wagner associated the leitmotif with literary antecedents and pointed out the fixed Homeric epithet as a parallel. Thus it is conceivable that Sibelius's use of a given musical germ for Lemminkäinen could stand as a symbol for *lieto Lemminkäinen* (reckless Lemminkäinen) and, consequently, as a representation of the hero only in abstract terms as a symbol for wantonness. This would justify the argument that the work is symphonic, spanning "the extreme poles of human existence: life raised to its nth power, and death to the utmost limit,"[21] even if the basically programmatic character of the suite is undeniable.

It was Lemminkäinen and his wanderlust that still intrigued Sibelius in the choice of the topic of *Tiera*, for wind and brass, which he composed for the send-off concert of the Helsinki Philharmonic Orchestra's trip to the Paris World Exhibition of 1900. We can see in the topic reflections of Sibelius's problems with temptations of good times with friends in Lemminkäinen talking his friend Tiera into sharing new adventures despite the warnings of the latter's family because of Tiera's recent marriage. However, wanderlust wins and Tiera grabs his spear defiantly, ready for another adventure with his friend.

Manifestations of personal concerns are equally evident in *Pohjola's Daughter* despite the fact that the work is, at least superficially, one of Sibelius's most programmatic tone poems. It is based on the same cycle of runos as the composer's would-be opera, *The Building of the Boat*, and it would seem to indicate that the wreckage still haunted Sibelius in 1906.

In runo VI Väinämöinen goes to Pohjola, where Joukahainen sees him riding across a river and tries to shoot him, hitting only his horse. Väinämöinen falls into the river and is carried by a strong gust to open sea, where he floats several days. An eagle spots Väinämöinen and wants to reward him for leaving a tree as a nesting place for birds while he was cutting his clearing. The eagle guides Väinämöinen to Pohjola, where the Mistress of Pohjola finds him sitting on a shore, hungry, crying, and homesick. Väinämöinen tells her that in one's own country even water from a birchbark shoe is better than mead from a golden bowl in a foreign country. The Mistress of Pohjola, a clever bargainer, promises to give her daughter to Väinämöinen in return for a magic mill, Sampo. The seer has to admit that only Ilmarinen, the mastersmith, is capable of forging a Sampo. When the disappointed suitor is leaving Pohjola, he sees a maiden sitting on a rainbow weaving. He falls in love with the girl and wants to take her along, but the girl tells him teasingly that a tomtit warned her about becoming a bride (runo VIII):

> A girl in her father's house is like a berry on good soil,
> A daughter-in-law in her husband's house like a dog in chains.

The girl reacts to Väinämöinen's persistent wooing by promising, in jest, to be his, if he can perform several tasks: make a boat from the fragments of her spindle, tie an egg into invisible knots, and so on. While working on the boat, Väinämöinen strikes his knee making a gushing wound. He has to give up wooing in order to look for a magician to cure his knee.

It is possible to interpret Sibelius's tone poem opening on a somber cello theme as a description of Pohjola. Väinämöinen's and the girl's appearances are announced and the sound of her spinning wheel is heard on the violins and the girl's teasing on the harp. In the second part Väinämöinen becomes more agitated and the girl ends up increasingly contemptuous. The tasks are beyond the hero's powers, and the tone poem ends in a delicate pianissimo to express Väinämöinen's sense of resignation.

However, in two short but important motifs, as confirmed by their reappearance at the end of the tone poem, the augmented fifth and fourth probably symbolize Väinämöinen's suffering, and we may therefore have an indication that the hero's suffering really is the topic of the work despite its title. This seems to be supported by the fact that in "Lemminkäinen in Tuonela" a variation of Lemminkäinen's theme with an added augmented fifth tenaciously repeated by the woodwinds seems to symbolize the hero's suffering and death. This might support the argument that both the *Lemminkäinen* suite and *Pohjola's Daughter* could be considered symphonic. Harold Truscott points out that Sibelius called *Pohjola's Daughter* originally *Symphonic Fantasia*, and he is of the opinion that the work "really is a genuine one-movement symphony."[22]

Although the *Kalevala* inspired Sibelius most often to write either orchestral or choral works, in 1904 he based a lengthy piano composition, his *Kyllikki* suite, on the same cycle of poems as the *Lemminkäinen* music. In the *Kyllikki* episode Lemminkäinen goes to Saari to court the fairest maiden, Kyllikki, and all the girls of the island laugh at him at first, but soon he becomes the hero of every girl, except Kyllikki, who is a proud girl with many suitors from as far away as Estonia and Ingria (runo XI). The girl rejects them, one after another, as she rejects Lemminkäinen who kidnaps her, pushes her onto a sledge and takes her home with him. When they come near Lemminkäinen's house, Kyllikki says contemptuously that the house is nothing but a miserable ruin. Encouraged by his mother, Lemminkäinen promises to build a better house. He takes an oath from Kyllikki never to go to young people's dances and promises in return not to go to war. Kyllikki breaks her promise, Lemminkäinen gets angry and sets out for Pohjola to find a new wife.

The failure of the *Kyllikki* suite can be ascribed to two factors: first of all, the piano was not Sibelius's instrument and, secondly, the episode was too vast a topic to be interpreted on one instrument. When Sibelius tries to depict the events of the poem realistically in his music, the result is tedious. On the other hand, in his choral works based on Finnish folk poetry, Sibelius had a wider range of possibilities at his disposal and, consequently, the results match his orchestral achievements in works based on the *Kalevala.*

An indication of the fact that inspiration derived from Finnish folk poetry was, in Sibelius's mind, closely associated with the vocal medium is an early choral suite, *Rakastava*, based on three short poems of the *Kanteletar*. The first movement, called also "Rakastava," is based on the poem "Missä armahani?" (Where is my beloved?) from the so-called Shepherd's Songs. The poems are typical of Finnish folk poetry in that the protagonist's mood is reflected in nature, as in the second part, "Armahan kulku" (The way of the lover), in which the significance of every object in nature is interpreted in relation to the lover's feelings:[23]

> Here my darling walked . . .
> The rock is much brighter, The boulder better than the others,
> The heath twice as pretty, The valley five times as gentle,
> The woods six times as luxuriant, The whole forest more pleasant,
> Because my beloved walked here, My darling stepped here.

In both parts of the suite Sibelius interprets the lover's longing in a gentle and restrained manner. The main motif of the first movement expresses love in an upward trend in the melodic line, which is in keeping with the composer's belief in love as sublime, not sensuous, as it is interpreted also in the madrigal-like setting of the third movement, "Hyvää iltaa, lintuseni" (Good evening, my little bird).

Sibelius also arranged *Rakastava* for male choir and strings as well as for mixed chorus *a cappella*. The work is known outside Finland in the transcription for strings, triangle and timpani from 1911. The style of the orchestration is subdued in keeping with the tone of the poems and is also typical of the composer during that period, approximately the time of the Fourth Symphony. The subdued character of *Rakastava* could be interpreted as Sibelius's way of stating that he intended his love music to be quite unlike the paragon of the genre in *Tristan und Isolde*. Sibelius considered Wagner too demonstrative with his characters shouting "Ich liebe dich" at the top of their voices, a declaration which, in Sibelius's view, had to be whispered tenderly.

Sibelius's view is also that of the *Kalevala*. Although there are references to carnal love in the work and passion is an important element in the episodes with Lemminkäinen and Kyllikki and Väinämöinen and Aino and there is condemnation of incest in the story of Kullervo — probably due to Christian influence, since pagan cultures in general do not condemn incest — the emotions are implied rather than stated. Therefore, Sibelius's interpretation of the seduction scene in *Kullervo* in an orchestral interlude is in keeping with the spirit of the *Kalevala*.

Something of the gentle atmosphere of *Rakastava* as well as of the quiet resignation of the ending of *Pohjola's Daughter* is expressed in *The Bard*, a short tone poem dating from 1913. Sibelius himself said of *The Bard* that it was not based on the *Kalevala* but rather that it referred to a bard in the Nordic sense. There is, indeed, a poem by that title by Runeberg, and Erik Tawaststjerna feels that Sibelius's *Bard* had to be inspired by the Runeberg work. He supports this theory by claiming that Sibelius himself mentioned that the brass theme built on ascending fourths and fifths was inspired by the sound of the *lur*, the old Scandinavian instrument. However, in refutation of Tawaststjerna's theory, it could be pointed out that the arpeggiated chords, which imitate the bard's instrument, would seem to be a reflection of Väinämöinen's kantele. This theory is also supported by the realistic mood of melancholy in *The Bard*, which is related to Väinämöinen's resignation at the end of *Pohjola's Daughter*.

From the point of view of the development of Finnish music, Sibelius's choral songs based on Finnish folk poetry are important, because with *a cappella* songs like "Venematka" (The Boat journey), "Saarella palaa" (Fire on the island), and "Min rastas raataa" (Busy as a thrush) Sibelius initiated a new style of choral writing in Finland.   Choral song has traditionally been an important part of the cultural life of Finland, and practically every community, no matter how small, has its own choral society. Since there has been a great deal of demand for music of this type, numerous church music directors and music teachers have been very productive as composers, frequently with easy opportunities of getting their creative efforts performed. Naturally the standards have not always been the highest, something Sibelius must have been aware of, since his earliest compositions included his choral entry, the *Rakastava* suite, at a contest won by the more traditional effort of Emil Genetz, his music teacher at the Hämeenlinna school.

However, Sibelius's choral suite of *Rakastava* was not anywhere as innovative as his later choral works such as "Venematka" and "Saarella palaa."   His setting of "Venematka," which dates from 1893, is based on runo XL of the *Kalevala*. According to the canto, Väinämöinen, Ilmarinen, and Lemminkäinen are returning from Pohjola, where they stole the magic mill Sampo, which they lost eventually.   After they survive a terrible storm conjured by the Mistress of Pohjola, the journey is now running smoothly.   Sibelius's setting picks up the story describing how Väinämöinen "singing he steered over the water, over the waves striking joyous music," and it renders marvellously the sense of joy, probably reflecting childhood memories of delightful boatrides at Loviisa, as well as the onward push of the craft.

"Saarella palaa" is based on a poem from the *Kanteletar*:

> There is a fire burning on the island; who is burning it?
> A suitor is burning a fire there.
> What is he working at? Decorating his sledge.
> What is he going to do with the sledge?
> (To bring) a maiden in the sledge
> What is the maiden working at?
> Weaving a cloth of gold, a cloth of silver.

We can see the familiar references to Lemminkäinen's abduction of Kyllikki and to Pohjola's daughter weaving her "cloth of gold" expressed in this version in the form of a riddle, a common type of expression in Finnish folk poetry. Sibelius's setting reflects the nature of the verse admirably.

A clear indication of a less personal, more cosmic approach to Finnish folk poetry on the part of Sibelius came with *Tulen synty* (The Origin of Fire), which he was commissioned to write for the inauguration of Kansallisteatteri (the Finnish National Theater) in 1902, where his daughter Ruth later became a leading actress, and with *Luonnotar*, which dates from 1913.

Tulen synty is based on runo XLVII relating the tale of the sun and the moon coming down in order to listen to Väinämöinen playing his kantele. Louhi, the wicked Mistress of Pohjola, captures them, hides them in a mountain and even steals fire from homes, and now there is perpetual night, pitch-dark. The climax of the work comes with Ukko, the chief god of the ancient Finns, striking light and fire from his sword like a Finnish Zeus as his gift to mankind, obviously an appropriate symbol for the occasion of the inaugural. Sibelius's *Tulen synty* is for baritone solo, chorus, and orchestra. The work is divided into two parts, which form an interesting contrast. After the monotonous recitation by the soloist, the male chorus takes over and the creation of fire is described in colorful orchestration, which includes a cymbal, triangle, and bells.

A companion piece to *Tulen synty* is an *a cappella* song, "Terve, kuu!" (Hail, Moon!), based also on the *Kalevala*. It represents a feeling of primitive worship of nature with an added Christian element. After the chief god, Ukko, struck fire with his sword, Ilmarinen, the master-smith, tried to forge a new sun and a new moon, but he could not make them cast any light. After Väinämöinen discovered that the sun and the moon were locked in a mountain in Pohjola, he and Ilmarinen went there in order to unlock the mountain. The Mistress of Pohjola panicked and released the sun and the moon. When Väinämöinen saw them back in their proper places, he greeted them (runo XLIX):

> Hail, to you, moon, for your pale glow!
> Hail, beauteous moon, for showing your face!
> Hail, lovely sun, for dawning! Hail, sun, for rising!

The lines at the end of the last poem of the *Kalevala* cycle on the three heroes, Väinämöinen, Lemminkäinen, and Ilmarinen, inspired Sibelius to write a polyphonic choral setting, which has as many as three texts being intoned at one time.

Another work representing Sibelius's interest in the cosmic issues as told in the *Kalevala* is *Luonnotar*, a tone poem for soprano and orchestra, premiered, strangely enough, in Gloucester, England, after several failed target dates.

Sibelius's composition is based on the story of Creation as told in the *Kalevala*. Runo I introduces Luonnotar, the Virgin of Nature, also called Ilmatar, the Virgin of Air, who got bored, came down and settled on the waves to be rocked by a gust of wind, which blew her pregnant. After the immaculate conception, as told in the *Kalevala*, she carried the fetus for seven hundred years and nothing was born. Finally she calls the chief god, Ukko, for help, and a bird comes looking for a nesting place. Luonnotar raises her knee, the bird lays eggs on it and sits on them for three days. When Luonnotar feels burning on her knee, she shakes it. The eggs fall and break, and the bits were turned into fine things:

> The bottom half of one egg/ becomes the earth beneath,
> The top half of another egg/ the heavens above.
> The top half of one yolk/ starts to glow like the sun,
> The top half of one white/ starts to gleam palely like the moon.
> Any speckles on an egg/ become stars in heaven,
> Any black spots on an egg/ become clouds in the sky.

The poem does not translate well into a foreign language, and despite — or perhaps because of — Sibelius's keen observation of the text, the Finnishness of the tone poem has prevented this fine work from becoming popular abroad, just as has been the case with the composer's choral songs.

In his choral settings Sibelius adheres to the ancient character of the runos with such old techniques as the *organum* effect in "Saarella palaa" with parallel 6-3 chords, the madrigal style in the last movement of his choral suite of *Rakastava*, and the polyphonic technique of "Hail, Moon!" Sibelius's fresh approach to the text, which is no longer subservient to the music, dictates the melodic flow in its observance of the rhythmic and cadential demands of the language. Therefore, many of his choral works, especially the numerous ones inspired by Finnish folk poetry, foreshadow the choral writing technique of Karl Orff in *Carmina burana* or of Stravinsky in such works as *Les Noces* and *Symphony of Psalms*.

Sibelius's early works based on the *Kalevala* were inspired by the spirit of nationalism and, consistent with romantic ideals, by the composer's identification with the hero. In *Kullervo* the composer expressed interest in the tragic fate of the protagonist, in *Lemminkäinen*, he makes reference to the Don Juan side of his own character, although the autobiographical element in the latter is by no means as obvious as in the former. In *Pohjola's Daughter* the personal element recedes even further, and the work probably expresses human suffering and disappointments on a level that is much less personal than in the previous works.

In *Tulen synty* and *Luonnotar* Sibelius wrestles with the cosmic view and with the eternal questions of man: where does it all come from? What is man's relationship to his origins? To what extent can man achieve harmony with nature? These issues are the basic substance of his symphonies as well as of *Tapiola*.

The connection between *Tapiola* and the *Kalevala* is so vague as to be almost in doubt. A rare "program" is provided by the composer in the form of a quatrain. In it he refers to the Forest's mighty god, who according to Finnish folk poetry, was Tapio, a grey-bearded old man and a fair king. Runo XIV describes Tapio's dwelling in the woods made up of three forts constructed of wood, bone, and stone. Contrary to the usual system of values in the *Kalevala* in which wealth is not a major concern, Tapio is described as an opulent fairy-tale-style king. The Mistress of the Forest, called Mielikki or Mimerkki, has bracelets on her hands, gold rings on her fingers, gold earrings in her ears, her hair braided with gold, and shiny pearls on her neck.

However, these external aspects are of no concern to Sibelius, and the key to *Tapiola* may be found in the fact that in runo XIV, Lemminkäinen is the main character. He has the task of catching an elk while skiing, and he tries huntsmen's charms as an aid:

> O, Ukko, god above, or heavenly father!
> Make me now straight skis, light runners,
> With which I will speed across the fens, across the fields
> To the Demon's lands, over the heaths of Pohjola,
> To the trails of the Demon elk,
> To the tracks of the reindeer.

Is this really Sibelius as a Faustian figure, realizing the drying up of his creative powers in his last major composition, making a pact with the Devil in exchange for musical inspiration, the one thing in his life that meant the most to him?

The idea that Lemminkäinen's skiing to "the Demon's lands" may have occupied Sibelius's mind seems to be supported by the fact that at the time the composer was working on *Tapiola*, he was also working on a melodrama with piano accompaniment based on his friend Bertel Gripenberg's poem "Ett ensamt skidspår" (A Lonely Ski Track).[24] The desolate mood of the poem is set forth in the statement about the answers to the questions in one's heart remaining far away, which seems to be compatible with the searching pessimism of *Tapiola*.

In light of the great extent to which Sibelius identified with his heroes Kullervo, Lemminkäinen, and Väinämöinen in *Pohjola's Daughter*, it is tempting to read Lemminkäinen in the kingdom of the forest god Tapio as Sibelius in his relationship to nature and ultimately through nature to the universe. This relationship is central to his symphonies. The "faith" that Sibelius struggled to attain crumbles in the pessimism of *Tapiola*.

This pessimism is partly attributable to the political circumstances in Finland in the mid-1920s. After the country fought for and gained its independence, it did not start the reconstruction work in a spirit of harmony. The polarization between the political right and left caused continual bickering, and finally led to the establishment in 1929 of an ultra-right organization, the so-called Lapua movement. On many occasions Sibelius expressed his disappointment about the country's lack of unity. He had made his contribution during the country's years of struggle only to discover that independence did not mean the end of Finland's problems. However, *Tapiola* is, above all, an introspective work, and we shall return to view its significance in the over-all picture of Sibelius's career.

Sibelius's works based on Finnish folk poetry span his entire career. They range from short choral pieces and a piano suite to tone poems and large orchestral works with choral or solo voice parts. They represent man's probing of eternal questions in the light of Finnish folk poetry. This questioning proved to be a most crucial influence on Sibelius, as he admitted: "I have drawn my inspiration from the poetry and legends of my native land, and I have then sung in my own way, often orienting my soul with the Kalevala."[25] Without the inspiration of the Kalevala, Sibelius's music would have lacked many of the characteristics we now consider specifically Sibelian.

Emphasis has been placed on the down-to-earth spirit of the *Kalevala*, characterized by Lemminkäinen's mother telling her son to forget all about his attempts to shoot the swan of Tuonela; Pohjola's daughter telling Väinämöinen that a daughter-in-law in her husband's house is like a dog in chains; or Aino's mother telling her daughter, unhappy at her prospective marriage, "God's sun shines elsewhere in the world!" In contrast, there is a fantastic fairy-tale element,[26] characterized in numerous episodes, such as the Mistress of Pohjola locking the sun and the moon in a mountain, Väinämöinen trying to build a boat from a spindle, and so on. This mixing of the natural with the fantastic became easy for Sibelius to understand during his years at Hämeenlinna, where the drudgery of the school years represented the realistic side of life and forays into the nearby woods and childhood games with his friends, the fantastic elements.

We have been seeking to detail the differences between the Finnish and the Finnish-Swedish nationalistic novements, which are not easy to understand for those unfamiliar with the culture of Finland.   Although Runeberg as a typical representative of Finnish-Swedish national romanticism was inspired by the same spirit as the collectors of Finnish runos, the manifestations of this spirit were vastly different.   Even if Runeberg frequently colored his poetry with touches of realism, he viewed the Finnish landscape and people through the rose-colored glasses of a learned romantic.   In contrast, the works that were inspired by Finnish folk poetry tend to view life from the point of view of a simple man guided by instinct rather than intellect.

This dichotomy is in evidence in Sibelius's *Kalevala*-inspired and Runeberg-inspired works, although an overlapping of influences does occur.   Sibelius's solo songs, chamber music, and piano music derive most clearly from the composer's Finnish-Swedish background.   His choral pieces, on the other hand, rely heavily on the Finnish Sibelius.   His orchestral works lean sometimes in one direction and at other times in the other.   If the later symphonies and *Tapiola* fuse the influences most successfully creating an idiom that we can with good reason call Sibelian, it was achieved with great effort.   In the search for a personal message and language, Sibelius was inspired by Finland's struggle for independence.   His participation in this struggle, even if indirectly, provided him with a sense of purpose at times when it was difficult for him to have confidence in his own value as an artist.

THE PATRIOT

Despite the fact that Finland's intellectuals were part of the Baltic community, they were, above all, Finns. For a better understanding of the conflict involving the country's intelligentsia, we will look briefly into the background of Finland's independence movement.

For centuries Finland was the battleground for numerous wars between Sweden and Russia. From 1570 to 1809 there were five wars lasting sixty years altogether. One of the most bitter was fought from 1700 to 1721, during which towns and villages of Finland were destroyed. In the peace treaty Sweden ceded most of Karelia to Russia.

When quarrels arose between Sweden and Finland about Finnish representation in the Swedish parliament, Empress Elizabeth of Russia appealed to Finland to break away from Sweden and become "independent." Nothing came of the appeal, but during the Napoleonic wars, Sweden was forced to surrender Finland to Russia in 1809. By then the idea of an independent Finland was strong enough for the liberal-minded Czar Alexander I to realize that Russia should not try to suppress it. He granted Finland semi-autonomous status as a Russian Grand Duchy and appointed a Finn, Yrjö Maunu Sprengtporten, as its first governor-general.

Russia argued later that what Alexander I had granted Finland "came from his magnanimity and omnipotence and that this gift could be withdrawn at any time." The Finns answered that it was not a gift but a contract binding both parties and reminded Russia that Alexander I had extended the binding powers of the agreement to include his successors when he pledged in 1816 to continue to uphold the fundamental laws of Finland "forever more . . . under Our scepter and that of Our successors."[1]

When the Czar's successors tried to curb Finland's autonomy, the Finns' desire for independence was augmented. Swedish speakers joined the Finns probably because of their resentment towards Russia for putting an end to Sweden's claim on Finland. With Lönnroth's collecting of ancient Finnish runos, Runeberg's poetry, and the Swedish-language patriotic works by Topelius— whose *Läsningar för barn* (Tales for children) was the first book Janne Sibelius owned— the ideological soil was well tilled. The independence movement also became a fight for the Finnish language largely due to J. V. Snellman, who persuaded his fellow citizens that a country in which the educated class spoke Swedish and the rest of the population spoke Finnish was "a country divided against itself."[2]

Czar Alexander II was aware of the trend in Finland. In 1863, he reaffirmed the autonomous status of the Grand Duchy and issued a decree stating that the Finnish language was to be equal to Swedish in official use. The Finns showed their gratitude to Alexander II by naming streets and buildings in his honor; even today the main business street of Helsinki is called Aleksanterinkatu. However, Alexander II received some of the gratitude of the Finns undeservedly,[3] as history later revealed that he had signed a law in 1881 that would have required Finland to send representatives to the Duma, which would have enacted the laws for the Grand Duchy as well, thus negating the power of the Finnish Senate.

With the rise of the pan-Slavic movement, Russification of the Baltic countries was undertaken vigorously and was soon extended to Finland. In resistance, the students, a politically alert group, became an important factor. Their inspiration had come above all from Snellman and Runeberg. Runeberg was indirectly engaged in political activity as a poet and more directly as the editor of *Helsingfors Morgonblad*, which had been initiated by some young academics who called themselves "Lördagssällskapet" (the Saturday Society) because of the day of their meetings. It is due to a large extent to Runeberg and the "Lördagssällskapet," whose motto was "two languages but one nation," that the Swedish-speaking and Finnish-speaking students were reasonably well united in their patriotic efforts. The Saturday Society's goals were expressed in Runeberg's best-known collection of poems, *Fänrik Ståls sägner* (The Tales of Ensign Stål), which had earned him the title of "national poet of Finland." The first collection was published in 1848 and the second in 1880. The opening poem of the first collection is *Vårt land* (Our Land), on which the Finnish national anthem is based. The colorful poems describe events from the 1808-09 Finnish-Swedish-Russian war, and the happenings and personalities are historically true, although much of the local color and some character portrayals are from the poet's imagination.

From the political point of view the *Tales* are naïve, but the students of Sibelius's idealistic generation viewed them as reflections of their own thinking. Every February they celebrated the anniversary of Runeberg's birth and every May, the memory of the first performance of *Vårt land* in 1848 to a tune written by Pacius. They set Runeberg on a pedestal on which he remained until after the Second World War. Much of their admiration of Runeberg was justified, and many character portrayals of the *Tales* are evidence of his keen powers of observation. For example, Runeberg describes the Finnish commander-in-chief W. M. Klingspoor as a man of two chins, one eye, and half a heart.[4]

Sibelius, like all his fellow students, loved Runeberg's *Tales*, but he seems to have steered clear of any active involvement in politics during that period. This, says Erik Tawaststjerna, was due to the fact that Sibelius was fundamentally apolitical by nature. Why was he then willing to become drawn into Finland's struggle for independence? The reasons are twofold. The first and most obvious one was simple peer pressure. This came from the *Päivälehti* (The Daily Paper) circle of liberal young men, including Kajanus. They were trying to resist by peaceful means the Russification that in 1890 took the form of a Postal Manifesto, making the Post Office of Finland dependent on the Russian Post Office. Russian was made a compulsory language in more and more schools, unlike in Sibelius's school days, when even Russian lads in Finland studied Finnish and Swedish.

After Sibelius's success with *Kullervo*, which meant more for the Finns as a nationalistic coup than as a work of art, he became almost overnight the symbol of the resistance movement in the eyes of the students. When the members of the Viipuri Student Corporation were planning their contribution to the movement with a series of historical tableaux, they wanted Sibelius to compose music for them. The idea of a resistance piece based on Karelian history appealed to Sibelius for whom history had been one of the few enjoyable subjects in secondary school. He began work on the incidental music during the summer of 1893, and the presentation of *Karelia* took place in November of the same year with Sibelius conducting.

The events of Karelian history in the tableaux included two runo-singers performing their recitation, the conversion of Karelia to Christianity and the founding of the city of Viipuri. The music ended with Pacius's "Maamme" (Our Land), the national anthem, in which the audience joined spontaneously, an indication that the propaganda aim of the presentation had been achieved beyond expectation. Later Sibelius combined "Intermezzo," "Ballade," and "Alla marcia" for the Karelia Suite, Opus 11, with the Overture published separately. The "Intermezzo" supplied the accompaniment for the third tableau, which described the Lithuanian Prince Narimont collecting tribute in the form of pelts, the currency of the period, from the Karelians. The "Ballade" was included in the fourth tableau with Torgil Knutsson, the founder of Viipuri, and his courtiers listening to a ballad singer at the castle. In the suite Sibelius scored the vocal solo for orchestral instruments. "Alla marcia" served as the orchestral illustration of the fifth tableau, which portrayed Pontus de la Gardie, who burnt the town of Käkisalmi (Kexholm) in 1580. It is said to be "a march on an old motif," but, as Harold Johnson points out, the old motif has never been discovered.[5] Whatever the inspirational sources of *Karelia* might be, there is no doubt about the enthusiastic spirit of the work. In contrast, there were several academic cantatas Sibelius was asked to write, and most of them clearly show the composer's lack of inspiration.

When the Imperial Alexander University, later the University of Helsinki, commissioned Sibelius to write a cantata in honor of Nicholas II, Chancellor of the University, the composer did not dare turn it down, although he was not happy about the request for political reasons. Nicholas II[6] caused more anxiety in Finland than his predecessor Alexander III did for his refusal to interfere in the activities of those who tried to curb Finland's autonomy. The text of the cantata by Paavo Cajander, based loosely on a German poem, did not inspire Sibelius. He put off the work until the last minute, and some orchestral parts were still missing at rehearsals. The performance was a disaster, and Sibelius claimed that the tuba player had been drunk and had started to improvise in the middle of a fugue, spoiling the piece completely.

What made matters worse for Sibelius was the fact that he was at that time competing with Kajanus for a professorship at the University, and neither the cantata nor Sibelius's only public lecture helped his chances. After a great deal of maneuvering, Kajanus was appointed to the post. This angered Sibelius's friends who felt that Kajanus did not need the money as badly as Sibelius did. As a consolation prize the latter was granted a government stipend soon afterwards.

After the appointment of Nicholas Bobrikov as governor-general and the issuance of the 1899 February Manifesto, depriving the Finnish Senate of most of its legislative powers, the political situation turned so grave that "the university students skied from farm to farm . . . and, in slightly more than a week collected 523,000 signatures [about half of the adult population of the country] on a protest addressed to the Czar, petitioning him to bring the provisions of the Manifesto into harmony with the constitutional laws of Finland."[7]   A deputation of five hundred men was sent to deliver the petition personally to the Czar, who refused to see them. Nor did he accept another petition on behalf of the Finns signed by over a thousand famous personalities, including Thomas Hardy, George Meredith, Herbert Spencer, Florence Nightingale, Henrik Ibsen, Theodore Mommsen, Anatole France, and Emile Zola.

Four days after the issuance of the February Manifesto, Sibelius set to work on a song of protest based on a poem by the Swedish writer Viktor Rydberg called "Dexippos" about the struggle between the Athenians and the barbarian Goths. Inspired by the parallelism of the situation in the poem to that in Finland, Sibelius set his song, "The Song of Athenians," for boys' and men's voices, wind septet, and percussion. It premiered in Helsinki in 1899 in a program that included the ecstatically received First Symphony.

Sibelius's most important contribution to the resistance movement after *Karelia* came with *Scènes historiques*, performed in November 1899 at one of the "Press Pension celebrations." Supposedly intended to raise money for the newsmen's pension fund, the celebrations in reality gave both moral and material support to the press whose freedom was being curtailed. The lyrics for *Scènes historiques* were written by Eino Leino, one of the greatest poets Finland has produced, and by Jalmari Finne. The tableaux started with "Väinämöinen's Song," with the "Bard" sitting on a rock playing his kantele and the people and "even the birds of the air" listening to him in ecstasy. The second scene, "The Finns are Baptized," depicted the conversion of the Finns to Christianity by Bishop Henry, and the third scene described Duke John and his court at Turku Castle. The next two scenes portrayed the Finns in the Thirty Years' War, the topic of Sibelius's matriculation essay, as we might recall. The last scene, "Finland Awakes," included the Finns' favorite Czar, Alexander II, Runeberg composing poetry, Snellman speaking to the students, Lönnrot compiling the *Kalevala*, and so on. The tableaux ended with "Finlandia."   Later Sibelius revised the "All' overtura" (Tableau 1), "Scena" (Tableau 4), and "Quasi bolero" (Tableau 3), which he renamed "Festivo," with "Tempo di Bolero" as a subtitle. These were published as *Scènes historiques* I, Opus 25. The finale was published separately as *Finlandia*.

The instant popularity of *Finlandia* can be understood in view of historical events. In June 1900 the Czar signed a decree making Russian the official language of Finland. In face of the accelerated efforts towards the Russification of the country, it is natural that the Finns found spiritual consolation in the piece. It was easy to interpret the opening fanfare as the Russian menace, the woodwind and brass motif of the Andante as the mighty oppressor, and the hymn as the oppressed for whom light would dawn after darkness.

In 1912, between the Fourth Symphony and *The Bard*, Sibelius added three more scenes to *Scènes historiques*, Opus 66, "The Chase," "Love Song," and "At the Drawbridge," which never matched the popularity of *Finlandia*, although they are good incidental pieces. Another patriotic composition, *Sandels* for men's choir and orchestra, also failed to gain popularity although it is based on one of the best poems of Runeberg's *Fänrik Ståls sägner*.

The effect of the February Manifesto was decisive for Finland. After it became clear to the Finns that the other Scandinavian countries would remain neutral and could not be counted on for help, they knew that they had to stand alone and united. They felt that calling attention to the achievements of the nation might create some good will towards the country. Music critic Karl Flodin suggested that this might be accomplished by making Sibelius's music known beyond the Finnish borders, and it was decided that the Helsinki Philharmonic Orchestra should be sent to the Paris World Exhibition of 1900.

A petition to send the orchestra to Paris was signed, among others, by Sibelius, but the Finnish Senate turned it down. Kajanus and Westerlund, a Helsinki music publisher, then tried to raise funds from private sources, but the moneys were far from sufficient even after Kajanus had organized a send-off concert at which a large choir sang a new patriotic song by Sibelius called "Isänmaalle" (To the Fatherland) to words by Cajander. Sibelius's *Tiera* also premiered at this concert. The Philharmonic Orchestra started its tour in Stockholm, where Sibelius debuted as a symphonic composer for the first time outside of Finland at the Olympia hall, a circus arena with poor acoustics and a lingering odor of horses. However, the First Symphony was well received, and the second concert was even more of a success with *Finlandia* and "Alla marcia" on the program.

After the encouraging start in Stockholm, the orchestra enjoyed only qualified successes in Oslo, Copenhagen, Lübeck, Hamburg, and Berlin and ended up in the Low Countries in the middle of an unusually hot summer season. Poor attendance was attributed to all the potential audiences being on the beaches. This was true also of Paris, where all the natives had headed for the seashore during their annual vacation, with only foreigners left in Paris. The Finns' spirits improved at the sight of their small but artistically impressive Pavilion, which Gallén-Kallela had decorated with frescoes, until they discovered the sign "Section russe" at the entrance.

Although the Philharmonic Orchestra was too small for the Trocadéro hall, Sibelius's First Symphony was, nevertheless, favorably received there, as were "The Swan of Tuonela" and *La Patrie*, the title the Finns used for *Finlandia* in order not to offend the Russians. The greatest personal success was achieved by Aino Ackté, the singer who was appearing at the Paris Opera at the time.

All in all, the Philharmonic Orchestra's trip probably did create some good will towards the country, but, judging from Sibelius's letters to his wife, the impact was not what had been expected. Meanwhile, the political situation in Finland gradually grew worse. For the first time the secretary of state for Finnish affairs in St. Petersburg was not a Finn but a Russian, Count von Plehwe, who started to dismiss top officials. The country's leaders were denied freedom of speech, and illegal searches by agents of a secret police force became commonplace. A number of patriots were sent to exile in Siberia, including Pehr Evind Svinhufvud, who later became president of Finland.

When the Finnish army was disbanded and a decree was issued ordering Finnish recruits to serve under Russian colors, an intensified wave of protest began in Finland. However, the Finns started to disagree on the course the country should take, and this was ultimately to lead to a split of the country into two factions: those who tried to defend the constitution and oppose any violation of it and those who were ready to make concessions to the Russians in the name of peace. Economic factors played a role in the decisions of individuals regarding the course the country should take, with the poorer classes in general opting for compliance and the more well-to-do, for resistance.

The more precarious the political situation in Finland grew, the more acute the Finns' need for spiritual leaders became. Sibelius's realization that he was a national figure inspired him. He worked diligently on his Second Symphony, which premiered in Helsinki on March 8, 1902. The concert was a success, as were two repeat performances which were sold out.

How much of the initial good reception of the work was due to genuine admiration of it? How much was due to the Finns' desire to read patriotic symbolism into the work is difficult to determine. At any rate, the Finnish musicologist and music critic Ilmari Krohn's characterization of the work as "our Liberation Symphony" was echoed by Kajanus and Georg Schneevoigt on their conducting tours around the world. Even today it is common to hear the usual patriotic connotations attached to the work, despite Tawaststjerna's — as well as Sibelius's — arguments to the contrary.

After the so-called Dictatorship Statute of 1903 gave the governor-general increased powers, including control of civil administration, illegal dismissals of judges and government officials were commonplace as Bobrikov determined to replace constitutionalists with compliant officials. Passive resistance finally took a violent turn in 1904, when Eugen Schauman, a government official, shot governor-general Bobrikov and then himself on the steps of the Senate building. It is believed that Sibelius's funeral march *In memoriam* was his memorial to Schauman.

Although the Finns gained some concessions after the general strike of 1905,[8] the Russo-Japanese war, and the internal unrest in Russia, in 1909 the Czar issued new illegal decrees. One of these established Finland's participation in Russian military expenditures on a permanent basis, perhaps punishment for the fact that Russia could no longer draft Finnish men into the army because of their lack of loyalty. In 1910 the Russian Duma passed a proposal for Imperial legislation subordinating essential matters of the economic, cultural, and political life of Finland to the decision of the Russian authorities, thereby putting an end to Finland's autonomous status.

After the post of governor-general was taken over in 1909 by Bobrikov's former chief of staff F. A. Seyn, who was even more severe than Bobrikov, the Finnish senators resigned: first the constitutionalists and a few months later those who had been for compliance. Upon his resignation Senator Paasikivi, a staunch supporter of compliance at first and later president of Finland, remarked that the mass resignation ought to have shown the Czar that all Finns opposed the illegalities. The political parties of Finland, which had fought each other during Bobrikov's regime, were once again united.

Sibelius's music reflects his country's political life quite faithfully. At first it was a symbol for patriotism and resistance to the Russians, then by 1906 the title of *Vapautettu kuningatar* (The Liberated Queen)[9] evoked for many Finns the idea of independence. Sibelius composed the piece for mixed chorus and orchestra to lyrics by Paavo Cajander for the hundredth anniversary of Snellman's birth. The symbolism of the story of *Vapautettu kuningatar* is naïve. After the chorus of men's voices sings a funereal theme and the lament of the captive queen is heard in the silent night, a women's chorus tells the country about the beauty of the queen. A young man hears the song and leads his countrymen's uprising to liberate the queen, who is led to her people to the tune of a joyous hymn.

When World War I broke out in 1914, Finland did not participate, but it suffered as a result of a commercial blockade which led to food rationing because of lack of imports and unemployment due to lack of exports. There were also restrictions on travel. Sibelius had not believed in the possibility of a world war. When it did start, it meant radical changes in his life-style. No longer could he travel to the music centers of the continent or England, as he was used to doing, and his contacts with his publishers were cut off. This meant a decrease in his income at the time when inflation necessitated increased earnings. For financial reasons during the first months of the war he composed sixteen minor pieces, including works like *Pensées lyriques*, Opus 40, for piano and Sonata in E Major for Violin and Piano, which he was able to sell easily to Scandinavian music publishers, while continuing work on his Fifth Symphony. It premiered at the composer's fiftieth birthday celebration in Helsinki in a program including *The Oceanides* and two violin serenades.

With Sibelius's birthday celebration the Finns were honoring the old tradition peculiar to all Scandinavian countries, where they celebrate a person's fiftieth, sixtieth, seventieth, and seventy-fifth birthday with great fanfare, while the other birthdays are virtually ignored in favor of a name day (saint's day) celebration. Sibelius's birthday was used also as an excuse for a national celebration to boost the country's morale. His old friend Werner Söderhjelm, the key-note speaker, emphasized the importance of Sibelius's contribution to the cultural life of Finland and the debt of gratitude that the country owed him as its cultural ambassador: "There is no power or time that can destroy what a nation has created in great spiritual works."[10]

Sibelius belonged to the bilingual middle class, which was fairly sizable by the time of the First World War. Although the middle class led a comfortable life, the tenant farmer and the rapidly increasing working class shared very little in the country's prosperity. When food shortages worsened during the war, they touched the working class more severely than the middle class, making the ground fertile for quick spreading of socialist ideology among the workers. By 1916 the well-organized Social Democratic Party gained a majority in the Finnish Senate, and when the Finnish communists went even further in identifying with the aims of the Russian communists, large numbers of Finnish workers joined the Russian Red Guard stationed in Finland. The middle classes, both Finnish-speaking and Swedish-speaking, turned to Germany for help, and about two thousand young men went there from Finland to receive military training and to return, with the aid of the Germans, as part of General Mannerheim's White Guard to liberate the country.

After the *coup d'état* in Russia, the provisional government which replaced the Czarist rule declared illegal all the measures taken against Finland and thus restored the country's autonomous status. Finnish political prisoners in Russian jails were released and governor-general Seyn imprisoned. The Russian *coup d'état* introduced anarchy into Finland, too, and, as a result, the idea of independence was no longer whispered about but discussed openly. On December 4, 1917, while revolutionary Russian troops held a noisy meeting in front of the Finnish Senate building, Svinhufvud submitted to the Senate a proposal drafted by K. J. Ståhlberg for a constitution for an independent Republic of Finland, and delivered a brief, simple speech for Finnish independence.[11] Two days later an even simpler declaration was added to this measure, its commemoration being celebrated annually as Finland's Independence Day.

With about forty thousand Russian soldiers stationed in Finland and Finnish Red Guards joining them, Finland's independence was only a meaningless word in a document. When the Red Guards tried to set up a Socialist Workers' Republic by a *coup d'état*, civil war broke out in Finland. Carl Gustaf Emil Mannerheim, who had served in the Czarist army, returned to Finland from Germany and was appointed commander-in-chief in January 1918 by the Finnish Senate. From the town of Vaasa, landing point for the Finnish troops trained in Germany and where thousands of Finnish young men joined them, Mannerheim launched a systematic attack against the Russians heading first towards Tampere and after liberating it, towards Helsinki. On April 3 some Germans who had promised assistance to Mannerheim landed on the coast of the Gulf of Finland and reached Helsinki in nine days while Mannerheim's White Guard was approaching the city from the north.

During these times Sibelius tried to turn to nature and music for consolation. His ability to find minute changes in nature as a source of comfort is amazing. On April 18, 1917, he wrote in his diary, "There are twelve swans on the lake [Lake Tuusula]. I saw them through my field-glasses. Strangely poetical, unique." A few days later he added, "A wonderful day, spring and life. The earth smells, mutes and fortissimo. An extraordinary light, reminiscent of a haze in August."[12]

By 1918 the war was becoming more and more a harsh reality for Sibelius. He had to start fearing for his life, but he carried on work with amazing tenacity. In early February 1918 he was put under house arrest by the military office of the Järvenpää district. On February 11 some Red Guard soldiers searched his house for hidden supplies of food and weapons. Sibelius did have a revolver hidden in the basement but, thanks to the loyalty of his servants who knew about it, his life was saved. The search was repeated two days later.

In March Sibelius's brother Christian and brother-in-law Eero Järnefelt found Ainola too dangerous for the Sibelius family, and they sent Kajanus there to persuade them to leave. They moved to Christian's living quarters at the psychiatric hospital of Lapinlahti, a suburb of Helsinki, the institution in which Christian Sibelius was the leading physician. In April they could hear fighting in the Helsinki area, which Sibelius recorded in his diary: "April 11 during the bombardment. Have never dreamt of anything so tremendous. Horrible, but grand! Shall I be alive tomorrow?"[13] The following day the first German troops entered Helsinki and the conquest of the city was completed in another day by Mannerheim's White Guard. Soon the rest of South Finland was liberated, and the Sibelius family returned home.

And with the above-mentioned quote from Sibelius's wartime diary we have come to the second reason why the composer, despite his allegedly apolitical nature, was willing to get so deeply involved in Finland's struggle for its independence. "Horrible, but grand! Shall I be alive tomorrow?" shows the sense of excitement and even danger that the romantic in Sibelius needed and also a typical romantic's self-centered reaction and concern with his own feelings. Obviously the composer became, without much persuasion, a more-than-willing tool in the hands of his patriotic friends, because he sensed intuitively that he needed them as much as they needed him. It was only towards the end of the War of Independence that conditions became such for Sibelius that they interfered with his work.

The romantic in Sibelius, the Sibelius who as a student in Berlin had been captivated by "two wonderful pieces by Berlioz," in fact — two scenes from *Lélio*, that truly romantic mixture of self-pity and protest, and overly sweet lyricism — needed ideals to fight for, and Finland's struggle provided him with those ideals. The true romantic's identification with a rebellious hero is seen in Sibelius's *Snöfrid*, an early work (1896) for recitation, chorus, and orchestra based on a poem by the Swedish writer Viktor Rydberg. Sibelius's approach, typical of romantic composers, is manifest in the chromaticism of the central theme in an attempt at portraying the conflicts of the hero.

However, despite the spirit of enthusiasm in *Karelia* and many other patriotic works, Sibelius is not a "military" composer in the style of, say Nielsen or Mahler. The occasional insert of an allusion to military music into the framework of a piece adds a somewhat unreal toy-soldier effect in Nielsen and a sense of haunting memories in Mahler. Although both Mahler and Sibelius grew up in garrison towns, the less direct influence of military music in Sibelius's works may be due to the fact that in his childhood the Russian military presence at Hämeenlinna was subdued and perhaps also to the national characteristic of Finns as good fighters but poor parade soldiers.

Even though there are truly inspired works among Sibelius's pieces connected with either patriotic topics or occasions, in general this part of his oeuvre does not represent the level of artistic achievement of his works based on Finnish folk poetry. However, the most important manifestation of the spirit of nationalism in Sibelius's output is in his musical expression, and it is in this area that he made his greatest contribution to Finnish music.

THE COMPOSER IN SEARCH OF HIS OWN VOICE

Sibelius became the founder of a new musical tradition in Finland with the creation of an idiom deriving strong influence from folk poetry and folk song. This fact is amazing in view of his Swedish home background and the status of serious Finnish music at the time Sibelius began his studies in Helsinki.

Despite Sibelius's early interest in music — his first composition "Vattendroppar" (Drops of water), written when he was eight — and violin lessons at Hämeenlinna, his pre-university days did not seem to point to a career in music, especially in the face of strong opposition from the Sibelius family. Although the family considered interest in music commendable, the grandmother, in particular, felt that trying to make one's living in that field was all right for a church musician or a traveling barrel organist, but not for a respectable middle-class youth. Nor was the Hämeenlinna of Sibelius's childhood likely to foster any serious interest in music. However, since the first railroad had been inaugurated in Finland between Helsinki and Hämeenlinna in 1862, there were occasions like the Swedish harp virtuoso Adolf Sjödén's rendering of his own arrangement of Finnish folk songs and performances by August Wilhelmj and Sophie Menter to enkindle Sibelius's ambition. Above all, the power of his artistic temperament[1] and his firm conviction broke the family's resistance, and after one year as an indifferent — and failing — law student he received his family's permission to study at Wegelius's Music Institute in the fall of 1886.

When Sibelius began his music studies in Helsinki, his training, apart from violin lessons with a mediocre teacher, had consisted of the school program of choral pieces by Bernhard Henrik Crusell, F. Ehrström, and other Finnish composers, who wrote in the typical romantic tradition with strong influence of German-Scandinavian music. The daily school prayers with emphasis on chorales fortified the power of the liturgical tradition. When we add to this the practicing of the Sibelius family trio with its repertory of continental music, it is obvious that the specifically Finnish influences on Sibelius's music were doomed to lie almost dormant for a while.

All of Sibelius's teachers in Helsinki — Wegelius, Kajanus, and Busoni — had received a strictly continental training. Unfortunately, due to one of the sorry chapters in the history of art music in Finland, the rivalry between Wegelius and Kajanus went to such ridiculous extremes that Sibelius heard relatively few concerts by Kajanus's orchestra, because Wegelius did not want Sibelius to show up on those occasions. This sad situation made Busoni's stay in Helsinki even more valuable for Sibelius than it might have been under different circumstances and, at the same time, strengthened the grip of the continental music tradition on him, as did such visiting pianists as Eugen d'Albert, Albert Reisenauer, and Alfred Grünfeld and the violinist Leopold Auer, who performed the Mendelssohn Concerto. Only the operatic fare was somewhat more varied: some Finnish amateur groups performed *Der Freischütz*, *Il Trovatore*, and *Carmen*, and a visiting Russian opera company presented Glinka's *A Life for a Czar* and Dargomiszky's *Russalka*.

Jean Sibelius was thinking of a career as a violinist after performing the David E Minor Concerto with the university's orchestra under the direction of Richard Faltin and receiving favorable press notices.[2] He also became intrigued by conducting and joined Faltin's orchestra as its assistant conductor. However, during his years as a student in Helsinki, it became increasingly clear to Sibelius that composing was what he really wanted to do; although a few years later, at the time of his engagement to Aino Järnefelt, when the thought of having to earn a living hit him for the first time, he thought of a career as a violinist.

Ironically, Sibelius's increasing interest in composing may have been due, indirectly, to Busoni. When Sibelius heard Busoni's keyboard mastery, for which he always professed greater admiration than for his compositions, he may have realized that comparable mastery of the violin was beyond his reach because of his late start. We should not feel, however, that Sibelius decided to major in composition only as a second choice. Rather, composition seems to have become a clear goal for him only after a few years of groping and indecision.

Because of Sibelius's German-oriented training in Finland, it is not surprising that most observers agree that the student compositions from this period adhere to what was "the accepted European idiom."[3]   However, there are the first signs of independent thinking.   There is an early String Quartet in E-Flat, which anticipates the finale of the Second Symphony, even including the Sibelian triplet, as Tawaststjerna points out. Similarly, an early violin sonata in the spirit of Grieg displays such specifically Finnish characteristics as an absence of upbeats and a trochaic repetition at the end of a phrase.

While Sibelius's student compositions are definitely in the German-Scandinavian tradition, we have to remember that they were written with a view to gaining Wegelius's acceptance.   It is fairly certain that Sibelius made numerous sketches along more independent lines.   Obviously he did not even want to show them to Wegelius, knowing that they would not meet with his approval. Wegelius, in accordance with his German training, believed in the virtue of discipline so strongly that when Sibelius wrote to him from Berlin complaining about the conservatism of his teacher, Becker, Wegelius answered categorically that discipline was good for Sibelius, because it would make it possible for him to write more freely later on.   When Sibelius, while visiting home from abroad told Wegelius that he was composing to a text from the *Kalevala* (his *Kullervo* Symphony), Wegelius, always skeptical of Sibelius's newfangled ideas, reacted with a grunt.

Had Sibelius been an obedient pupil and adhered to his teachers' guidance, what kind of composer would he have been? On the basis of his early attempts at composition, we can conclude that he probably would have continued to cling to the German-influenced Scandinavian style of his student compositions in which he wrote a fair number of romances, humoresques, and other pieces of this type later on.

As a typical composer of this school we might cite Franz Berwald, a Swede who died three years after Sibelius was born, sometimes mentioned as a possible influence on the Finnish composer.   It is, indeed, likely that Sibelius knew at least some chamber music works by Berwald, but how much influence on Sibelius's works could be ascribed specifically to the Swedish composer is difficult to say because of the fact that the works of Berwald adhere to the trends common in Scandinavia at the time: the tendency to write "romances" or romance-like slow movements with easy-flowing melodies in a nostalgic spirit.   This type of writing, propagated by Grieg particularly in his chamber works, prominently employs the triad, or the superimposed third, in the construction of melody, as is seen from the Norwegian master's admission that for him harmony frequently dictated melody. However, if Grieg's music is vitalized by influences of Norwegian folk music, we can also detect occasional innovative details in Berwald's works due to his familiarity with Swedish folk music.

As a representative piece by Grieg we could cite the well-known "Valse" from his Small Lyric Pieces, Op. 12:

Example 5 Used with kind permission by Edition Wilhelm Hansen AS, Copenhagen.

If we compare the opening of Grieg's "Valse" with Sibelius's minor piano piece, "Etude," Op. 76 we can see similar modal touches in harmony. We might recall the frequent use of Lydian F-sharp by Chopin for "Slavic" flavor.

Va - ka, van - ha Väi - nä - möi - nen

tie - tä - jä i - än - i - kui - nen

Example 6 Used with kind permission by Edition Wilhelm Hansen AS, Copenhagen.

However, there is one area in which Sibelius's approach differs markedly from Grieg's: in the field of rhythm and, as a corollary, in phrase construction. Where Grieg preferred easy-flowing melodies in 3/4 time, often progressing in chains of three notes, such as the well-known "Morning Mood" from *Peer Gynt*, Sibelius liked two-beat and four-beat bars with strongly marked rhythms for decisive masculine effect. Naturally there are exceptions like Grieg's *hallings* in his Norwegian dances in 2/4 time and a number of waltzes and other pieces by Sibelius in 3/4 time, but the basic preference of each composer is clear. As pointed out by Eino Roiha, even in Sibelius's symphonies two-beat and four-beat phrases are much more common than three-beat or six-beat phrases; in other words, the influence of the Finnish language and Finnish folk music is marked in his idiom, including his symphonies.

Related to rhythm is the matter of phrase structure. We can see the effect of four-line stanzas of poetry frequently in the music of Schumann, Brahms, and many others. This phenomenon, to which Gerald Abraham refers as *folklore imaginé*, is manifest in Grieg's "Valse," whereas Sibelius's strong beats in his "Etude" indicate clear adherence to the *Kalevala* verse, and it would be easy to sing, for example, the typical introductory lines, "Vaka, vanha Väinämöinen/ tietäjä iänikuinen," to Sibelius's phrasing. This evidence of Finnish influence is all the more surprising considering the fact that, in general, his piano compositions represent the genre that remained affected the least by the influence of the runo-song. However, there is also indication in some early piano pieces of attempts at more characteristically Finnish writing for the piano; for example, in *Six Impromptus*, Op. 5 (1893), No. 3 introduces a theme vaguely reminiscent of *En Saga*, and No. 4 employs a melody moving within the range of a fourth and reflecting the insistence of runo tunes. This faint promise of more typically Finnish pianistic writing was never fulfilled, and Sibelius's idiom for the instrument remained curiously void of progress.

In another early work, Sonata in F for Piano, Op. 12 (1893), there is some indication of the type of theme development of which Sibelius was capable in his orchestral writing. However, the orchestral impact — which was to be the main weakness of his piano writing — is so strong that in the Andantino one can almost hear the pizzicato strings in the accompaniment, a common Sibelian orchestral device.

Reference was made above to one of Sibelius's major piano works, *Kyllikki*, inspired by the *Kalevala*. The subtitle, "Three Lyric Pieces for Piano," gives an indication of the structure in which the outer movements are spoiled by dense writing. Only the middle movement, based on a simple folk-like theme, offers some relief. Three Sonatinas for Piano, Op. 67 (1912), on the other hand, are much shorter than the previous works and are of considerable interest because of somewhat better pianistic writing. No. 2 in particular, with its joyful outer movements contrasted by a lyrical song-like tune in the middle movement, is enjoyable and it almost manages to convey some humor, which is unusual for Sibelius. The thematic treatment is more complex in the Third Sonatina with a tongue-in-cheek kind of march as a middle movement and a rather joyous rondo as a finale. Despite some fascinating details in the thematic development and hints at interest in canons and fugues, it is easy to see even from these pieces that the piano was not Sibelius's instrument.

The Liszt-Schumann-oriented writing tends to dominate the Finnish orchestral master's pianism, of which we might cite by way of example his "Caprice," Op. 24 (1894) the opening of which owes too great a debt to the Hungarian master of the instrument, while the middle section derives influence from the Scandinavian folk song-hymn style with simple strophic construction. Liszt's influence is still in evidence in the Sonatinas of Op. 67 (1912), and No. 1 could even contain a recollection of Liszt's *Transcendental Etude* No. 3, known as *La Campanella*, which used to be considered a high point of pianistic achievement in student association performances in Finland.

There is a vague hint at a more interesting approach to keyboard writing in Sibelius's "tree pieces" of Op. 75 (1914). In "Granen" (The Spruce):

Example 7 Used with kind permission by Edition Wilhelm Hansen AS, Copenhagen.

we can detect a suggestion of some type of austere northern variety of impressionism and also some relatedness to the Fourth Symphony, but the effect of the piece is spoiled by the naïve middle section, which is, once again, too orchestral. Perhaps Sibelius in his piano writing could have benefited from a few lessons with Erik Satie!

In addition to the piano pieces, the other popular forms of entertainment of the continental salon tradition in the bourgeois homes of Finland, solo songs and chamber music, remained in Sibelius's compositions fairly firmly tied to the Baltic style of writing. This "Italianate" tradition, as Stravinsky called it, was so universally accepted all over Europe that Grieg became popular from Russia to France, loved not only by audiences but admired even by composers like Rimsky-Korsakov and Debussy.

Sibelius composed a large number of chamber works in this tradition and one of them, his *Canzonetta*, Op. 62a (1911), originally written for strings, was arranged by Stravinsky for eight instruments, four horns, two clarinets, harp, and double bass.[4] As Stravinsky stated, he was fond of that kind of "northern Italianate melodism," which was a part, "and an attractive part of St. Petersburg culture." This was the element in Tchaikovsky's music that Stravinsky remained fond of all his life, and it is in the manifestation of this spirit in Sibelius's output that numerous people outside of Finland have seen influence of Tchaikovsky on Sibelius, in addition to certain similarities in the orchestral sound.

There are certainly passages, say, in Sibelius's First Symphony which bring Tchaikovsky to mind, but, in general, the Finnish composer's orchestral coloring is more austere than that of the Russian master.   We might recall that, by Sibelius's own admission, his orchestral writing was connected with the firmness of Finnish granite, and it was such an integral part of his act of creation that in many cases his inspiration included the orchestration, with frequent dialogues between the strings and the woodwinds and the use of divided strings as characteristic features.

Burnett James, in his recent study of Sibelius's music, wonders whether there is "a relevance to the historic organ aesthetic" in the composer's use of long sustained pedal points which he used in order to compensate for the lack of an orchestral pedal, a fact Sibelius deplored. Aside from the possible influence of Anton Bruckner and the use of pedal points by such pre-Sibelian Scandinavian composers as Grieg and before him Ludvig Mathias Lindeman, in this writer's view, the answer to James's question has to be affirmative.

Mention was made earlier of Sibelius's exposure to church music as a daily routine in school. Traditionally, the most common musical instrument in Finnish schools was the harmonium, admittedly a poor substitute for the organ, and obviously the instrument on which Sibelius heard school songs and hymns. One of his earliest youthful quartets was written for the strange combination of violin, violin-cello, harmonium, and piano, evidently indicating which instruments were available.

What is the function of a pedal point? The main purpose is to halt the flow of harmony, and it can be used either to increase tension or as a final resonance to release tension. When harmony has thus been "demoted,"[5] our senses are allowed to concentrate on other aspects of music, such as the themes.   Now, in "homophonic art ... the essential thing is the *development* arising from the basic motive."[6]   Thus Sibelius in his frequently homophonic writing uses pedal points, a reflection of childhood influences, as a means of emphasis on the development of themes. We have a good example of this in the largely monothematic work, *Tapiola*, in which the pedal point is often a major second, one of the most characteristic intervals of the Finnish folk song. Needless to say, it enhances the atmosphere of Finnish forests in the work. Another feature of Sibelius's orchestration, the frequent use of string pizzicato accompanying woodwinds could be a reflection of the plucked strings of the kantele, the national instrument of Finland.

Although Sibelius's early String Quartet in B-flat Major (1890) is generally considered the first work in which the composer's own voice started to emerge, the main subject of the first movement, the *Allegro*, is based firmly on the triad, representing the thinking that was to prevail in his chamber music works.

The grip of triadic harmony was so firm in the countries in which continental influences prevailed that Bartók concluded a composer whose ear was tuned to it was not capable of appreciating "the true peasant song."[7]   Therefore, it is not surprising that Sibelius, whose background included early exposure to Finnish folk song, was not able to receive any sympathy from his teachers, all trained in Germany, when he started to show Finnish influence in his choral and orchestral writing.   Even his choral songs of *Rakastava* won only second prize in competition with the more traditional entry of his teacher.   However, it is difficult to see the justification of the jury's thinking, because the work is quite traditional, representing the kind of delicate writing that characterized love music of the Romantic period, and it has a clear affinity with the slow movement of the B-flat Major Quartet.   In the 1911 string arrangement of *Rakastava*, only the phrasing is indicative of the *Kanteletar* inspiration of the work.

After being continually advised by Wegelius to refrain from using Finnish elements in his compositions, Sibelius had a similar reaction from Robert Fuchs and Karl Goldmark.   The latter, however, was less categorical than the former in condemning the use of folk material in Sibelius's sketches for *Kullervo*.   He admitted that the folk element had greater significance for a Finn than for others.   Yet, direct encouragement to probe new areas was something Sibelius failed to get from anyone.   Consequently, he had to rely on his own instinct.   In this search his only encouragement came from Finnish nationalism.   Inspired by this spirit, Sibelius kept rereading the *Kalevala* while in Vienna.   He was fascinated in particular by the music inherent in the poetry and wrote to his fiancée that it was to his ears "pure music, themes and variations."[8]   Thus he was led to Finnish folk music as a means of enriching his own musical vocabulary through folk poetry.

Although Sibelius, unlike Bartók and Kodály, was no folk song specialist, he had been exposed to Finnish folk songs ever since his childhood, because at Hämeenlinna, just as in any Finnish-language town, the later-type folk song must have been as omnipresent as opera is in an Italian community. The old Finnish runo-song survived better in Karelia than in western Finland, but the later type was naturally influenced by the earlier, thanks largely to the demands of the language. Thus Sibelius's statement to Karl Ekman, "First I composed *Kullervo*; then I went to Karelia to hear, for the first time in my life the *Kalevala* runos from the lips of the people,"[9] has often been misinterpreted as a claim that the composer did not know anything about the Finnish folk song before composing *Kullervo*. This is, of course, not true. Sibelius was present as a young student in Helsinki when Larin Paraske recited her runos and Sibelius was observed there taking notes on her inflections in particular. Besides, even if the later-type Finnish folk song was influenced by the folk song and the art song of the other Scandinavian countries and by church music, the rhythms and cadences of Finnish folk songs were something Sibelius was exposed to in his childhood environment.

We have to remember also that at the time Sibelius grew up, there was a lively interest in Finland in collecting folk songs, and many a student went to Karelia in the hope of making new discoveries, as did Sibelius. Tawaststjerna takes a skeptical view of Sibelius's trip to northern Karelia and claims that for him it was a way of financing his honeymoon on a scholarship, but the rigors of the trip could hardly justify the financial benefit: for the last leg of the trip Sibelius's grand piano had to be loaded on two rowboats.

An indication of Sibelius's awareness of the significance of folk music in his art lies in the choice of the topic of his only public lecture, "Some Reflections on Folk Music and Its Influence on the Development of Art Music," when he was competing, unsuccessfully, for the professorship in music in Helsinki.[10] Although Sibelius's lecture was not a cohesive presentation of his ideas, there were many interesting points he emphasized, as, for example, the intricate rhythms of Finnish folk songs. As we have seen from the Finno-Ugric folk song, there were two main rhythmic tendencies: the flexible rhythms following the demands of the languages in question and the monotonously repetitive rhythmic patterns. Based on the latter trend, Sibelius created primitive rhythmic effects, for example in *Tulen synty* (The Origin of Fire), which are comparable to those in works like Bartók's *Allegro Barbaro* or Prokofiev's *Scythian Suite*.

The earliest composition by Sibelius hinting at the kind of synthesis of the standard Western idiom and native Finnish influences that the composer was aiming at is *Kullervo*, whose nationalistic significance is referred to earlier in this study (see chapter 3). Sibelius liked to call *Kullervo* a symphony, although the title page of the original score subtitled the work a "symphonic poem for orchestra, soli, and chorus." The inclusion of a male chorus was obviously due to the Finns' fondness for choral singing. The orchestra is of modest proportions reflecting what instrumental performers happened to be available in Helsinki at the time, but the composer's ability to create beautiful orchestral color even with limited means is eloquent testimony of his innate gift. However, Robert Layton sees Tchaikovsky's influence in particular in the coda of the first movement, the slow movement, and the finale, while others have pointed to Wagner's influence in the orchestral palette and to Bruckner's in the long sustained pedal points, as in the chord of E major in the first movement. If various outside influences can be discerned in Sibelius's orchestral writing, there is a determined effort on the part of the composer to put his own imprint on the themes of *Kullervo*. The initial ideas were obviously in Sibelius's mind associated with Finnish folk song since the first sketch was, according to a letter the composer sent his fiancée from Vienna, based on an actual folk tune. Yet, firm determination was not enough to get the composer started on his work. After a complete impasse he had to abandon the idea of using a folk song as his main theme.

However, with *Kullervo* Sibelius establishes a feature that was to be characteristic of his oeuvre. While the opening theme of the first movement with a strong upward sweep represents a melodic line typical of many romantic composers, a clear Finnish impact is seen in the main theme of the second movement, "Kullervo's Youth," opening on a strong stress, repetition of tones, and a limited melodic range, typical features of Finnish folk melodies. The first two movements are important in establishing a contrast that was to become one of the cornerstones of Sibelius's idiom. The middle movement "Kullervo and his sister," a baritone representing Kullervo and a soprano his sister, is important in establishing genuine Finnish recitative with sensitivity to the demands of the language. The mostly syllabic writing for the soloists and the choral writing chiefly in unison enhance the primitive atmosphere, as can be seen from the opening line of the chorus in which Kullervo is introduced:

Example 8 (C) by Breitkopf & Haertel, Wiesbaden.

"Kullervo's Lament" after his sister's death introduces a theme reminiscent of Karelian laments (*Largamente*). Although Layton discerns "an unmistakably Slav ring"[11] about it, the opening of the Kalevalaic duple-unit theme displays such typical characteristics of Finnish folk song as a descending melodic line ending in a falling cadence and trochaic repetition of the final tone. However, the accompaniment is firmly rooted in triadic harmony. Thus we have in *Kullervo* a feature that was to become typical of Sibelius's idiom: a scheme of contrasting themes, one of which can be characterized as "romantic," the other as "Finnish." This tendency is seen even in compositions not inspired by Finnish literature. A case in point is his incidental music to a Swedish translation of Maeterlinck's *Pelléas et Mélisande* by the composer's friend Bertel Gripenberg. The "Pastorale" and "Death of Melisande" of the suite represent the Nordic, elegiac mood so familiar to us from the works of any Scandinavian composer of the period, while "In the Park" derives from the Finnish Sibelius:

Example 9 Reprinted by permission of the original publisher Robert Lienau, Berlin.

Layton feels that many composers would have omitted the sixth bar in favor of a well-balanced eight-bar phrase, and he obviously considers the asymmetrical phrasing a stroke of Sibelian originality. However, the construction is, indeed, symmetrical from the point of view of runo-song construction with prolongation of the final tone of the second half of the duple phrasing, in order to facilitate the second singer's assuming of the recitation despite the fact that the two phrases appear asymmetrical. Evidence of this type of flexibility of construction was observed by Kodály in Hungarian folk music.   Likewise, Sibelius's melody winding around the pivotal tone of E and the falling final cadence ending in a prolonged tone reflect the influence of Finnish folk song, as does the monotonously insistent melodic line of "The Three Blind Sisters" based also on parallel dual construction:

Example 10 Reprinted by permission of the original publisher Robert Lienau, Berlin.

The limited melodic range and the rigidity of construction suit poorly the fluidity of the original French text.   Although Sibelius's Finnish style enhances the gloomy atmosphere of the Maeterlinck work, the heaviness of the writing is not compatible with the play in the way Fauré's and Debussy's lighter touch is.

With *Kullervo* Sibelius established another feature that was to be important in his idiom: the use of modal coloring within the framework of major-minor tonality.   For example, the opening theme is in E minor with an Aeolian flavor and the runo-style theme of the second movement includes the tones of the Dorian sixth, with the exception of C-sharp.   In the climactic third movement, the orchestral introduction is in the Lydian F major, the first scene between Kullervo and his sister in Dorian D minor, shifting to Dorian E minor in the scene of Kullervo meeting another maiden and to Dorian C-sharp minor, which is also the key of the orchestral interlude representing Kullervo's seduction of his sister.

As we know, modal coloring was used by many Russian composers, but *Kullervo* was more of a pioneering work than most compositions by the "Russian Five" with their incorporation of folk tunes.   In *Kullervo*, the penetration of folk influence is deeper than in most works by the Russian nationalistic composers, except for Mussorgsky, and Sibelius's achievement in *Kullervo* is comparable to Mussorgsky's in Russian music even in the creation of genuine native recitative and in the observance of the requirements of the languages in question in their musical idioms.

Kullervo was a landmark in the Finnish nationalistic movement and it was important for Sibelius as a composer in forcing him to decide between native and foreign influences in his music. However, basically *Kullervo* is still a romantic composition. The fact that the work opens on a romantic theme, possibly characterizing the hero as an ambitious man, and the fact that "Kullervo's Youth" presents a Finnish-style theme establishes a typically romantic conflict of the protagonist as a man of the world and as a Finn; in other words, the composer as the protagonist. Thus we are dealing with a romantic, subjective view, and many of the weaknesses of the work as well as its greatest strength, the genuine inspiration, are attributable to this basic view. A more objective approach to composition is manifest in *En Saga*, which Harold Truscott, justifiably, considers the key to the composer's symphonies.

We can do no better than to let Sibelius provide us with a key to the ensuing discussion with a short quote from the opening of *En Saga* (oboe, clarinet, and bassoon, pp. 2-3):

Example 11 (C) by Breitkopf & Haertel, Wiesbaden.

An obvious feature in the example is the emphasis on dissonance after the chords in solid triadic harmony; we shall return to this issue. The other important matter concerns rhythm.

With *En Saga* Sibelius establishes rhythm as one of the key factors in his idiom. Why is this important? Because with the work the composer proclaims his opposition to the Wagnerian ideal the German master had established in *Tannhäuser* and stated in "On the Performance of *Tannhäuser*": "I urge that the strict

observance of the musical beat be given up almost completely . . .
Let the singer give absolutely free rein to his natural feeling, yes,
even to the physical necessities of his breathing in the more
agitated phrases . . . ."[12] This was in keeping with the trend of
romantic music towards instinctive, or intentional, introduction of
speech rhythms and intonations into music, as, for example, in
Fauré, Elgar and Vaughan Williams,[13] and the effect of language
can be seen in such cases as the difference between Liszt's
German and French settings.

Now, Sibelius was a bilingual Finn. Which language was it
that affected his musical idiom? He showed great sensitivity to
the Swedish lyrics of lieder like "Säv, säv, susa" in taking
advantage of the dark vowels of the final line "våg, våg, slå." On
the other hand, he showed keen sensitivity to the runo text in
Kullervo and in setting Kivi's lullaby to a dead child, "Sydämeni
laulu" — before the death of his own little daughter — he was
inspired by the sound of the Finnish language in giving the line
"Siell' on lapsen lysti olla" (It is lovely for the child there) with
repetition of the sonorous consonant [l] and the closed vowels [e],
[i], [y] by the tenors, with the line "kaitsea Tuonelan karjaa" (to
tend to the herd of Tuonela) with the open vowel [a], the
diphthong [uo] and the harsh consonants [k], [t], [r] given to the
basses in the choral setting, as Tawaststjerna points out.

When Sibelius composed a setting for Runeberg's Swedish-
language poem "Till Frigga" (To Frigga), he set it in 9/4 time,
which reflects the compound rhythm of four and five beats, or
2+2+2+3, of Finnish folk songs, whose influence can be detected
also in the slowly rising melodic line. If we believe in the theory
of an interrelationship between language and music, how could
Sibelius then have been influenced by the characteristics of
Finnish folk song and the Finnish language in setting a Swedish
text?   Very easily, indeed, because of the fact that Finnish
Swedish, which Sibelius learned as his first language, uses the
falling intonation of Finnish, unlike that of the Swedish of
Sweden with its tendency to rising intonation. Thus the marked
Sibelian trend of descending phrases like those of his solo-voice
setting of the Swedish poem "Säv, säv, susa" (Sigh, rushes, sigh)
could be attributed to either Finnish or Finnish-Swedish
intonation, although the harp-like accompaniment, which could
reflect the kantele, might point to specifically Finnish influence.
One example of *Luonnotar*, a work in which Sibelius's sensitivity
to the runo text is superb, will suffice to illustrate this
phenomenon from the point of view of the language:

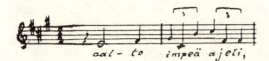

aal - to   impeä ajeli,

Example 12 (C) by Breitkopf & Haertel, Wiesbaden.

Because Finnish orthography indicates both long vowels and geminated consonants with double letters, it is possible even for a non-Finn to see Sibelius's principle.

Given the composer's high degree of sensitivity to the Finnish language, it is easy to see his common melodic pattern of a long note followed by a triplet as a reflection of enclitic personal endings of verbs and case endings or possessive endings of nouns, as Tawaststjerna mentions in passing. Thus the parallel between *saa-rel-la-ni* (on my island) and the rhythm of the opening of the swan's theme in "The Swan of Tuonela" (𝅝. 𝅘𝅥𝅯𝅘𝅥𝅯𝅘𝅥) is obvious.

As typical examples of the influence of the Finnish language on prominent themes in Sibelius's symphonies, we might cite the main theme of the first movement of the First Symphony:

Example 13 (C) by Breitkopf & Haertel, Wiesbaden.

and the *Tranquillo* theme, which is a variation of the main theme, of the first movement of the First Symphony and the second subject of the first movement of the Second Symphony:

Example 14 (C) by Breitkopf & Haertel, Wiesbaden.

Tawaststjerna refers to it as "this recitative-like figure" but fails to emphasize that with the agogic accent on the first tone followed by a triplet it is definitely Finnish-accented recitative.

An extreme utilization of the properties of spoken language for the enhancement of music is, of course, that of Wagner's sound-painting, whose value from the purely musical point of view has frequently been contested. According to Wagner, an artist could be aided in "feeling back" his sensations by suggestive rhythmic patterns or by alliteration (*Stabreim*) in which the kindred speech roots (obviously from the point of view of sound, not grammar, etymology, or any such considerations) are fitted to one another in such a way that, "just as they sound alike to the physical ear, they also knit like objects into a collective image in which the feeling may utter its conclusion about them."[14]

The Wagnerian *Stabreim* of "Ross und Reiter," "froh und frei," and so on, has its ready-made equivalent in the poetry of the *Kalevala*, starting with the stock epithets of *vaka, vanha Väinämöinen* "steadfast, old Väinämöinen" and *lieto Lemminkäinen* "reckless Lemminkäinen," a feature with which translators obviously can never hope to cope successfully.

Examples of building into an emotional climax by verbal means abound in the *Kalevala*. One example is the passage in which Väinämöinen and Joukahainen have a singing contest to find out which of the two is more knowledgeable and has a better memory.   Väinämöinen,   after   having   been   insulted   by Joukahainen, gets really angry and begins to sing with the following effect (runo III):

> Järvet läikkyi, maa järisi,
> Vuoret vaskiset vapisi,
> Paaet vahvat paukahteli,
> Kalliot kaheksi lenti,
> Kivet rannoilla rakoili.
> (Reprinted by permission of Suomalaisen Kirjallisuuden Seura)

The following is the writer's rendering of the passage into English, with the effect of the propulsive rhythm and much of the impact of the sound painting with plosives of the original lost in the translation:

> Lakes swelled up, the earth shook,
> The copper mountains trembled,
> The mighty rocks cracked,
> The crags burst,
> The stones on the shore split.

If we compare the *Kalevala* poetry's sound-painting, its method of parallelism mainly in two-line divisions, and the rhythmic monotony of the eight-syllable lines with a typical excerpt from a Wagner opera, for example, of *Tristan und Isolde* (act III, scene I), in which Tristan describes his place of birth to Kurwenal:

> Wo ich erwacht, weilt' ich nicht;
> doch wo ich weilte, das kann ich dir nicht sagen.
> Die Sonne sah' ich nicht,
> nicht sah' ich Land noch Leute;
> doch was ich sah,
> das kann ich dir nicht sagen.

it is easy to see that repetition is suggested as a key feature both by the *Kalevala* text and Wagner's lyrics, although in a completely different manner. While Wagner's verbal repetition suggests the use of leitmotifs whose occurrence depends on the meaning of the text, the *Kalevala*'s monotonous rhythmic repetition suggests rhythmic firmness in music and the parallel structure of two-line units leads naturally to duple-unit phrasing.

While Sibelius wrote competent Finnish recitative in *Kullervo* and while a common melodic pattern of his idiom opens on a prolonged tone on the strong beat followed by a triplet in adherence to the Finnish intonation, the most important discovery the composer made while working on *En Saga* was that in *Kullervo* the influence of Finnish language and poetry was not yet fused into his idiom. He realized that the use of the leitmotif, which he called "too purposive," was not the answer. He concluded that despite the ancient connection between music and poetry the two art forms had drifted so far apart that the independence of each had to be respected. We can see the shift in Sibelius's thinking when we compare the five-beat measures and the adherence to the *Kalevala* text in *Kullervo* with the rhythmic steadiness of *En Saga*.

The rhythmic monotony of Finnish folk songs found its echo in the insistent rhythm of the following themes of *En Saga*:

Example 15 (C) by Breitkopf & Haertel, Wiesbaden.

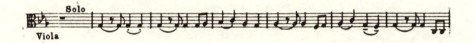

Example 16 (C) by Breikopf & Haertel, Wiesbaden.

They are based on the rhythmic motif of ♩ ♪ 𝄾 ♩ ♩ ,varied to ♩ 𝄾 ♪ ♩ ♩ . They are self-repeating and they could be carried on endlessly just as in the cases of the runo songs mentioned earlier. As an example of a runo tune with rests within a bar, "Kullervo, Kalervon poiga" (Kullervo, Kalervo's son) could be pointed to as an indication of the open-end quality:

E: Kul - ler - - 'vo Ka - - ler-von   poi - ga, *(J:)* Ši - ni-

šuk-ka   hie - no - hel - ma.

Example 17 Courtesy of Suomalaisen Kirjallisuuden Seura.

As in the folk song sample, in Sibelius's *En Saga*, emphasis on rhythmic monotony is felt throughout the work and it is clearly manifest at the end with the music gradually dying and the only thing remaining, the steady beat, "morendo"

Example 18 (C) by Breitkopf & Haertel, Wiesbaden.

A different type of emphasis on rhythm is manifest in the competing theme group in *En Saga*. The theme is based on an extremely simple phrase ending in a prolonged note:

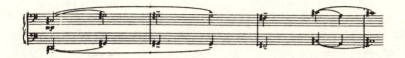

Example 19 (C) by Breikopf & Haertel, Wiesbaden.

It is clearly reminiscent of runo tunes, as is its variant:

Example 20 (C) by Breitkopf & Haertel, Wiesbaden.

The relatedness of these themes is even more obvious from the point of view of Finnish folk song than from pure theory. Both tunes are based on two bars of emphatic tones of equal length. The variation of the final two bars of the second example can be understood from the point of view of folk song as a representation of the same time value divided in a different manner in each case. The typical eight-syllable line of the *Kalevala* verse could easily be sung to these tunes (cf. Example 6). This is in keeping with Kodály's observation of Hungarian folk songs: "Rubato does not so much mean sudden changes of tempo as different lengths of fermata, the pauses between the lines; the time-value of parlando sections does not generally show much variety."[15]

Thus *En Saga* is the first work in which Sibelius used rhythm both as a cohesive force and as an element of construction in a manner reflective of both Finnish folk song and folk poetry. Just how intent the composer was on the use of an amalgamation of various devices for cohesion is seen in the final version of the work which retains the same basic tempo, whereas in the first version new thematic material was introduced in the development section, the tempo was slackened, and there was a series of chromatic modulations, not unlike those of Wagner. However, in the revised version Sibelius cut out the lyric episode, thus subjecting the work to greater discipline.[16]

In the First Symphony, there is clear evidence of attempts at thematic unity by means of short motifs in which rhythmic factors play a prominent role. The opening clarinet theme suggests two motifs:

2 Clarinetti in A

Example 21 (C) by Breitkopf & Haertel, Wiesbaden.

Numerous variants of motif *a* create more thematic logic than the work is usually given credit for (cf. Example 13).

An interesting use of a rhythmic motif ♩. 𝄾 ♪ , for coherence occurs in several themes of the finale of the Second Symphony, and the cohesive power of the motif is anticipated in the previous movement, the scherzo, in two themes. The fact that the figures with short rests occur in the bars preceding the end of phrases in the bridge passage between the scherzo and the finale made Cecil Gray attribute their use to the influence of the *Atempause*, the breathing rest, of the Viennese waltz. However, as far as the Second Symphony is concerned, the same rhythmic figure occurs also in the beginning of phrases, and thus it is easier to see its use as an application of Sibelius's germ motif technique rather than as a reflection of the *Atempause*, even if the composer was fond of the Viennese waltz.

Sibelius's germ motif technique evolved far beyond mere repetition and variation. Just as the composer discovered during the year he finished *Kullervo* that the main weakness of the work was its lack of thematic cohesion, he realized at the time he was concluding his First Symphony that the thematic growth in the work did not satisfy him. The first sign of the composer developing further his germ motif technique came with his solo song "Illalle" (To the Evening) from 1898, one of the rare ones by the composer based on Finnish lyrics. There are clear indications that, once again, the basic idea for a further development of Sibelius's method came from the poetry of the *Kalevala*, as we can deduce from a closer scrutiny of Sibelius's song in the light of Kalevalaic poetry.

The idea of using repetition and variation to build to a climax occurs commonly in the incantations of Finnish folk poetry where they are frequently woven into epic poems. Incantations were recited to hold back the dangerous forces of nature or to give a sailor a favorable wind for his voyage, a fisherman good luck, and so on. The following from runo XXIX, used on this occasion by Lemminkäinen on starting on his trip to Saari to woo Kyllikki, occurs in several variants:

Wind, inflate my sails above me
Wind of spring, push on the vessel,
Drive the boat of pine wood forward
To a nameless isle, and a nameless promontory.

Concurring with Tawaststjerna's view, it is this writer's conviction that the invocational character of the Forsman-Koskimies sonnet entitled "Illalle" brought to Sibelius's mind the Kalevalaic method of repetition and made him associate it with the incantations of Finnish folk poetry. In this setting, which dates from 1898, he used the runo-technique of building to a climax. It is no longer a matter of repeating a phrase but rather of creating a sense of growth by means of simple variations. In other words, Sibelius turns the self-repeating force of the Finnish folk song, which depends only on minor variation, into something organic and growth-giving like the power inherent in a seed. Thus he manages to create the sensation of an elemental force at work.

Sibelius's Second Symphony depends on this sense of organic growth and not only on repetition and variation as the concepts were established in earlier art music. The growth process starts with the opening motif:

Example 22 (C) by Breitkopf & Haertel, Wiesbaden.

The following theme is introduced by the oboes and clarinets and commonly referred to as the first subject:

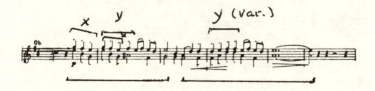

Example 23 (C) by Breitkopf & Haertel, Wiesbaden.

It is important in crystallizing the opening motif into a germ (*x*), which gives rise to another germ (*y*). The self-perpetuating power of the germ is seen in the way it gives rise to two fairly long phrases whose parallelism seems to reflect the duple units of the *Kalevala* poetry.

Practically all important themes of the Second Symphony are traceable to the germ motif. When the finale repeats the germ in a macrorhythm, the listener cannot fail to sense the thematic unity of the work, which is subjected to the strict discipline of the usual ternary structure (exposition, development, recapitulation) in the first movement and the finale and a binary structure in the middle movements.

In *Luonnotar*, we have an excellent example of the growth process expressed with the germ motif technique. After the violins introduce the germ, the soprano opens her intoning on the same motif:[17]

Example 24 (C) by Breitkipf & Haertel, Wiesbaden.

With the clarinets introducing a variant of the germ motif, a new dimension has been added:

Example 25 (C) by Breitkopf & Haertel, Wiesbaden.

This, in turn, gives rise to a syncopated rhythm, which opens the climax:

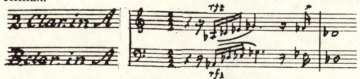

Example 26 (C) by Breitkopf & Haertel, Wiesbaden.

Renewed emphasis is placed on the original germ motif, when the trumpets and trombones announce the act of creation in a majestic macrorhythm:

Example 27 (C) by Breitkopf & Haertel, Wiesbaden.

The growth of the germ motif itself can be considered a parallel for the story of *Luonnotar*, the act of Creation, as told in the *Kalevala*'s symbolism in the form of the birth of the earth from a bird's egg.

With the Second Symphony Sibelius carried his method of creating a work of complete thematic unity considerably further than in the First; with the Third Symphony, on which he worked from 1904 to 1907, he reached still another stage. The symmetry (4 x 4) and firmness of rhythm of the opening bars of the Third Symphony has led many observers to compare them to Haydn and Mozart:

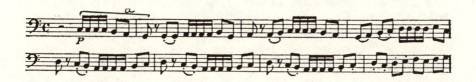

Example 28 Reprinted by permission of the original publisher Robert Lienau, Berlin.

Edward Garden, on the other hand, attributes the opening theme to influence of a theme of the first movement of Balakirev's First Symphony.[18]   However, Sibelius's motif is based on an actual Finnish folk theme:

Example 29 Courtesy of Suomalaisen Kirjallisuuden Seura.

which was collected in the Rautalampi district, not very far from the area where Sibelius had spent his honeymoon writing down folk songs. Since the distribution of a folk tune is hardly ever limited to a small area, it is possible that on that trip he heard the folk theme, which then remained in his subconscious. Sibelius did change the five-beat theme into a four-beat one, a change that is easily understood on the basis of the composer's problems with five-beat tunes in *Kullervo* and their omission in *En Saga*.

After the opening of the symphony, a pentatonic tune is introduced:

Example 30 Reprinted by permission of the original publisher Robert Lienau, Berlin.

Although it is somewhat folk-like, it is clearly in the romantic tradition in contrast with the opening of the work, and thus the basic conflict is established at the outset. The opening of the pentatonic tune could even contain a quick rhythmic recollection of a theme of the coda of the first movement of Beethoven's Pastoral Symphony, ♫ ⌐ ♫♫ *etc.* , another justification for the characterization of the Sibelius work as "pastoral." In addition to consisting of triadic sequences and Sibelius's motto theme (x), a matter to which we shall return, the end of the theme contains a pendant that harks back to the opening theme. The logic of the themes of the first movement is further emphasized by the fact that even the next important theme, a nostalgic cello theme accompanied by the violins and violas in pizzicato:

Example 31 Reprinted by permission of the original publisher Robert Lienau, Berlin.

is derived from the opening theme.

The conflict between classicism and romanticism is accentuated by the fact that the first part of the development section is dominated by motifs related to the opening theme and the second part by those affiliated more closely with the theme of Example 31. If the first movement states a conflict, the second, *Andantino con moto, quasi allegretto*, is simple, although more can be read into it than in most performances, as an excellent

interpretation by Kajanus in an early recording proves.[19]   The
flute theme, which is the basis of the movement, reflects the
stepwise progression of the opening theme of the first movement.
Sibelius emphasizes the folk-like atmosphere by letting the flute
theme   dominate   the   movement   practically   unvaried,   while
contrapuntal and orchestral coloring counteracts any threat of
feeling of monotony. A wonderful, faintly dance-like background
is created by the motion of the bass parts, in contrast to the more
commonly occurring pedal points.

The third movement, a fusion of a scherzo and a finale,
centers on a theme whose descending stepwise progression reflects
the opening theme of the first movement, as does the concluding
theme of the work:

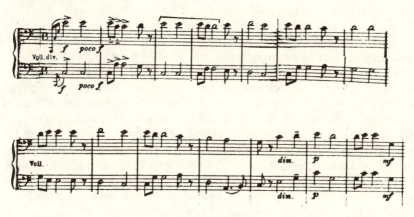

Example 32 Reprinted by permission of the original publisher Robert Lienau, Berlin.

It consists of thirteen nearly isorhythmic phrases, and it is a
splendid example of use of the *Kalevala*-style self-repeating tunes
that became one of the hallmarks of Sibelius's idiom.   From a
simple chant in two-bar units the composer was able to create a
logical ending to a symphony, which, unfortunately has been
underrated.

Thus Sibelius's early symphonies continue to refine the basis
of composition established in *En Saga*.   The method is
characterized by two principles: emphasis on rhythm and on
Sibelius's individual approach to the method of variation of a
theme.   However, rhythm is more an implied than a dominant
feature in *En Saga*, and it is the principle that Sibelius adheres to
in the works that followed. Rhythm is an important feature in the
Third Symphony from the opening bars through the slow
movement to the concluding theme of the finale, but Sibelius does

not allow his interest in rhythm to dominate the work in the way it often does for composers like Bartók, Prokofiev, and Stravinsky.

In Sibelius's use of rhythmic effects, there are two seemingly opposing trends, both of which are related to the use of rhythm in Finnish folk song: emphasis on a steady beat, even to the point of monotony, on the one hand, and on flexibility, on the other. These are not necessarily opposing forces in folk song, which may use compound rhythms and yet maintain a steady beat. This is seen, for example, in the so-called Bulgarian rhythm, which can occur as an alternation of two-beat and three-beat measures, say, in a pattern of 2 + 2 + 3 + 2 in a rhythm marking of semiquavers. We might recall the constant changes of rhythm in some sections of Stravinsky's *Sacre du printemps* as a reflection of Russian folk music while the basic beat remains firm, and as early as 1862 Borodin had introduced in his C Minor Piano Quintet in the first movement alternation of two bars in 3/4 time and two bars in 2/4, which could also be interpreted as a 10/4 beat. A somewhat similar occurrence is Borodin's construction of the G-sharp minor trio of the scherzo movement of his First Symphony, often suggested as a possible influence on Sibelius's First Symphony, on a Russian folk motif of alternating three-beat and four-beat measures. As an example of rhythmic firmness despite change of marking in Sibelius's compositions we might cite his "Love Song" form the *Scènes historiques* II, Op. 66 (1912), in which by insertion of a two-beat measure into a steady three-beat tune, the composer creates a wonderful sense of the lover's passion and feeling of urgency with extremely simple means.

Compared to the exploitation of the rhythmic features of folk song by such composers as Bartók and Stravinsky, Sibelius's method could be characterized as an understatement. Sibelius considered the use of rhythm in his variation technique more crucial than rhythm *per se*. What caused Sibelius to look for revitalization of the continental idiom with means derived from folk music in the creation of his "themes and variations"?

Wagner's influence may have been important in reawakening Sibelius's interest in Finnish folk poetry and through it folk song. Wagner, who was not interested in folk poetry except for its unusual topics, recognized the ancient connection between music and poetry, starting with the Greeks, and made music subservient to his poetry to the extent that he considered the vocal line in *Tannhäuser*, the *Ring* cycle, *Tristan und Isolde*, and *Parsifal* so sacrosanct that he placed his word-painting mostly in the imitative effects of the orchestra in order not to disrupt the vocal line dictated by speech.[20] Sibelius, on the other hand, like Bartók and

Stravinsky, realized that music and poetry had drifted so far apart that their independence had to be respected.

In *Kullervo*, there is no evidence of use of leitmotifs, even if a melody of the coda of the first movement reappears in the finale; nor is there any indication as yet of the exploitation of a germ for development of new ideas characterizing *En Saga*. Just as Bartók's and Stravinsky's methods of composition have been compared to the *talea* and *dragma* techniques of older music, we can sense in Sibelius's variation method and in the construction of parallel phrases in duple units, the influence of old Finnish music and its close relationship to the text.

Although the method of variation of a theme as a form of thematic unity is found as early as Haydn, it was Beethoven, Sibelius's idol, who made the principle the cornerstone of his idiom. Naturally every composer is influenced by the past, and certain similarities do, indeed, exist — for example, between Sibelius's Second and Third Symphonies and Beethoven's Fourth and Fifth[21]— in the importance of short motifs as the bases of these works. But the motifs themselves, as well as their employment, display fundamental differences between the composers. In Beethoven's motifs the third interval plays an important role (as in the Fourth and Fifth Symphonies) as do arpeggios (in the Third and Sixth Symphonies, in particular), while Sibelius's motifs are chiefly conditioned by the second and fourth intervals, familiar to us from Finnish folk song, which he juxtaposes with those dependent on triadic harmony. Likewise, in Beethoven's method the employment of these motifs relies mainly on "academic" techniques (for example, diminutions in the Fourth and Fifth Symphonies), while Sibelius's method reflects also the variation techniques of Finnish folk song and poetry.

Inspired by Beethoven's example, Brahms created his own style of variations based on short motifs, which he usually starts to develop almost immediately without repetition or considerations of symmetry.[22]   Although Brahms's method, naturally, included repetition, such as the descending second in the opening of his C minor Quartet, Op. 51 No. 1, his frequent dispensing with "small scale rhythmic or metrical symmetry" suggested to Walter Frisch, following Schoenberg's observation, that the composer had created "genuine musical prose." Brahms's method of variations, although influenced by folk song, was more "academic" than Sibelius's and it is easy to see why Brahms has had numerous imitators, perhaps even Aaron Copland.

Sibelius never professed much admiration for Brahms, but a performance of Bruckner's Third Symphony, which he heard while he was a student in Vienna, made an enormous impression on him.   He admired in particular "its youthful quality,"[23] although it was composed by "an old man."   What did Sibelius mean by "its youthful quality"?   He probably sensed the feeling of growth and dynamism in the way the climax is built starting from the opening trumpet theme.   Yet Sibelius observed that from the point of view of form the work was "ridiculous."   He was evidently aware of the fact that Bruckner builds his theme before the *crescendo* and, in order to create a climax, Bruckner could not go any further with the theme and, instead, had to introduce a new theme.   In other words, the work alerted Sibelius to the conflict — and the possibilities of its exploitation — that existed between the demands of themes and those of symphonic structures.

Although Sibelius's First Symphony uses certain short rhythmic and melodic motifs as a unifying force and, in particular, the first movement points to the Sibelian brand of organic growth, it was only in the Second Symphony that the composer created the variation method that can be characterized as his own.   To what was the change due?   It may have been due to Sibelius's extended trip to Italy in 1901-1902, when he heard older church music and became an admirer of Palestrina.   This was crucial in assisting Sibelius to rid himself of the ghosts of Wagner and Tchaikovsky.

In order to understand Sibelius's thinking, it might be useful to recall Debussy's reaction after he heard a Palestrina mass at Saint-Gervais: "Even though technically it's very strict, the effect is of utter whiteness, and emotion is not represented (as had come to be the norm since) by dramatic cries but by melodic arabesques."[24]   It is easy to see that the same features of Palestrina's music that fascinated Debussy must have made an impression on Sibelius.   The strict discipline, which Sibelius found frequently lacking in Bruckner, is much more in evidence in Sibelius's Second Symphony than in his First, and the "dramatic cries" of the First Symphony are replaced by "melodic arabesques" in the Second, represented by germ motifs whose basic features hark back to Finnish folk music.

In the Third Symphony Sibelius was finally able to build his variations on an actual folk tune, thus accomplishing what he had set out to do in *Kullervo*, while the thematic antithesis, typical of romantic composers, also remained a feature of the work.   Thus, with the Third Symphony Sibelius refutes Schoenberg's statement: "I cannot remember a single case of deriving subordinate ideas from a folk song by this method [the method of developing variations]."[25]   When Schoenberg stated in his discourse entitled "Folkloristic Symphonies" (1947), "The discrepancy between the requirements of larger forms and the simple construction of folk tunes has never been solved and cannot be solved,"[26] he obviously was not aware of the fact that in his Second Symphony Sibelius had used as the backbone of the work a motif that could have been suggested by a typical progression of Finnish folk songs and that in his Third Symphony he had used an actual folk tune for the same purpose. After achieving in the Third Symphony what Sibelius had set out to do in *Kullervo*, the creation of a symphonic work based on a folk tune, what caused the collapse of his world in the Fourth Symphony?

THE WATERSHED AND ITS AFTERMATH

Although a period of only four years, from 1907 to 1911, separates Sibelius's Fourth Symphony from his Third, the works seem to originate in a completely different world. What were the reasons for the change from the most optimistic symphony to the most pessimistic?

The reception of the Third Symphony in cities like St. Petersburg, Moscow, and Berlin was not as favorable as Sibelius had hoped for. A young Russian music student, however, Sergey Prokofiev, was impressed enough by the cello introduction to present immediately an exercise in composition featuring a solo cello to Rimsky-Korsakov, to the latter's consternation. At any rate, Sibelius was by this time trying to ignore reviews as much as possible, although evidence of hurt feelings is a common occurrence in his diaries.

Political reasons have frequently been cited for the pessimism of the Fourth Symphony. However, while Sibelius was working on the Third, one of the worst crises in Finno-Russian relations occurred: the assassination of the Russian governor general in Finland in 1904, followed by a general strike and the constitutional crisis of 1905. Although this resulted in concessions to the Finns, efforts at Russification were resumed in 1908. The Czar's prime minister, Stolypin, was against any negotiations with the Finns and Paasikivi considered the situation more serious than in 1904-1905. When the 1910 legislation concluded that all important matters concerning Finland had to be decided by the Duma, Sibelius, like any Finn, felt apprehensive. However, just as at the time when he was working on the Third Symphony, he tried to stay above day-to-day developments.   Besides, he had many more pressing problems with his precarious health and his chaotic financial situation.

After surgeons in Helsinki were unsuccessful at removing a throat tumor, they advised Sibelius to consult a German specialist. The composer was so deeply in debt after building his house that he simply did not have the money for the trip to Germany and even the banks considered him a poor risk.   The humiliation of having to make the rounds begging for a loan for a hospital trip, while his pregnant wife was waiting on a park bench, compounded with no bright prospects of royalties for his compositions was traumatic enough to give Sibelius nightmares even in later years.   Let the composer's own words interpret his state of mind, when he referred to "dessa stämningar som födas ur tomhet och smärta!!" (these moods which are born of emptiness and pain).[1]

These moods are reflected in the opening of the Fourth Symphony in the prominence of the tritone:

Example 33 (C) by Breitkopf & Haertel, Wiesbaden.

Most observers have referred to the similarity of the opening to Wagner's *Tristan*.   However, in view of the remarks in the previous chapter of Sibelius voicing his objection to Wagner's use of the leitmotif by means of the technique he employed in *En Saga* and his first three symphonies, the idea of possible Wagner influence in the basic motif of Sibelius's Fourth Symphony has to be viewed with caution.   We might also recall that dissonance played an important role in the opening of *En Saga*.   Likewise, the tritone figures prominently in the main theme of the Violin Concerto as well as in the Third Symphony, which followed it.

The prominence of the tritone is established in the Third Symphony right in the first movement in various themes.   For example:

Example 34 Reprinted by permission of the original publisher Robert Lienau, Berlin.

The theme introduces the tone of F-sharp, which in the key of C is the tritone, the destroyer of harmony, and a sense of conflict is enforced by a broken triad in the following:

Example 35 Reprinted by permission of the original publisher Robert Lienau, Berlin.

An interesting difference is observed in the melodic use of the tritone between the Third and Fourth Symphonies. While the theme of Example 34 of the Third uses the tritone in the traditionally accepted way as the leading tone to G, the theme of Example 33 of the Fourth has the F-sharp as the highest tone, obviously introducing a desolate mood. However, the most significant use of the tritone in the Third Symphony is its use as a harmony note.

The often-repeated claim that the Third Symphony is "classical" is supported by Sibelius's treatment of tonality. The progression from C to F-sharp (p. 7, measures 1-6), the tritone, "forms a parallel to the modulation from tonic to dominant in the classical symphony, a change of tonality made in order that the second subject [Example 31] might provide an area of contrast with the opening by being in a key one degree sharper."[2] Thus Sibelius writes the key signature with one sharp for the second subject, although the music has to be one degree sharper still, since the first group of themes already included many F-sharps. "Hence, Sibelius writes a second subject in B minor — a key one degree sharper than Lydian C major." Then the composer returns the second group of themes to the "correct" key of G. Thus the first movement does, in fact, adhere to the "classical" concept of tonality.

The key of the second movement, G-sharp minor, seems unusual for a C major symphony, but, as Lionel Pike indicates, the choice of key follows logically from the fact that C and F-sharp were the pivotal notes of the first movement to create tonal areas opposed to C and that F-sharp acts as the dominant of B, as we saw from the second subject of the first movement. With the creation of a new tritone, F to B, and with the prominence of B established, the choice of the relative minor of B as the key of the second movement is logical. However, the result of the prominence of G-sharp as the tonic presented a considerable challenge for the composer regarding the finale, in which the opening octave G-natural and the tritone F to B in the harmony help to reestablish the key of C major. The task was not easy and, as Pike points out, the uncertainty about the key is accentuated by rhythmic irregularity, a feature that was to be important in the Fourth Symphony.

After a complicated manipulation of the keys between F-sharp and F-natural and C-sharp and C-natural, the resolution of F-sharp into C major is established only in the last four bars of the finale, where the C major triad, C-E-G, is played in octaves, a device used prominently both by Sibelius and Bartók for emphasis and probably influenced by monophonic folk song. The conflict between B and C, which was also to play an important role in Sibelius's Seventh Symphony, is obstinately maintained in the strings almost to the end, when B is finally resolved up to C.

In addition to the prominence of the tritone in the Third and Fourth Symphonies, there are numerous characteristically Sibelian features present in the latter work. The usual thematic antithesis is seen in various themes in which the tritone figures prominently, on the one hand, and in those that depend on the triad, on the other. A thematic dialogue is established between the opening theme containing a tritone and the following, introduced in measure 6 of the Fourth Symphony:

Example 36 (C) by Breitkopf & Haertel, Wiesbaden.

A double pedal point, E and F-sharp, with its dissonance, affects the interplay between the A minor and C major triads. Thus the basic conflict is a reversal of that of the Third Symphony: in the latter work the tritone destroys harmony and the triad is broken in the first movement whereas in the Fourth Symphony harmony is in disarray right from the start, and there is an attempt to restore it.

The second movement opens with an oboe theme centered on the major triad and it is followed by a delicate theme, in which the triad also figures prominently, played by a string quintet together with the oboe. The mood is changed by the introduction of this theme, which depends largely on second and fourth intervals:

Example 37 (C) by Breitkopf & Haertel, Wiesbaden.

The contrast between triadic thinking and the stepwise progression of folk music is mirrored in the switch from triple time in the previous themes to duple time. The change in rhythm and the presentation of the theme by violins and violas in unison clearly suggest the influence of Finnish folk song as well.

Was it Sibelius's purpose to insert some folk-song material in the manner of Rimsky-Korsakov? Certainly not, because the theme leads again to atonality by the use of several augmented fourths followed by long chords in the wind instruments and, once again, both the tonality and the regular pulse are destroyed. Thus the second movement is important in showing the incompatibility of a tune in the style of genuine folk melodies with the major-minor tonal system.

In the first movement there is tonal uncertainty between the key centers of C (A minor) and F-sharp, with the "development" section (pp. 6-10) being completely atonal. After several augmented fourths play havoc with both the tonality and pulse, the return to the tonic in the last two bars is a mere whisper. However, continuity is established with the tone of A, in which the second movement begins. The fairly settled mood of the opening cannot be maintained; the movement ends with harmony in disarray and the lack of direction is reflected in the third movement, *Il tempo largo*, at the outset in an augmented fourth. The movement presents several motifs based on unrelated triads with no firmness in either rhythm or tonality and a C-sharp major climb comes crashing down three octaves. After a short whole-tone theme, a hint at the main theme of the last movement forms a transition to the *Allegro*. As with the first two movements, only a weak link is suggested with the finale opening on C-sharp, the tone on which the third movement ends. Even though the last movement opens with the key of A major quite well established, uncertainty prevails despite the glockenspiel's attempts at establishing the key. While the strings are playing in E-flat and the wind instruments in A, the tritone (C and F-sharp) opening the coda indicates destruction of tonality, and the key of A major is reached only in the final bars.

A sense of groping is reflected in the symphony's formal structure, and analysts have disagreed on the nature of the movements. William C. Hill calls the first and last movements a "sonata-allegro form, not deviating too far from regularity,"[3] whereas Tanzberger considers the first movement a three-part song preceded by a prologue and the last movement a sonata-type form without restatement. While Hill considers the second movement a rondo "with a richly developed coda," Tanzberger considers it a three-part song rounded off by an epilogue. Robert Simpson, on the other hand, considers the first movement "a clear and simple sonata movement"[4] and the second a scherzo "with the merest hint of a reprise." While most commentators characterize the third movement as a rondo, Simpson describes it as "an unclassifiable growth where a theme forms itself by a *quanta*." He agrees with most observers on the sonata-like nature of the last movement.

In this short summary of the thematic and tonal scheme of the Fourth Symphony two facts stand out: the incompatibility of the folk-like theme in the second movement (Example 37) with the triadic system the work is trying to establish, and the fact that with the tonality in disarray, the only thing to cling to is a given tone. Despite a few periods of stability, everything in the work is on the point of falling apart any moment and, therefore, the emphasis on a given tone as a fragile cohesive link is appropriate symbolically.

In the first movement, the slow-moving pace of the themes is held together by pedal points, and their prolongations and shifts support the thematic development, which is kept within the bounds of a sonata form. As Simpson points out, "for the first time in a symphony [Sibelius] made practical application of a means which had always been to hand if anyone could have thought of using it."[5] Thus Sibelius used the simple principle of the folk song's emphasis on a given tone as the support of a symphonic structure within a movement and between movements. And when we peel the symphony to its core, the main issue is the struggle between C and F-sharp, the former representing the key of A minor and stability and the latter, instability and destruction.

The thinking is clearly foreshadowed in the finale of the Third Symphony in which the tonic, C, is "like an obelisk with different faces — from one angle it reflects the light of A minor, form another that of F minor, and at moments when we see it edgeways there is no easily definable reflection (see Figures 8 to 12 in the score)."[6]

Already during his student years in Helsinki, Sibelius started to have doubts about the chromatic harmonies of Liszt and Wagner, composers whom Wegelius revered. Then during his year of study in Vienna, Sibelius was so overwhelmed by *Siegfried* that he joined the Wagner Society. But while he was reading Wagner's prose works, towards the end of his stay in Vienna, he again started to have doubts about the Wagnerian method. Yet in *Kullervo*, despite the introduction of a few runo-style melodies, we have clear evidence of Wagner's influence both in the orchestration and harmony, with frequent use of chromaticism. In *En Saga* we sense, for the first time, independent thinking. The tones of the opening of the work include (Example 11) C, E, E-flat, F-sharp, G, A, A-flat. The work has been criticized for a random use of tonalities. It opens in A minor (the key of the Fourth Symphony) and the most important key areas are C minor and its relative major, E-flat. Before ending in E-flat minor, the work touches such remote keys as E major, F-sharp minor, and G-sharp minor, which in the context is really A-flat minor. In other words, the tones important in the work are presented in the opening and, consequently, the criticism of lack of tonal cohesion in the work is valid only form the orthodox point of view. The fact that the modulations were even more frequent in the original version of *En Saga* than in the revised version is clear indication of inspiration derived from folk music, with its idea of tonality different from that of the established Western idiom prevalent at the time.[7]

Sibelius's First Symphony appears, at first blush, quite traditional, yet many of the conflicts in the work are indicative of development in the composer's thinking. The slow introductory clarinet solo should be in E minor,[8] the key of the work, but it opens in B minor, touches G major and cadences in G minor, which, with the roots of the keys a third apart — typical of the so-called nationalist composers — gives the opening a modal flavor. The key of B minor is finally established with the aid of an F-sharp pedal, a device which points clearly to later works, in particular to the Fourth Symphony. The significance of the fact that G (F-double sharp) remains a persistent note throughout the first movement of the First Symphony becomes clear with the opening of the second movement in E-flat, in which the G remains the third of the key:

Example 38 (C) by Breitkopf & Haertel, Wiesbaden.

The elements of G major (D, G, B) in a predominantly E-flat passage indicate the kind of emphasis on a pivotal chord that Sibelius was to explore more fully in the Second Symphony. In the third movement of the First Symphony, the scherzo, the G becomes dominant and thus the key of the movement, C major. The work foreshadows the kind of thinking that the composer explored in his later symphonies and it prepares the way for the emphasis on a few pivotal notes in the Fourth Symphony.

A conflict in the First Symphony between the keys determined by modality and the classical concept of a fourth or fifth apart, results in a dichotomy between C-sharp and C-natural and D-sharp and D-natural. On page 3 of the score (measure 13) Sibelius prevents the music from heading to a major key by a C-natural in harmony thus counteracting the C-sharps of the tune, which is, in fact, a conflict between the modal minor seventh and the more tonal leading-note. This pull of tonal forces in opposite directions foreshadows an important feature of the later symphonies, especially of the Sixth.

If the First Symphony establishes a clear trend in Sibelius's approach of emphasis on certain pivotal notes, this view is obvious in the Second Symphony right from the opening upward progression of repeated notes (cf. Example 22), which establishes, in addition to the fundamental tone of D, also F-sharp. A double use of the basic germ

Example 39 (C) by Breitkopf & Haertel, Wiesbaden.

opens on B-natural and B-flat, thus emphasizing the conflict inherent in the keynotes, D, F-sharp, and B-flat.

As Pike points out, the choice of these keynotes, which are a major third apart, presents a problem in that a continuous circle of modulations based on those fundamentals would return the music to the tonic. Since B-flat does not fit into the key of D major, there can be no such tonality in the classical sense that would include all three pivotal notes. The struggle of fitting the B-flat into the key of D major results in a conflict between D minor and D major, which goes on even in the finale necessitating numerous repetitions; this has caused many critics to characterize the finale as the weakest movement of the work. As Pike suggests, the whole-tone scale would have offered a solution, but since it lacks the perfect fifth and fourth, as well as the minor second, Sibelius rejected that alternative. This can be understood in view of the importance of seconds, fourths and fifths in his idiom. Thus the use of tonalities is linked with the thematic material and much of the tension in the work results from the requirements of the themes and the traditional view of tonalities.

Naturally, no composer works in a vacuum, and Sibelius's view of harmony and tonality certainly was influenced by that of his idol, Beethoven, who had already expanded the classical Haydn-Mozart concept in his First Symphony by strengthening the dominant at the expense of the tonic. In his Fifth Symphony, Beethoven suggests the tonal and thematic relationships in the opening and lays out the tonal design in the beginning of the Seventh, but he stays in the tonic-dominant orbit. While there is some indication of exploration of key relationships other than the tonic-dominant in the *Pastoral* and Eighth Symphonies, it is only the Ninth Symphony that clearly shows the trend towards the use of D minor and B-flat as pivotal keys and thus of key areas a third apart.[9]

The Ninth Symphony by Beethoven made an enormous impact on Sibelius, when he heard a performance of it during his student years abroad, and he commented that he felt "so small, so small." Therefore, it is not surprising that, inspired by Beethoven's example and by a liberated view of harmony and tonality derived from folk music, Sibelius in this First Symphony started to explore tonalities a third apart and to place emphasis on certain keynotes, expanding his view from one symphony to the next.

Tracing the development of Sibelius's thinking from *En Saga* through the early symphonies, we can see the trend towards emphasis on pivotal notes, which was compatible with Sibelius's desire to be "a slave" to his themes. It has to be admitted that, superficially, the romantic flavor of the First Symphony is obvious, suggesting Borodin's and Tchaikovsky's influence to many a listener. This somewhat uncontrolled romantic spirit, evident in such features as the less than successful emphasis on rhythm in the finale and the "lurid" chord[10] in the introduction to the trio of the scherzo, is counteracted by the surprising assurance in the handling of the tonalities which, particularly in the first movement, contributes to the sense of movement, one of the greatest assets of Sibelius's writing. The trend towards a more controlled expression in the Second Symphony is established even more clearly in the Third.

The distance from the "classicism" of the Third Symphony to the rhapsodic passages and the lack of development of themes in the usual Sibelian sense in the Fourth seems, on the surface, difficult to understand. However, when we delve deeper into these works, we realize that the continuity is there in the form of the central position of the tritone and of concentration on certain pivotal notes.

The ultimate paradox of the Fourth Symphony lies in the fact that, after Sibelius had found in the Third a reconciliation between a folk tune and the idea of developing a work of art from it, in the Fourth Symphony that victory is meaningless. Music is destroyed and neither the triads nor the whole-tone scale reappearing from time to time in the work could reestablish it. Thus Sibelius abandons tonality sporadically for valid reasons, namely, the crisis atmosphere of the work. There is a definite desire felt throughout the symphony to stay within a given tonality.

Sibelius's liberated view of the idea of keynotes concurs with the thinking of composers like Bartók and Stravinsky, who were influenced by the folk music of their native lands. As early as 1908 in the eighth of his Fourteen Bagatelles for piano, Opus 6, Bartók uses the intervals of a minor second, major third, and perfect fourth for the construction of a non-symmetrical cell in his radical departure from the harmonic use of the triad.[11] Both Bartók and Stravinsky abandoned the use of key signatures altogether. Sibelius, on the other hand, seems to believe in abandonment of the diatonic system only if there is a valid reason for it.

It is easy to see why Sibelius's Fourth Symphony was considered avant-garde at the time of its première and only gradually did it find its proper place among the composer's greatest achievements. As a typical early reaction we might cite an admission of incomprehension by Heikki Klemetti, a Finnish music critic and choral director: "Everything was strange. Weird, transparent creatures are soaring back and forth and speak to us in a language that we do not understand."[12] A strange evaluation was that of the critic for *Tidning för musik* in Helsinki, who concluded his review of the work: "His [Sibelius's] art represents . . . an orientation towards a fusion of Classicism, Romanticism, and Modernism, which might well become the ideal of the music of the future."[13] Despite the fact that the reaction of the audiences and of most critics was at first hesitant or negative (in Sweden it was received with hoots), there were a few who were able to see the significance of the symphony for future trends in music.

Undoubtedly there are reflections of trends prevalent in music at the time of the Fourth Symphony in Sibelius's use of the tritone, and the conflict between tonal and whole-tone elements, introduced in the opening by the C, D, E, F-sharp, is well-known, for example, from the works of Debussy. Likewise, the tension in the opening of the Fourth between C major with a Lydian fourth and F-sharp major exploits the trend to create conflict by introduction of modality, and by replacing the usual tonic-dominant tension of the sonata form by key relationships a tritone apart, Sibelius suggests bitonality, which is known from the works of such composers as Stravinsky and Bartók. What makes Sibelius's achievement unique is the sense of organic growth he manages to create from the varied ingredients. By his basic nature he was not an experimenter, and he even warned against excesses along those lines despite the fact that he found "much that [was] interesting in present-day music."[14]

To this writer, the highest achievement of the Fourth Symphony is its demonstration of courage, artistic integrity, and clarity of vision. Although Sibelius was in worse financial straits than at any point in his life either before or after, he composed exactly according to his beliefs.

After proving in the early symphonies that he had learned from Beethoven the significance of conflict in a composition, Sibelius showed with his Third Symphony that he could use song not only as a source of conflict but also as a generator of growth. Now his artistic integrity forced him to admit with the Fourth that he was a Kantian, for whom "free beauty," the highest manifestation of beauty, did not depend on an object and its perfection, and the beauty of music did not depend on words. Thus the themes of the Fourth no longer have the relationship to song they do in the Third. Although Sibelius seems to undermine the accomplishment of his Third Symphony with the Fourth, the latter does not necessarily mean rejection of the former but rather an artist's quest for something even higher and purer. Does the return of the Fifth Symphony to some principles of the Second and Third thus negate the Fourth? In a sense this is true, and several external circumstances may have contributed to this state of affairs.

In early 1914 Sibelius went to Berlin after a quiet year at home. As usual, he initially enjoyed hearing a great deal of new music, of which many pieces, in his view, showed influence of his own music. He was impressed enough by Schoenberg's Second String Quartet to state later that year to an interviewer in New York that Schoenberg was a composer he admired greatly. However, in the final analysis he concluded, upon reflection on Schoenberg's *Chamber Symphony*, that the work, important though it was, was the result of too much "cerebration,"[15] and he became convinced that his own music had infinitely more natural feeling and life than the works that represented the new direction. The activities of the independence movement in Finland also contributed to the trend towards greater externalization in his music.

The onset of the First World War and, as a result of growing unrest in Russia, the faint stirrings of Finland's independence movement must have brought back to Sibelius's mind some of the moods of *Karelia* and his other patriotic works. This makes the somewhat nostalgic return to the world of the early symphonies in the Fifth easily understood. However, the composer's powers of expression had undergone changes and, despite some similarities between the early symphonies and the Fifth, there is also a new Sibelius in evidence in the latter.

The Fifth Symphony in E-flat premiered in Helsinki on December 8, 1915, at the composer's fiftieth birthday celebration. Sibelius revised the work in 1916 and 1919. In the final revision, as the composer stated, the symphony was "så godt som ny-komponerad" (as good as composed anew),[16] and apparently he made radical changes, including the fusion of the original first and second movements into one, despite Harold Johnson's claim that the only difference between the second and third versions was the reorchestration of the slow movement and the grand capitulation of the finale.

Although there are similarities between the Third and Fifth Symphonies, there are differences as well. In the Third Sibelius fused the scherzo and the finale in such a way that the transformations from the scherzo generated the finale replacing the customary recapitulation.[17] In the Fifth, in the definitive version, the composer has a new movement integrated into the music between the end of the development and the recapitulation in order to create a combined first movement, with the scherzo of the earlier version replacing the recapitulation. This was the result of the natural growth of the thematic material, which was always paramount in Sibelius's thinking.

Thematically the composer puts his signature to the opening horn motif, which is characterized by an ascent of two fourth steps, separated by a full step (*x*), followed by a triadic descent (*b*).

4 Corni in F.

Example 40 Used with kind permission by Edition Wilhelm Hansen AS, Copenhagen.

We might recall that the fourth and fifth intervals, as well as seconds, are common in Finnish folk music, as they are in Hungarian folk tunes. Bartók makes ample use of these intervals, as does Kodály, and the latter's Sonata for cello and piano, Opus 4, uses the sequence C-sharp, F-sharp, G-sharp, C-sharp as a characteristic motif. Thus the thematic conflict in the horn motif of Sibelius's Fifth Symphony appears to state the antithesis between influence of folk song and standard triadic thinking (cf. Example 30).

The main theme of the first movement, presented by the flutes and oboes, is built on the basic ingredients of the opening motif. After a modulation to G major, a chromatic motif prepares the way for a woodwind theme (starting on p. 6, measure 3 of the score), which consists of two nearly identical periods, thus reflecting the parallelism of the two-line divisions of runosongs. After a change of tempo to *Allegro moderato* (*ma poco a poco stretto*), a change of key to B major and of rhythm from 12/8 to 3/4, the scherzo, which takes the place of recapitulation, opens on a theme that includes all the important germ motifs of the main theme, thus indicating logical growth. After several manipulations of the key, the climax is reached with repetitions of the opening horn motif.

The slow movement, *Andante mosso, quasi allegretto*, is strophic, as is the slow movement of the Third Symphony. The main theme of the movement

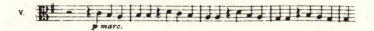

Example 41 Used with kind permission by Edition Wilhelm Hansen AS, Copenhagen.

with repeated tones at the end of short phrases and rhythmic monotony suggests the open-end quality of Finnish folk song so accurately that it could very well be one. The accompaniment by pizzicato strings and flutes in staccato, perhaps reminiscent of the plucked strings of the kantele, fortifies the folk song atmosphere. Although the major seventh, first appearing on the flutes (70.6), causes some disturbance, the composer, as usual, keeps the emphasis on the melody with the aid of a double pedal point, G and D, on the horns and woodwinds.

If the slow movement is simple with strong influence of folk song, the finale, *Allegro molto*, is dynamic. The sense of movement balanced by countermovement points to Sibelius's interest in polyphony in the Sixth Symphony. After the famous "Thor's hammer" theme of wide steps, a more typically Finnish-style theme progressing in seconds is introduced on the woodwinds (106.5). The former is doubled in thirds, the latter in octaves, thus underlining the difference in the nature of the themes. The more Finnish-style theme makes a hymn-like appearance, reminiscent of the end of the Third Symphony, and it is played by the strings in unison. The work ends in five powerful chords (one for each decade of the composer's life?) in *fff*, followed by a sixth flourish bringing the work back to the tonic.

Does the Fifth Symphony show any growth on the part of the composer? Certainly the handling of the thematic material is carried out with a great sense of logic. As in the case of *En Saga*, the earlier version of the Fifth shows even stronger influence of Finnish folk song than the later, as can be seen in the prominence of the fourth interval, for example, in the finale of the earlier version. Sibelius even tried to use trumpet calls of a fourth interval, which he later eliminated.

As Pike points out, Sibelius announces his interest in rhythm and speed right in the opening motif, whose pattern of ♩ ♪♪♩ suggests acceleration of speed just like the two-beat bar inserted into a three-beat tune of "Love Song" in *Scènes historiques*, II. Contrasting speed, ♪♩ ♩ ♪, also included in the opening horn motif, is used to maintain both rhythmic and tonal balance. Contrasting speeds are also suggested by the opening of the work with three accompanying horns playing two chords in long notes.

A good example of the slow-fast contrast occurs in the finale, in which the hymn-like theme suggesting the slow-fast-slow pattern of the opening motif is counteracted by the "Thor's hammer"-theme moving in steady rhythm. The latter, in turn, becomes a macrorhythm of groups of bars on the final pages of the score.[18] Thus the slowing down at the end of the symphony is a reversal of the acceleration of the opening. Perhaps this could be interpreted as an expression of the fifty-year-old composer's slowing down following youthful quickening of pace and thus, symbolically, as a mirror of human life.

With this symphony the composer wishes to reaffirm his belief in the constructive power of rhythm, which he had already stated in *En Saga*, and to prove the basic simplicity behind apparent rhythmic complexities, as in folk music, applicable to larger structures as well. As a matter of fact, the entire rhythmic scheme of the Fifth Symphony could be characterized by Kodály's statement about typical rhythms of folk song: flexibility and yet firmness of rhythm. If Bartók's and Stravinsky's rhythmic techniques inspired by folk music could sometimes be accused of overstatement, Sibelius's could be characterized as an understatement in this area.

Whereas, as Simpson sees it, in the Fourth Symphony Sibelius still keeps the two extremes of pace apart, "the next step was to find a way of incorporating [them] in a continuous form."[19] This is what the composer achieved in the Fifth Symphony. While the first movement of the Fourth Symphony manages to compress a genuine sonata form at a slow pace into some ten minutes of music by "short-circuiting" the recapitulation and by shifting the pedal points, the two extremes of pace, fast and slow, are not yet integrated as they are in the Fifth Symphony. While, in Simpson's view, it is not likely that this was Sibelius's intention, yet the reworking of the original version's first two movements solved the problem by shifting gradually from slow pace to fast in the original scherzo. Since both the thematic logic, as we saw earlier, and also the tonal cohesion contribute to the shift in pace, the fusion becomes a show of the composer's technical mastery. In fact, Simpson considers the transformation of "a colossally slow tempo into a Beethovenishly fast one" such a stroke of genius that "it must be accounted one of the crucial discoveries in music."[20]

While the rhythms and tonalities, affecting each other, threaten to run out of control in the Fourth Symphony, everything gives a sense of strict discipline in the Fifth. The working out of the tonalites in the latter is governed by three pivotal notes — G, G-flat, B — of which G is stated in the opening. B occurs only later as the dominant note of the first chromatic tone, G-flat. Thus the important keys are B major and minor, G, C, and G-flat, in addition to the tonic key, E-flat. Tonal tension prevails to the very end with G-flat still being dominant even in the reprise of the finale, which makes the final return to the tonic all the more dramatic.[21]

The use of tonalities a minor or major third apart is characteristic also of the First and Second Symphonies and harmonies in thirds particularly of the Third, in keeping with the "pastoral" atmosphere of the latter. Thus the return in the Fifth to the tonal scheme of the so-called "nationalist" composers, which was characteristic of Sibelius's Second Symphony, may indicate the composer's desire to emphasize the nationalistic aspect of his birthday celebration. Because of its nature, the Fifth Symphony has been more of an audience piece than the Fourth, and it has been, after the Second, the composer's most popular symphony.

Considering the reasonably optimistic spirit of Sibelius's Fifth Symphony, it is surprising that, judging from the genesis of the Sixth Symphony, Opus 104, the original ideas for the Sixth must have been closer in mood to those of his Fourth Symphony. In his statement regarding the early sketches for the Sixth, the composer characterized the work as "wild and passionate" and "gloomy with pastoral contrasts," and in describing the final climax he said that the orchestration was "somber."[22] By the time of the première in Helsinki in 1923, the spirit of the work must have undergone a drastic change towards more pastoral. On another occasion Sibelius referred to the symphony as "a poem." Later he admitted that the work was somehow incompatible with the trends in music at the time, but he was proud of it and claimed that the time would come when it would be appreciated.

After the composer conducted the Sixth Symphony in Stockholm later in 1923 at his debut as a conductor in the Swedish capital, the Stockholm critic William Seymer characterized the work as almost "modern Mozart."[23] Pike confirms the classical approach in the treatment of the themes, because he sees the opening bars containing the important motifs in a "pre-motivic" state. However, the composer himself deemphasized the "classical" label, stating that, despite the traditional division into four movements, the music flowed freely without following "the usual sonata form."

The opening of the Sixth Symphony, with prepared and resolved suspensions, is suggestive of late Renaissance polyphony, and the very first sound of the work, a major third, announces the tendency of much of the material to be presented in parallel thirds, a sign of a settled mood. The opening oboe motif (p. 4)

Example 42 Used with kind permission by Edition Wilhelm Hansen AS, Copenhagen.

and the following flute motif

Example 43 Used with kind permission by Edition Wilhelm Hansen AS, Copenhagen.

suggest the typical Sibelian thematic conflict between stepwise and triadic progressions. However, what Sibelius does in this work with the basic thematic ingredients is new, as suggested by the additional conflict inherent in the oboe motif between influence of Renaissance modal music and of Finnish folk song.

There are no first and second subjects in the traditional sense in the first movement. The motifs are tossed about in a manner that we could perhaps characterize best as impressionistic until they crystallize into a lengthy theme (14.5ff). When the theme has been constructed and we expect the movement to end, the composer adds another theme (18.2), which is derived from the end of the previous one. However, the new theme suggests the movement-counter movement principle of polyphonic music and thus it is important in showing a continuous process of growth.

In the second movement the thematic development is, once again, polarized between stepwise and triadic thinking. The climax of the *Poco vivace* movement centers on a theme that firmly reestablishes the stepwise progression, both ascending and descending (p. 56). This supplies a logical transition to the finale, in which the upward and downward stepwise progressions dominate the thematic material. Does Sibelius wish to confirm with the movement his belief in the validity of Renaissance

polyphonic music for our age?   The answer seems to be given in
the violin and viola theme (p. 77):

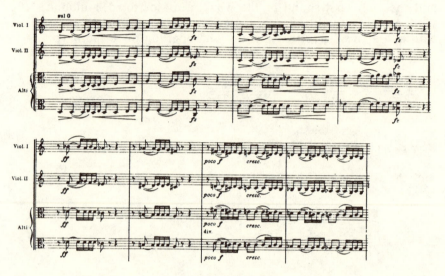

Example 44 Used with kind permission by Edition Wilhelm Hansen AS, Copenhagen.

It opens on an elaboration of the opening oboe motif of the
symphony which, in Sibelius's view, also represented the basic
scale of Finnish folk songs, "with *h* and *c* added, when the melody
grew in intensity," as in this instance. This time the downward
motion presents a broken line with chromaticism, perhaps as an
indication of the incompatibility of folk song with polyphony.

As Harold Truscott points out, the logical growth of the
thematic material in the Sixth Symphony is such that it "might
almost be said to replace normal tonal processes."[24] While the
opening oboe motif could represent the Dorian diapente, thus
suggesting the Dorian mode, much of the material of the first
movement is, in fact, in a pentatonic C major — reflecting the
first movement of the Third Symphony — and yet the work is said
to be in D minor. Thus the conflict inherent in the opening is
thematic as well as tonal.

Modality was suggested in the main theme of the first
movement of Sibelius's First Symphony, and a conflict between
modal and diatonic approaches to tonality is an essential feature of
the work. The modal flavor caused by the use of the minor
seventh in a major scale and the major sixth in a minor to form
the Mixolydian and Dorian modes points to the Sixth Symphony.

While there are modal passages in the First Symphony, in the
Sixth, the approach to modality is structural with much of the

first movement in D Dorian, of the second in G Dorian, and of the third chiefly in D Dorian, the key of the finale.[25] While the Renaissance composers did not modulate between different pitches in the same mode, Sibelius used subdominant for the second movement, mostly a dominant for the third, and the dominant in the fourth. However, by using the same mode instead of a key at these pitches, he was able to produce harmonic and melodic modality.

In its pure, so-called Greek, form, the Dorian mode is a minor scale, with the sixth degree major and the seventh degree minor. Renaissance polyphony brought the mode closer to the modern D minor scale, with the sixth degree made sometimes minor and the seventh sharpened. In the untransposed mode, B-natural could be replaced by B-flat and C-natural by C-sharp. This alternation is one of the characteristics of the Sixth Symphony and Sibelius used it as a unifying force to fortify the thematic logic; for example, in the transition from the first movement to the second (with the coda of the first movement including notes E-flat and D) and in the transition from the second movement to the third, with the pivotal notes in the coda in both major and minor versions.

In the finale, the continual tension between the major and minor pivotal notes is seen in the numerous semitone progressions. The tension reaches its climax towards the end of the movement, supported by dynamic markings of *fff*, only to culminate in the *fff* unison (typical of Sibelius) B-natural. After that the tension caused by the semitone is exhausted, although both B-natural and C-sharp occur occasionally almost to the end. After F-natural eliminated the power of F-sharp in the third movement and the fourth movement returned to D Dorian, the tension is solved.

Thus Sibelius was able to adapt his use of keynotes or pivotal notes to a symphony whose structure is linked with modality. In order to realize the significance of the idea of keynotes for the work, we should take a look at the conclusion of the work in which the only tone remaining is the D:

Example 45 Used with kind permission by Edition Wilhelm Hansen AS, Copenhagen.

The emphasis on keynotes is indicative of the composer's novel view of the concept of tonality and we realize that he was able to approach modality with a different view from that of the Renaissance masters. Although Sibelius relies on such techniques known from Renaissance polyphony as stepwise movement, familiar to him also from Finnish folk music, which he uses in the complementary upward and downward motions as well, frequent use of antiphony (for example on p. 5 in the score), there are also innovations, in addition to those related to the structural use. An interesting innovation is the reversal of dissonances and resolutions in such a way that they appear on weak and strong beats respectively. This could be ultimately related to the fact that in the Finnish language a stressed syllable can be short and an unstressed long. Sibelius also entered parts on dissonant notes and allowed parts to move in syncopation, features that were unknown in Renaissance polyphony.

As is known, in Renaissance music a seventh used as a harmony note had to resolve downward. In Sibelius's Sixth Symphony, when C-sharp occurs for the first time in a seventh chord (C-sharp, G, E, B, p. 4, measure 5), it is resolved to D, but on page 5 the C-sharp is repeated, in crescendo, and left unresolved. These occurences of unresolved sevenths are repeated and thus tension is created between resolved and unresolved seventh chords. Since the tension between B-natural and B-flat, C-natural and C-sharp, and F-natural and F-sharp is inherent in the Dorian mode, as mentioned above, the tension between the resolved and unresolved seventh chords is a manifestation of the semitone tension inherent in the modality. When in the final bars of the symphony the violins play a downward stepwise motif in thirds and the final chord is resolved down to D, all the thematic and tonal conflicts of the work are brought to a conclusion.

We may recall that dissonance plays an important role in every work by Sibelius, starting with *En Saga*. While the Third and Fourth Symphonies concentrate on the tritone, the tension in the Fifth between longer and shorter delays of resolutions, either up or down, foreshadows Sibelius's interest in the issue in the Sixth and Seventh Symphonies. We might cite an important occurrence of the seventh chord from the Fifth Symphony. In the development section of the first movement (p. 20), the chromatic motif (after B) and the woodwind theme (6.3) are reintroduced. The polyphony of the strings fades to *ppp*, and the rhythm loses. its steadiness, but the music is stabilized by motifs on the solo bassoon and solo clarinet developing into a theme. The intensity keeps growing to *fff* and breaks off suddenly on the tonic E-flat. A seventh chord, A, C-sharp, E, G, together with the tonic note, creates a melancholy mood, which is changed by all the strings, except for the double basses, in unison.

The finale, *Allegro molto*, of the Fifth Symphony opens on an A-flat above the sustained tonic, E-flat. As Pike states, "A feature is made of this at the recapitulation in G-flat, for at that . . . stage the . . . dissonant note is the enharmonic equivalent of one of the most important notes in the symphony (from the tonal point of view), B-natural"[26] Thus Sibelius views dissonance as an "application of dissonance to tonality rather than chords" in an approach which seems to indicate influence of folk music with its view of tonality and dissonance different from that of the standard Western idiom. This is confirmed by Sibelius's observation in his 1896 public lecture.[27]

As in the case of Hungarian folk music, there is an obvious influence of the old pentatonic scales in Finnish folk music, even if pentatony by now occurs only rarely in it.   In pentatonic melodies the modal diminished seventh takes on the character of a consonant interval.   Bartók points out in his essays on Hungarian folk music that a visible sign of the consonant character of the seventh is the fact that the regular resolution down to the sixth degree does not occur, indeed, cannot occur because the sixth degree is missing.   In fact, the third, fifth, and seventh degrees are of equal rank.   Thus the tension in Sibelius's music between resolved and unresolved seventh chords is, once again, the result of influences of folk music on the one hand, and of the standard Western idiom on the other.   It is significant that in the Sixth Symphony emphasis on leading-notes is mostly avoided, and they appear after the climax in *fff* in the finale, as do perfect cadences.

While dissonance is important in the Sixth Symphony, it is a key issue in the Seventh, and it is easy to see why the composer worked simultaneously on the two symphonies.   For Pike, the key to the Seventh is the initial G stroke in the timpani followed by a rising scale in the strings, culminating in the semitone D, E-flat, and the chord including A-flat, forming together with the timpani stroke another dissonance, as well as their resolutions.   Thus the work continues the exploration of semitone relationships, which had intrigued Sibelius already in *En Saga*.

However, in the Seventh Symphony the themes have a more important role than in the Sixth, as can be seen from the weighty germ contained in the first theme:

Example 46 Used with kind permission by Edition Wilhelm Hansen AS, Copenhagen.

It opens on a typically Sibelian prolonged tone followed by a stepwise descent.   The construction of the theme, played by the flutes and clarinets alternating, is a model of symmetry based on the idea of a motif (*a*) and its variant. Although the symmetry would seem to point to a classical construction, it could also reflect the duple-line units of the *Kalevala* runos. The ambiguity may be intentional, as in the opening of the Sixth Symphony with the main germ motif.

An important theme is introduced by the first trombone (9.2), and it reflects the essence of Finnish folk tunes in its dependency on second and fourth steps. The reappearance of the theme in the key of C is used almost like a *deus ex machina* introduced to solve problematic situations.

A typically Sibelian thematic antithesis is set up in the third part of the symphony, the *Allegro moderato*, between the following curt theme:

Example 47 Used with kind permission by Edition Wilhelm Hansen AS, Copenhagen.

and these themes:

Example 48 Used with kind permission by Edition Wilhelm Hansen AS, Copenhagen.

The spirit of almost Viennese nostalgia of the last two offers an interesting contrast to the previous theme, which is clearly Finnish in essence with its limited ambitus. Although Sibelius called the work originally *Symphonic Fantasia*, there is the usual logic in the handling of the themes, which include some that could even be characterized as "beautiful melodies." This somewhat deceptive atmosphere of beauty of an earlier era is achieved irrespective of the unsettling effect of dissonance.

Sibelius's liberated view of dissonance is manifest in various ways in the symphony. The dissonance of the opening timpani stroke, the rising scale on the strings as well as those in the woodwinds and horns, are temporarily resolved up; however, the bassoon theme displays a stepwise resolution down, as expected in the traditional view. Despite the fact that the dissonance of the opening is resolved down, later on this is not necessarily true, neither is a dissonant note always prepared for. Thus uncertainty about the resolutions contributes to tension, which prevails from the introduction of the C-flat in measure 3 to the last chord of the work, which brings back C-natural.[28] In other words, the semitone tension, which is important in *En Saga*, is one of the main issues in the composer's last symphony.

In addition to temporary resolutions in a new dissonance, a practice known already in Renaissance music, Sibelius also uses a series of dissonant chords (around Cue E) or repeated chords which are, in fact, dissonant, as late as on the final page of the score starting in *dolce* and growing more powerful before the final resolution.

After the Seventh Symphony Sibelius composed only one major work (except for incidental music for *The Tempest*), *Tapiola*, which is still centered on dissonance. Although *Tapiola* is a tone poem, it is related to the symphonies in the sense that most themes derive from a basic germ motif. The themes of the tone poem also show such characteristics of Finnish folk tunes as stepwise motion and 2/2 pulse. With the change of pulse to 12/8, a whole-tone theme changes the restlessness into a more peaceful mood, which, however, turns out to be as elusive as the evocation of Viennese nostalgia in the Seventh Symphony. The ominous woodwinds of measure 352 of *Tapiola* create havoc, and in three bars the dynamics change from *p* to *fff*. Several motifs are repeated in a vain effort to establish order. The attempt is carried on to measure 569, but the result is a defeat in the chromatic descent in the strings. Although parallel thirds try to establish harmony, the efforts are counteracted by the effect of G-sharp and D, which in the scale of B minor is the tritone. The final cadence resolves the conflict of the tritone, D and G-sharp, by sharpening the D to form a perfect fourth in B major, and thus the semitone solution, which the composer had already suggested in *En Saga*, is applied in his final work.

Simpson claims that *Tapiola* is not a symphony, because the essence of symphony is action while *Tapiola* in its monothematicism and in its "vast monotonality" stands "motionless as the sinister forests it depicts."[29] Now, reference has been made to the unsettling effect of G-sharp and, as a result of it, much of the music is not in B minor. Because of the fact that the major sixth in a minor key is Dorian, there is the usual Sibelian uncertainty between major-minor tonality and modality. The Seventh Symphony, which Simpson considers a true symphony, does not observe the common symphonic requirement of contrasting keys either, although it, too, wanders away from the home key of C and even opens with a Lydian subdominant (F-sharp) in the key of C. In any case, *Tapiola* pursues many of the same issues that intrigued Sibelius in the Seventh Symphony, and with its subtle scoring and rich orchestration the tone poem is a glorious epilogue to the composer's career.

If Sibelius declared in *Kullervo* for the first time his independence, albeit in a limited way, of the continental music tradition, *En Saga* employs influence of Finnish folk song in a more subtle and yet more profound manner. Although there are no appreciable stylistic changes between the composer's early and late salon-type pieces, the major works, by contrast, are studies of different aspects of music and their reconciliation with ideas derived from folk music.

Since German folk music is of fundamental importance in the Western tradition of art music, introduction of folk themes into art music was easier for composers like Beethoven, Brahms, or even Dvořák than, say, for Borodin or Tchaikovsky, who hailed from a different culture.

Rimsky-Korsakov, who was genuinely interested in folk music, experimented, in true romantic fashion, with a new scale of alternate tones and semitones in *Sadko*, *Mlada*, the third movement of *Antar* and the finale of the *Maid of Pskov*,[30] and yet his musical language remained untouched by folk song in any fundamental sense. Then there are composers like Wagner, who did not have any interest in folk music but yet arrived at a different conception of dissonance from that prevalent at the time, obviously by the academic route. And, lastly, there are those like Mussorgsky, Stravinsky, and Bartók, whose musical language has basic features in common with the folk music of their native lands. Sibelius belongs to the last group, although the penetration of folk music into his idiom was more subtle than in the cases of Bartók and the two Russian composers.

Rimsky-Korsakov was aware of the "different" sound in Sibelius's music without being able to realize to what it was due, when he stated after hearing the Finnish master's Third Symphony in St. Petersburg in 1907: "It sounds different, somehow, not like our music, and this is good."[31] He had a vague feeling that national differences were involved: "And yet, maybe this originality is purely superficial and no more remarkable than it is that from the day he's born, the French peasant speaks French, not Russian. Who knows?"

It is easy to see why Rimsky-Korsakov had no way of understanding Sibelius's thinking, since he did not even know what his countryman Mussorgsky was accomplishing and he saw to it that he "corrected" many of Mussorgsky's "wrong" harmonies. On the other hand, Debussy had the perspicacity to see the significance of Mussorgsky's efforts.

In 1880 and 1881, when Debussy visited Russia, he obviously became acquainted with Mussorgsky's music, in which "each chord is conceived as a sonorous unit in a phrase whose structure is determined more by melodic shape or color value than by the movement of harmony."[32]   As Donald Jay Grout points out, the chord progression of the bass line of Mussorgsky's song "Les jours de fête" must have impressed Debussy, since a similar progression characterizes the opening of the French master's *Nuages*. Evidently Debussy saw in this approach his answer to Wagner's influence, just as Kodály's purpose was to help Hungarian art music "to recover from the influence of iambic melody and Wagnerian opera."[33]

If Sibelius in *En Saga* declared his protest to Wagner's view of rhythm as being subservient to the vocal line, he stated with the work his opposition to Wagnerian chromaticism as well.   As Norton states: "On the one hand, *harmony* is the result of linear causes — simultaneous melodic motion in several parts; on the other hand, harmony is the result of conscious selection."[34] Sibelius's, just as Bartók's and Stravinsky's, view of dissonance and of harmony is based on a "practical" view derived from folk song with their linear harmonies.

While Bartók and Stravinsky emphasized the interval relationships of folk song in their pitch cells without regard to key relationships, Sibelius insisted on an application of the intervals of Finnish folk song within the diatonic keys. While the Second and Third Symphonies concentrate on refining his variation method with influences of folk song incorporated into the technique, the Fourth is a watershed both musically and emotionally, and the sporadic destruction of music is symbolized in temporary abandonments of tonality. In the Fifth Symphony sanity returns and the work is an interesting study of rhythm and speed, just as the Sixth is of polyphony and the Seventh of dissonance. *Tapiola*, on the other hand, is in many respects a continuation of the train of thought of the Fourth Symphony. We shall return in the next chapter to this work and its significance as the composer's musical last will and testament and as an expression of Sibelius's view of nature and, by implication, of cosmic issues.

THE SIBELIAN LEGACY

By nature Sibelius was a romantic and it is not surprising that at the beginning of his career he was attracted to romantic music and literature. *Svartsjukans nätter* (Nights of jealousy), a cycle of poems by Runeberg representing the poet at his worst while under the influence of Stagnelius and other Swedish romantics, inspired Sibelius to compose in 1888 an accompaniment for the recitation of these poems. During his year of study in Berlin, two years after *Svartsjukans nätter*, he heard episodes of Berlioz's *Lélio*. In view of such influences, why did Sibelius turn away from continental romanticism to the world of the *Kalevala* during his year of study in Vienna? The strongest reason was the spirit of the Finnish nationalistic movement and, as a result of it, Sibelius's discovery of the *Kalevala* and its possibilities for a composer. The movement was also responsible for Runeberg's appreciation of Finland's folk poetry and his turning away from *Svartsjukans nätter* to a more simple, more realistic view of people and nature expressed in a style that used devices like parallelism and repetition taken over from folk poetry. It was in these two manifestations of the nationalistic movement of Finland that Sibelius found an ingredient for revitalizing romantic music, which was still being represented in a true Viennese tradition by Richard Strauss and Gustav Mahler.

On the basis of a superficial hearing of Sibelius's works, many have considered them typical of the romantic tradition, largely because in his orchestration there is continental influence with the young composer's admiration of Beethoven, Bruckner, and Wagner clearly in evidence. Although *Kullervo*, to this writer's knowledge, does not quote actual Finnish folk melodies, many of the tunes could be of folk origin, and the composer's sensitivity to the Finnish language is such that we can be justified in referring to Sibelius as the creator of genuine Finnish recitative.

With *En Saga* Sibelius reached the stage where Finnish influences are no longer a matter of superficial techniques. The work uses, for the first time, the method of the *Kalevala* runos, to which the composer referred as "themes and variations." He uses outright reiteration and also repetition of the runos, usually in the form of parallelism, in the creation of his self-repeating motifs in order to produce themes which, in turn, create their own structural logic. Sibelius referred to this structural cohesiveness on the occasion of a rehearsal of his Fourth Symphony in Helsinki, when he remarked to a young musician: "You see how Kajanus builds up my symphony . . . He actually makes you feel the construction of the work like a huge building."[1]

En Saga is also a crucial work in giving a vague suggestion of a new approach to harmony and tonality. Sibelius absorbed from genuine Finnish folk music a liberated view of harmony according to which the significance of each tone stands in relation to the basic tone. This "democratic" view, which regards each one of the twelve tones of the scale as equals, resulted in a fresh approach to the interval, both melodic and harmonic, and, as a corollary, to dissonance. This is the view that Stravinsky absorbed from Russian folk music and Bartók from Hungarian. While the influence resulted in abandonment of the major-minor tonal system in the music of Bartók and Stravinsky, Sibelius never broke completely with the continental tradition, although he came close to it in his Fourth and Seventh Symphonies and in *Tapiola*. While Bartók and Stravinsky came to regard the triad as equal to any harmony, Sibelius's view is one of conflict. On the one hand, he respected the traditional diatonic system of tonality; on the other hand, he adopted a liberated view of harmony and tonality from folk music, and the struggle between the two opposing forces is one of the major sources of tension in his symphonies.

With the Second Symphony Sibelius created a work in which the specifically Finnish element was strong enough to have caused the work to be hailed as avant-garde at its premières outside Finland. For example, in Boston the critics were puzzled by it, and Olin Downes observed forty years later that in 1904 at its American première the symphony had been before its time.

It is ironical that Tawaststjerna feels that in the Third Symphony "Sibelius turned his back on his 'nationalist' past," and he continues: "In contrast with the earlier symphonies, there is scarcely any specifically Finnish flavouring as far as the thematic substance is concerned," and he concludes: "In this work Sibelius is Finnish in the same sense that Beethoven or Brahms are German, indeed, from this time onwards one can say that he becomes more international."[2]

Was Sibelius aware of the fact that he used a Finnish runo tune as the basis of his Third Symphony? The employment of the tune could have resulted from a subconscious memory flash dating as far back as his honeymoon trip to North Karelia, the remembrance perhaps being brought back by the domesticity of his new home. On the other hand, when several foreign critics referred to influences of Finnish folk music in Sibelius's early works, the composer was annoyed, because he did not want to be classified as just another national composer. In February 1906, while he was working on the Third Symphony, he wrote to Rosa Newmarch: "I would be pleased, Madame, if you would correct a general misconception. I often find in newspapers abroad that my melodies are spoken of as folk tunes; up to this point I have never used any themes other than those that are entirely my own."[3] Did the remark "up to this point" mean an admission that he was now consciously using a folk theme? Be that as it may, despite Tawaststjerna's claim that in Sibelius's total output the folk element plays a fairly insignificant role, it is, indeed, next to his continental musical inheritance, the most vital force in his compositions.

Already in 1896 Sibelius emphasized in his only public lecture the value of the properties of folk music in its tonal system and melodic construction for revitalization of art music.[4] He even went as far as to state that such art music practices as modulations, and so on, are only of passing value if the "germ cell" of the music is not founded on folk music. Yet the view of no — or hardly any — influence of folk music on Sibelius's output has been propagated from one study to another. As an example we might quote Grout's statement in *A History of Western Music*: "He [Sibelius] does not quote or imitate folk songs and there is small evidence of direct folk song influence in his works, the best of which depend little, if at all, on qualities that can be concretely defined as national."[5]

With total integration of folk song and the symphonic form in the Third Symphony, Sibelius reached the goal that had escaped him in *Kullervo*. With the conflict between the thematic material derived from folk song and the rigidity of form solved, there was a threat of thematic, harmonic, tonal, and structural collapse in the Fourth Symphony. After Sibelius had studied the conflict between thematic material and the symphonic form with special emphasis on rhythm in the Fifth Symphony, on polyphony in the Sixth and on dissonance in the Seventh Symphony and *Tapiola*, the only step he could have taken was complete abandonment of the diatonic system.   This the romantic in Sibelius could not and would not do.   Certainly he could have written competent music with his technical prowess based on this or that principle, but, to him, composing without inspiration would have been tantamount to a court councilor composing works which "made one think of doctors' dissertations."[6]

Sibelius believed in strict discipline in composition.   After exhaustive studies of the conflict between the diatonic and the "liberated" view of tonality, his refusal to accept a Bartókian type of freedom in which "a key" chiefly means adherence to a keynote as a form of discipline, meant that the basic struggle that fired his inspiration was over.   However, the human struggle between the romantic and the realist in the composer continued, witness his Six Songs to words by Runeberg from 1917, five piano pieces, *Romance*, *Chant du soir*, *Scène lyrique*, *Humoresque*, and *Scène romantique*, as well as some other short works, in which the return to the romantic-nostalgic world of Loviisa lacks the poignancy of many of the early songs and the Violin Concerto.

As for the romantics in general, for Sibelius the human struggle often found its expression in images derived from nature. The conflict between the educated Baltic's view of nature, derived from the Enlightenment, the Sturm und Drang, and Darwin, on the one hand, and the Finnish peasant's attitude towards his surroundings, on the other, was reflected even in Sibelius's natural environment.   For him, the dark spruce forests around Hämeenlinna with their somber mood represented the Finnish peasant's view of nature as something savage and, at the same time, the only eternal thing around man, as he described the Northland's "dusky forests . . . ancient, mysterious, brooding savage dreams" in his "program" for *Tapiola*.   Loviisa, on the other hand, represented the change of seasons from the melancholy beauty of summer nights to the icy monotony of the winter and thus in its symbolism the cycle of life and death and the eternal renewal of life, which appealed to the Baltic romantic in the composer.   Always sensitive to his environment, the change of seasons was one of the most important events in Sibelius's life, just as it is a dominant theme in Scandinavian literature and in the songs by Grieg, Crusell, Ehrström, Collan, and many others.

But if continental romanticism tended to see the dark recesses of man's mind in conflict with the beauty of nature, Scandinavian romanticism saw man's moods reflected in nature, as in the lyric poems by Swedish writers like Fröding, Rydberg, Snoilsky, and by Finnish-Swedish writers like Runeberg, Wecksell, and Karl-August Tavaststjerna.

In addition to many solo songs, a number of orchestral works by Sibelius are expressions of the Runebergian view of nature. These include *La Tristesse du printemps*, an early work entitled originally *Vårsång* (Spring song), and the Violin Concerto. The romantic spirit of the latter is evident especially in the well-known opening theme and the slow middle movement. However, this folk song-type theme of the first movement of the Violin Concerto

Example 49 By permission of International Music Company, New York.

as well as the following solo violin theme of the finale

Example 50 By permission of International Music Company, New York.

which with its marked accent, insistent rhythm, and limited range is reminiscent of *En Saga*, reveal the typical Sibelian conflict.[7]

Two short tone poems by Sibelius, *Pan and Echo* (1906) and *The Dryad* (1910), lean clearly towards the composer's Runebergian side, as reflected in the central theme of *The Dryad* in the Grieg-style melodic line with emphasis on the tonic, leading note, and dominant. However, something of Sibelius's Bellmanesque approach to nature is evident in these works, especially in the construction as a series of details, which never acquire the sense of dynamic growth typical of many of Sibelius's works based on the *Kalevala*.

Although the Finnish title, *Aallottaret*, of the tone poem known internationally as *The Oceanides* refers to the water-sprites of Finnish folklore, the composition, which Sibelius originally called *Vågornas rondo* (The Rondo of the waves), has generally been considered his most impressionistic composition. It is a rare work by Sibelius in that the specifically Finnish influences are, on the surface, hardly in evidence, although a closer scrutiny of the score reveals the typically Sibelian growth process from the opening motif.

Even if there is also a strong impressionistic element in *Nightride and Sunrise*, the work is not Debussyan the way *The Oceanides* is. The first part of *Nightride and Sunrise*, which premiered in St. Petersburg in 1909, is Sibelian in that it consists chiefly of an interplay of five related germ motifs, while the ride is rendered in a trochaic rhythm for almost four hundred bars. The interesting feature of the first section is the sense of intimacy and interaction between the rider and nature, which is reminiscent of the people of the *Kalevala* communicating with a natural object, such as a bird or a tree.

The first ray of the sun in *Nightride and Sunrise* is introduced on the piccolo and the bass clarinet in a somewhat impressionistic manner. Yet the subsequent section, which mixes some motifs of the introduction with the motif of the solar ray in a polyphonic texture, is a description of a slow, Nordic sunrise and quite unlike, say, Ravel's sudden outburst in *Daphnis et Chloë*. When the trumpets finally announce the triumph of daylight in octaves, the elemental power interpreted in the work brings to mind those Sibelian works whose inspiration derives from the *Kalevala*. One cannot help but think of the words of the narrator in runo I describing how the cold told him a song and the rain, wind, and waves of the sea brought runos, with birds adding songs and treetops, magic sayings.

Wilfrid Mellers saw in Sibelius's approach to nature the composer's desire to "relinquish his personality in the impersonality of Nature,"[8] but, in keeping with the animism of the *Kalevala*, it is no longer a matter of a sympathetic mood in nature in whose impersonality the viewer can abandon his persona, but rather man's identification and communion with a natural object that has its own personality.

The people of the *Kalevala* created a religion in which trees, birds, and animals showed human characteristics and thus formed a link between man and the universe. They believed that as long as they did what was right they were protected by their *haltiat*, the resident spirits of their homes, barns, lakes, and forests. W. F. Kirby, whose first edition of his translation of the *Kalevala* appeared in 1907, characterizes the religion of the work as "peculiar; it is Shamanistic animism overlaid with Christianity."[9] Since, according to the *Kalevala*, man could look for assistance in the forces of nature, it stands to reason that man tries to study omens, good or bad, around him.

Sibelius's attitudes were greatly affected by primitive beliefs, by the study of omens, reliance on a sixth sense. For him, cranes and swans seem to have represented messages from another world. When he was applying his last pen strokes to his Fifth Symphony, he glanced from the window of his study facing Lake Tuusula and saw some swans settling down on the lake. Curiously enough, on the day Sibelius died, Sir Malcolm Sargent was conducting the Fifth Symphony in Helsinki. Because the spiritual essence of man's interaction with nature is a key element in Sibelius's music, it is hardly ever musical *pleinairisme*, with a few notable exceptions like a bird call, barely recognizable, after the sunrise in *Nightride and Sunrise*.

It is in his turning away from continental-Nordic romanticism towards the *Kalevala*'s pantheism, which is not unlike that of Wordsworth, that we can see the reason for Sibelius's music turning from typically romantic to a more disciplined style. The heightened sense of discipline has caused many observers to emphasize Sibelius's indebtedness to Haydn, Mozart, and Beethoven in his string quartet, *Voces intimae*, which dates from 1909. Certainly Sibelius's enthusiasm for Beethoven's last quartets, which he heard performed by the Joachim Quartet during his student year in Berlin, has a great deal to do with the introverted character of the work. It seems logical to believe that in the first movement, *Andante — Allegro molto moderato*, the "intimate voices" are interpreted in the musical dialogue and in the mysterious E minor chords of the middle movement, *Adagio di molto*, above which the composer wrote in pencil "*voces intimae*" in a copy of the miniature score. Even if the Quartet derives clearly from the continental side of Sibelius, there are features like the dominant theme of the fourth movement with its rhythmic monotony and the insistence with which the melody at first hovers around a given tone that point to specifically Finnish influence. The remarkable feature of the work is the sense of discipline that controls the emotional conflict despite the intimate nature of the work, even if the effect is at times too orchestral pointing to an affinity with the *Lemminkäinen* music.

Like the ancient Greeks, the man of the Enlightenment, and the Finnish peasant, Sibelius considered a violation of the laws of nature a form of hubris, insolence towards the gods. He saw in the shape of a snowflake or the brightness of a wild violet more perfection than man was ever capable of creating. It is in his respect for details in nature as symbols for the non-phenomenal world that we can see the reason for the Anglo-American understanding of the essence of Sibelius.

For Sibelius, the appreciation of the beauty of details in nature made it even possible for him to see beyond the prevalent monotony of the Finnish landscape, which is most often short on color and not particularly dramatic in its outlines, as a traveler approaching the airport of Helsinki can observe. Therefore, it seems to require the element of time in order to find an adequate artistic expression. Sibelius must have been aware of this, judging by the fact that as a young man he dreamt of a new art form, a combination of sculpture and music, that would have given life to line and shape by means of sound, that is, by adding to the three dimensions of sculpture the concept of time. Thus it is not at all strange that Sibelius's music has captured the essence of Finland's nature better than have most of its sculptors and painters. Marc Vignal was aware of Sibelius's achievement, when he stated in reference to *Tapiola* that in the work Finnish nature is not described but "saisie dans son essence."[10]   And therein lies the genius of Sibelius: he was able to capture the essence of Finnish nature and turn its negative feature, its monotony, into a growth-giving force.   How did he do it?   By relying on a musical technique whose essence is the monotonous repetition of Finnish folk song and on a variation method characterized by an affinity to Finnish folk poetry. This sense of harmony between what the composer says and how he says it gives his best works that indefinable something that we have in the sense of heroism in Beethoven's works or in the unreserved veneration of God in Bruckner's. Just as Mahler took the sense of Viennese nostalgia, in itself a negative feature, and turned it into a positive force for his own purposes, Sibelius took the most essential characteristic of Finnish nature and the Finnish folk song, their monotony, their sense of endlessness, in itself a negative feature, and turned it into something positive in defeating monotony by a sense of constant renewal.

In turning a negative aspect of Finnish nature, its monotony, into a thing of beauty, Sibelius expresses his own personal victory over the romantic, who concentrates on the beauty of nature and mourns its loss in the change of seasons. In this way, *Tapiola* is born out of the typically Finnish realistic attitude of man towards his environment, but it is not a sense of confrontation, as Burnett James suggests, but a sense of search of harmony based on realism.

When in the end of *Tapiola* respect for natural laws is restored — even if only barely — it could be construed either as a warning for man against tampering with the environment or even as a vague hope of victory in the present-day conservationists' search for balance between industrial progress and respect for nature. In that sense we could call Sibelius a realistic visionary, who was able to foresee the possibility of modern man in harmony with nature, not the human spirit "in a hostile environment"[11] as Burnett James claims in his unfamiliarity with the spirit of cooperation between man and nature in the *Kalevala*.

For Sibelius, as to the romantics in general, the artist was a privileged person for whom it was possible to achieve what Goethe described as "dem Augenblick Dauer verleihen." Sibelius expressed his belief in the artist's ability to penetrate beyond the phenomenal world when he stated about his Sixth Symphony: "...I don't consider a symphony only music in so many bars but rather an expression for a principle of living, a phase in one's spiritual life."[12] This is not an avowal of belief in biblical dogma nor is it a view of man and his universe based on scientism but simply an acceptance of music as an expression of everything that relates to man's life. Therefore, if music is to express what is important to man, it has to have an intimate connection with everything around man, including nature.

The amalgamation of nature and music is the unity of nature and art and cosmos that was emphasized already by Crusell and Runeberg. This fusion of the concrete element of the environment with its spiritual essence is the basis of Alvar Aalto's work, as it is for so many Finnish artists. We might cite by way of example Erik Bryggman[13] whose greatest design, the burial chapel at Turku cemetery, harmonizes architecture with the surrounding landscape in a unique manner. The lateral wall of the chapel is made entirely of glass, giving the audience the impression of being in a pine forest. The simple altar with a wooden cross tinted faintly by a purplish stained glass window above it transports the viewer to a meeting-place of this world and the world beyond.

It is this unity of life, death, art, and nature that is the starting point of *Tapiola*. It is not a descriptive work, but it is not a static work either despite Simpson's view that "it stands motionless as the sinister forests it depicts."[14] In order to show that the work is static, Simpson claims that it never really leaves B minor and that it is monothematic. Despite a short core motif, the work is not really monothematic, and since it does not dwell essentially in B minor, it is not monotonal either. Despite the fact that it is the only major work for which Sibelius provided a "program," it could be considered a symphony, because it "treats modality in modern symphonic terms."[15] In short, it is a paradoxical work, which uses the image of Finnish forests as a symbol of man's life. As the forests are mysterious, "brooding savage dreams," so is man's life. The crystallization of the essence of man's life in the finale of the Third Symphony is the main focus of the Fourth, while the Fifth, Sixth, and Seventh Symphonies view the same focal point from different angles. The purification of the Fourth leads to the feeling of life as an orderly process moving towards a goal in the subsequent symphonies. However, the goal, which had already proved elusive in the Fourth Symphony, becomes unattainable in the Seventh, and it dwindles into a series of paradoxes in *Tapiola*. It is in the disillusionment of *Tapiola* that we must look for answers to "the silence of Järvenpää"[16] and not in Sibelius's intemperance, since there is no correlation between his creative powers and his early years of indulgence and his years of total abstinence.

While the romantic in Sibelius was engaged in a fervent pursuit to "know it all," so to speak, a privilege of the artist, the Finnish peasant in him was resigned to nature's superiority over man and to man's inability to comprehend its mystery. The Kullervo-Sibelius, the romantic hero who had begun his search in the first major work was transformed into the rebellious Lemminkäinen of the first two symphonies. In the Third Symphony, Lemminkäinen gradually acquires some of the wisdom of Väinämöinen, the seer, whose painfully honest search in the Fourth Symphony culminates in a barely admitted resignation in the end of the work. In fact, without the sense of capitulation in *The Bard* and in the end of *Pohjola's Daughter*, we almost believe that the romantic hero could still be resuscitated. Indeed, Sibelius himself seems to have believed that a faint flicker of the patriotic flame of the bygone years could bring this about in the Fifth Symphony. If the Sixth Symphony examines life calmly and philosophically in its effort to reconcile the past with the present, the Seventh Symphony and *Tapiola* have to admit the defeat: Lemminkäinen, the romantic hero, is dead. The only consolation left is nature, which can understand man's language as well as man can nature's, but nature can only be a sympathetic communicator and not a source of conflict, and without conflict, music is dead.

Because of this Finnish-based sense of harmony between the matter and the manner in Sibelius's works, it has been easier for the Finns, thanks to their physical and cultural environment, than for others to grasp emotionally the essence of Sibelius's music, and he has been a giant and a cult figure in his own land, even if the understanding of his symphonies has been beyond the man on the street.

It is curious that the Finns who have been increasingly capable of viewing their situation between East and West with realism and pragmatism, have not adopted the same attitude towards their heroes. In their hero worship the Finns even today respect Sibelius's desire to use many masks in his human relationships and to appear as the enigmatic Olympian. Despite their practical attitude in present-day politics, the Finns tend to sentimentalize the past and to portray Sibelius as the great patriot marching with a banner to the tunes of *Finlandia*. Perhaps this is understandable, because for an entire generation of Finns the country's greatest composer in his citadel of Ainola was as mysterious a figure as Santa Claus is for Finnish children in Mount Korvatunturi in Lapland. Despite occasional rumors and good-humored jokes about Sibelius's drinking habits, it has been difficult for the Finns to regard the composer as a human being, a very real human being, who needed Finland's fight for independence as much as Finland the music it inspired. Courageous he may have been but, feeling wounded, he was not able to convince himself that a statue had never been erected to a critic and turned back from the innovativeness of his Fourth Symphony after critics expressed their doubts and audiences, their hostility. Had the Finns, and with them the world, been willing to accept Sibelius as a complex human being and a great composer who at times reached unique heights working out his own musical thought and idiom from various influences, perhaps a new understanding would have resulted from such a reconsideration. Valuable works like the Third, Fourth, and Sixth Symphonies, as well as *Tapiola*, which have not been fully appreciated even in Finland, would have found their rightful place among the great achievements of the human mind in the search for divine perfection in the harmony of art and nature.

The romantic in Sibelius also wanted to prove that the creative imagination could reestablish a harmony of being between man's soul and the cosmos. His open-ended theme fragments tried to reach to infinity and found only nothingness, as proved by *Tapiola*, but, as in a late Picasso work, the beauty is in the frankness of the statement. Thus Sibelius ended with the aesthetic credo that beauty is experienced not only in proportion and harmony but also in something negative like monotony and dissonance, as long as that negative quality is true to the content of the statement. This result is one of the many paradoxes connected with Sibelius who, like his countryman Alvar Aalto, hated theorizing. When Aalto answered all questions about aesthetics by saying "I build," Sibelius's reply might have been "I compose." But Aalto said also: "With every construction I write ten volumes of philosophy."[17] This is what Sibelius did with every major composition. Yet, above all, like Aalto's designs, Sibelius's works are a cultured man's expressions of man's basic instincts, his yearning for light, and for harmony with nature, which is the ultimate Sibelian paradox.

Thus Sibelius's weightiest works have a single "meaning" at a very basic level, even if the treatment of the issues may have different connotations for Finns than for others. In probing those issues the composer displays universal insights that give these works the essence of greatness.[18]

Has the shadow of a great predecessor been a positive or a negative factor in post-Sibelian music in Finland?   In the next chapters we shall look for answers.

POST-SIBELIAN INSTRUMENTAL MUSIC

Many of Sibelius's incidental pieces, tone poems, and the first two symphonies aroused admiration from St. Petersburg to London,[1] not to speak of the Scandinavian capitals, while the Third, Fourth, Sixth, and Seventh Symphonies were slow in acquiring recognition. Although approval was by no means universal, in England, in particular, there was a firm group of Sibelius fans, thanks to the efforts of Ernest Newman, Sir Donald Tovey, Sir Thomas Beecham, Rosa Newmarch, and many others. Ralph Vaughan Williams dedicated his Fifth Symphony to Sibelius, as Arnold Bax had done. Vaughan Williams stated in his dedication that Sibelius's "great example was worthy of imitation,"[2] but the Bax symphony actually shows closer affinity to Sibelius's Fifth than the Vaughan Williams work does to anything by Sibelius. In the United States, Olin Downes, Theodore Thomas, Walter Damrosch, Eugene Ormandy, and others were active in spreading Sibelius's reputation, and several composers gradually came to show influence of the Finnish master's music. Foremost among these is Howard Hanson, who has jokingly become known as "the American Sibelius." Some Sibelius influence can be detected also in certain Russian composers, including Shostakovich.

One would tend to think that the younger Scandinavian composers would have started to imitate Sibelius and Nielsen *en masse*, but this has certainly not been the case, obviously because of the highly individualistic style of each master. Naturally, tangential influence can be detected frequently, but no close imitation of the languages of the two composers has occurred comparable to, say, that of numerous Brahms clones.   Even a Scandinavian like Wilhelm Stenhammar, whose studies in Germany initiated him into the Wagner and Brahms traditions, started only gradually to show influence of the textures and the tight control of the material typical of Sibelius, although he frequently conducted works by both Sibelius and Nielsen.

Other Swedish composers like Wilhelm Petterson-Berger (1867-1942), also a music critic and at times a harsh reviewer of Sibelius's music, and Ture Rangström (1884-1947), continued the Swedish Romantic tradition.   Kurt Atterberg (1887-1974) a music critic of the influential *Stockholms Tidningen* 1917-1957, attempted to turn from romanticism to neoclassicism in his compositions.   Despite his efforts, Sibelius's shadow is often discernible in his music and, for example, in his suite for violin, viola, and string orchestra composed for Maeterlinck's *Pantomime* the Finnish master's *Valse triste* lurks in the background.   Lars-Erik Larsson (b. 1908) has acquired international fame chiefly with his *Pastoralsvit* (Pastoral suite), which is in keeping with the post-Griegian Nordic tradition, although direct influence of Sibelius can be detected in the work.   After a spell under the influence of Alban Berg and Hindemith, Larsson's thinking turned towards neoclassicism.

A search for an individual idiom under various influences has characterized also the career of Hilding Rosenberg, likewise from Sweden (b. 1892), who, by his own admission, was strongly influenced by Sibelius's First Symphony, which he heard in Gothenburg.   However, later on Rosenberg was impressed by Schoenberg, with whose works he became familiar on a visit to Dresden in 1920.

A Swedish composer whose music displays the powerful individual character reminiscent of Sibelius and Nielsen is Allan Pettersson (1911-1980); his works have slowly started to gain international recognition.   Although the introverted quality of his oeuvre harks back to the two Nordic masters, his idiom is more modern than that of his predecessors with almost complete lack of melody and textures that are not as tightly controlled as those of Sibelius.   However, definite influence of Sibelius's Fourth Symphony can be heard, for example, in Pettersson's Seventh Symphony.   Perhaps a conscious effort to put some distance between himself and his Nordic predecessors led Pettersson to use an alto saxophone obbligato part in his Sixteenth Symphony, in which the instrument plays throughout the work.

Pleasant but not remarkable music in the Scandinavian late romantic tradition has been composed by Dag Wirén, a Swede (b. 1905), whose best known work, *Serenade for Strings*, shows strong influence of folk song and by the Estonian Eduard Tubin (1905-1982), whose works are strongly in the Baltic post-Wagnerian tradition. Many of the latter's works have been recorded by his zealous countryman Neeme Järvi.

Sibelius's ambivalent attitude towards music critics — he claimed to be indifferent to criticism while, at the same time, taking careful notice of the attention he was receiving in the press — gave many of them the idea that the composer guarded jealously his fame as Finland's, and Scandinavia's, most prominent composer. However, while there was a streak of naïve pride in Sibelius in his own achievements, he was also generous in his evaluation of younger composers' works in vivid remembrance of his own struggles at the beginning of his career. In particular two of his younger contemporaries, Toivo Kuula (1883-1918) and Leevi Madetoja (1887-1947), received strong encouragement from Sibelius.

Madetoja, a native of northern Finland, was a pupil of Sibelius during the latter's brief teaching career and, thanks to the similarities in their personalities, a warm relationship developed between them. Madetoja, like Sibelius, was an introvert and this is reflected in his musical expression, but he did not have the strong sense of conflict between the introvert and the extrovert that is characteristic of Sibelius. Like Sibelius's idiom, Madetoja's language is in general restrained, but the power of imagination and the quickly changing moods that make Sibelius's music so interesting despite a degree of monotony are not in evidence in Madetoja. As an indication of Madetoja's conservatism, we might cite a short piano piece, "A Little Romance," Opus 17, number 2, which indicates in a small form influence of both church music and Ostrobothnian folk music manifest in a large form in particular in his Second Symphony (see Example 51). The unimaginative harmonies and the strict observance of the strophic constuction of phrases in imitation of folk song are indicative of a talent that in no way is comparable to that of Sibelius.

Although Madetoja's Second and Third Symphonies have remained in the symphonic repertory in Finland, they have not gained wide international recognition. It is easy to understand why, say, the first movement of Madetoja's Third Symphony, despite its somewhat Sibelian sense of motion, appears monotonous, perhaps even boring, to a foreigner unable to relate to the composer's background.

Kuula, a native of the province of Ostrobothnia like Madetoja, began his career like Sibelius with chamber music

2. Pieni romanssi.

Kleine Romanze.

Leevi Madetoja, Op. 17. No. 2.

Example 51 (C) Fazer Music Inc., Helsinki.

compositions. His violin sonata and piano trio were regarded very favorably and John Horton characterizes his chamber music in general as having "great vitality and passionate spontaneity."[3] Unfortunately, Kuula's life ended prematurely in a shooting accident during the First World War, and a projected symphony, for which he had completed an introduction, never materialized.

The impact of the melancholy folk song of Ostrobothnia and its pulsating rhythm is the most characteristic feature of Kuula's idiom, in addition to influences derived from standard continental writing and from Sibelius. As an indication of the use of folk song-type material we might mention Kuula's short piano piece entitled "A Sheep's Polka" (see Example 52). The piece shows much more direct exploitation of moods of Finnish folk music than Sibelius's piano music ever did. The rhythmic vitality of folk songs — almost reminiscent of Prokofiev or Stravinsky — and their somber atmosphere, features which usually appear in the Bothnian folk song separately, are combined quite successfully in this piece by Kuula.

As early as 1907 Sibelius encouraged his occasional pupil Kuula to adhere to his inspiration derived from folk song and warned him not to start composing "in evening dress."[4] The master thought highly enough of his pupil to recommend a performance of Kuula's Piano Trio in A major to Alexander Siloti, who included it in a concert program in St. Petersburg. However, Sibelius's attempt at getting the Trio performed in England failed.

Unfortunately, Kuula's death, like the premature demise of two earlier promising Finnish composers, Philip von Schantz and Ernst Mielck, left behind more promise than accomplishment, and we are left wondering what course his career would have taken. In light of the fact that after Kuula's short stay in France and Italy clear impressionistic influences are in evidence in such orchestral works as *Rain in the Forest*, *Demons Lighting Will-O'-the Wisps* and in the orchestral song *Maidens Bathing in the Sea*, it is doubtful whether he did heed Sibelius's warning in his orchestral compositions.

In the final analysis we can conclude, however, that Kuula probably would have remained a more "Finnish" composer than Uuno Klami (1900-1961) because of the fact that the former had absorbed influences of the Ostrobothnian folk song in childhood, whereas the latter came from an area around Kotka on the Gulf of Finland where the tradition of folk music was much poorer than in Kuula's Bothnia.

Lampaan polska.

Toivo Kuula.

After entering the Helsinki Conservatory (later the Sibelius Academy) at the age of fifteen and studying there on three different occasions, Klami headed for Paris, where he studied composition with Florent Schmitt, also receiving occasional instruction from Maurice Ravel. Paris proved to be the right choice for Klami, and he discovered there that after his German-oriented training in Helsinki he could now develop his own musical language under impressionistic influences in order to express his love for the sea in his native area. Many find it difficult to believe that in 1927–1928 Klami composed Nos. 2 and 6 of his *Sea Pictures* (in anticipation of Ravel's *Bolero*) under the inspiration of Paul Valéry's poetry without having heard the famous Ravel work.

In Paris Klami composed also his First Piano Concerto subtitled *A Night in Montmartre*, which combines influences of both the waltz and jazz. It is one of the earliest works by a Finnish composer to show influence of jazz, even if a rather tame variety, and it has enjoyed great popularity in Finland.

In the 1930s Klami combined *Kalevala* inspiration with impressionistic influences in his five-part *Kalevala* suite. The "Maidens of Terheniemi" section brings to mind Sibelius's *Oceanides*, and strong influence of Sibelius is discernible in particular in the "Forging of the Sampo" section, which is reminiscent of Sibelius's Fifth Symphony in the insistence of a short runo-like tune, as well as in the orchestration. A persistent repetition of a short motif in the manner of Sibelius is characteristic also of Klami's short orchestral work, Concert Overture, Opus 23.

If Klami's compositions have only recently started to attract international attention, the works of Väinö Raitio (1891–1945) are hardly known outside of Finland. A clear indebtedness to French impressionism is characteristic also of Raitio's orchestral sound. His best known instrumental works include a Double Concerto for violin, cello, and orchestra and such tone poems as *The Swans* and *Lemminkäinen's Mother*, which echo Sibelian interests. However Raitio's range of topics went far beyond the scope of nationalism, as indicated even by the titles of symphonic poems like *Moonlight on Jupiter* and *Fantasia estatica* and his biblical operas *The King of Lydia* and *Jephta's Daughter*.

If a certain international flavor is characteristic of Klami's and Raitio's output, the same is true also of that of Selim Palmgren (1878–1951), who studied at the Helsinki Conservatory as well as in Germany and in Italy with Busoni. He taught at the Eastman School of Music in 1923–1926 and later at the Sibelius Academy. He gained international reputation around 1913 with his Second Piano Concerto subtitled *The River*. It is a typical romantic concerto, basically a set of variations of the theme of the river. He composed five piano concertos and a number of piano miniatures. His idols were Chopin and Schumann, and he is often referred to as "the Finnish Chopin."

However, Palmgren's affinity to Liszt rather than to Chopin is in evidence both in his piano concertos and shorter piano pieces, such as *Gondoliera veneziana*, Opus 64, Number 1, and in particular in *The Sea*, Opus 17, Number 12. If we consider Liszt, rather than Debussy, "the father of Impressionism," then Liszt's influence could be discerned in such impressionistic miniatures by Palmgren as *May Night*, Opus 27, Number 4 (see Example 53).

Palmgren's piano music epitomizes the basic problem of early Finnish piano music: it lacks the originality of the continental models, which it tends to imitate too slavishly. Although these early piano composers have, by and large, failed to arouse international interest, the Japanese pianist Izumi Tateno has been intrigued by their works and he has recorded several disks devoted to the piano music of Oskar Merikanto (1886-1924) and Ilmari Hannikainen (1892-1955), both better known in Finland for their vocal works, as well as pieces by Heino Kaski (1885-1957). All these composers represent the late romantic tradition, although, for example, Hannikainen's *Variations fantasques* show impressionistic influence in the writing for the left hand. In 1917 Hannikainen composed a piano work which he called *Thème original et neuf variations*. The "original theme" is simple and built on fourth-chords, which in 1917 must have appeared even more "original" than today. Thus the preference of Finnish folk music for fourth steps is obviously represented by the harmony of the simple folk-like tune. Hannikainen must have thought highly of his "original theme," judging by the fact that he reworked the variations later on and increased the number to nineteen. He called the final version *Variations fantasques*.

If Sibelius was not able to reach the highest internationally accepted standards in his piano compositions, the same is true, by and large, of his younger contemporaries, although their output in the genre was huge in Finland due to the popularity of the instrument. The style of composition with strong cosmopolitan influence, in general true of early twentieth-century Finnish piano music, dictated younger composers' approach to orchestral composition. The meager following of Sibelius's nationalistic line

Majnatt.

Mainacht. Kevätyö.

Selim Palmgren, Op 27 No 4.

Example 53 (C) Fazer Music Inc., Helsinki.

of works based on inspiration derived from the *Kalevala* or the *Kanteletar* is probably partly due to the different political situation. After Finland had gained its independence, there was, naturally, no longer any compelling need to compose works like Sibelius's *Karelia*, *Finlandia*, and his patriotic cantatas.

The tendency towards internationalism in evidence already in Klami's and Raitio's output and, to a certain extent, in Kuula's and Madetoja's orchestral works, was of crucial importance in the career of Aarre Merikanto (1893-1958), the son of Oskar Merikanto, due to his influence as a teacher of younger Finnish composers.

After taking courses in Helsinki, Merikanto continued his music studies abroad under Max Reger in Leipzig and also at the Moscow Conservatory. As a young composer he was prolific without gaining any recognition whatsoever for his works. Finally in 1925 he had his first break when he won a competition sponsored by the Schott Publishing House with his Concerto for Violin, Clarinet, Horn, and String Sextet. Although Merikanto won several other international composition competitions, his three symphonies, three piano concertos, four violin concertos, two cello concertos, a number of chamber music works, and — inevitably — a tone poem entitled *Lemminkäinen* have failed to gain international recognition. Merikanto is, regrettably, remembered best as a teacher of several better-known younger composers, including Einojuhani Rautavaara and Aulis Sallinen.

However, Aarre Merikanto's compositions have at least recently aroused a little more interest than those of Lauri Saikkola (b. 1906), whose five symphonies have remained in virtual oblivion. His *Divertimento* for wind quintet and a string suite entitled *Musica per archi* are his best known works. If the latter work contains influence of folk music, it is more in a style reminiscent of Bartók than of Sibelius. One would be hard put to detect any significant Sibelius influence in the works of Nils-Erik Ringbom (b. 1907) either, who is better known as a conductor, music critic, and Sibelius biographer.

The fruitful impact of Aarre Merikanto's restless experimenting under various international influences can be seen in the works of Erik Bergman (b. 1911 at Uusikaarlepyy [Gamla Karleby], Finland). He began his career in the late 1930s with songs in the romantic tradition, the only type accepted in Finland at the time. Later he became an expressionist probably as a reaction to the disillusionment caused by the War.

Bergman's initiation into the modern techniques came with his studies of the twelve-tone method with Vladimir Vogel in Switzerland. Bergman's *Burla*, an orchestral work, his Sonatina and Three Fantasies for Clarinet were preparation for twelve-tone composition, first adapted in a major work in Finland in his *Tre aspetti*. After a period of "neo-impressionistic"[5] serial works, he reached the high point of experimentation in the *Concertino da camera* and the orchestral work *Circulus*. In the latter, the significance of intervallic processes is reduced in favor of rhythmic and coloristic, which points to the composer's return to impressionistic influences. Side by side with this trend there is a tendency towards homophonic chord sequences and small intervals in several works.

An important work in Bergman's output is his *Colori ed improvisazzioni* (1973), which he, surprisingly, did not call a symphony. While it owes a great deal to Aarre Merikanto's *Orchestral Fantasy*, it declares boldly the composer's attitude towards modern trends in composition. Particularly striking is the slow middle movement, a study of the sound of a falling drop of water. Important works from Bergman's later period are several concertos; in particular his cello concerto entitled *Dualis* is one of the composer's most original works. In this one-movement concerto the guiding principle is, as the title implies, the dialogue between the soloist and the different orchestral groups in the form of various motifs integrated into a whole. Monothematicism woven into a complex structure is the principle in his *Dialogue* for flute and guitar, a short but important work, in which Bergman's fellow composer Heininen sees influence of Bartók.

In Bergman's approach to composition, he follows several principles which are those Sibelius emphasized: importance of certain intervallic, and rhythmic or coloristic figures, monthematicism and dialogue between different instruments and instrumental groups; however, Bergman's means, naturally, are colored by those of his era and include refined orchestration and careful use of percussion. Bergman closely follows the tradition established by Aarre Merikanto, but the opposite trend in Finnish music is represented by Ahti Sonninen (b. 1914), in whose Four Suites for orchestra reflections of folk song both in rhythm and melody have been compared to Kodály's use of folk music.

Sonninen represents the tradition of Sibelius's nationalistic works through the intermediary of Madetoja while Einar Englund (b. 1916) is more of an innovator and closer to Aarre Merikanto with, at the same time, a clear link to Finnish nationalism. Englund was an early figure in Finnish "new music," and he has sometimes been referred to as "Finland's Hindemith."[6] However, he is also a Nordic composer whose concise expression typically consists of thematic blocks. In principle this is somewhat reminiscent of Sibelius's variation method, but Englund's large leaps and sudden harmonic flashes give his idiom something of an impressionistic character.

While Englund's Second Symphony has been considered a cultural milestone in Finland, many have found his First Piano Concerto somewhat facile. After a long silence, during which Englund concentrated on teaching, he finished his Third Symphony in 1971. To many observers the work was a disappointment, because in it the intensity caused by the harshness of daily living in the years immediately after the Second World War characteristic of Englund's earlier output is replaced by masterly technique. In Heininen's view, this is the effect of the spirit of the welfare state that is also manifest in the smartness of Aalto's architecture. Technical prowess is in evidence likewise in Englund's Fourth Symphony (1976) for string orchestra and percussion, with passages reminiscent of Shostakovich. In Englund's later works especially, as well as in those by Joonas Kokkonen, there is a tendency to build a work from a small cell, a method that in principle recalls Sibelius. However, Englund's technique did not incorporate serialism as Kokkonen's did in many instances.

This is the essence of Kokkonen (b. 1921): a member of the Finnish Academy, who grew up and still lives in the vicinity of Ainola at Järvenpää. As a high school student, he knew Sibelius's symphonies by heart and avowed admiration in particular for the Fourth, Sixth, and Seventh Symphonies, as well as for *Tapiola*, but felt disappointed with the Fifth Symphony. Sibelian echoes are clear in Kokkonen's statement of his method of composition: an "evolution from a seed, which takes root, grows a stalk, leaves and blossoms."[7] Depending on the qualities inherent in the seed, it might grow to be a tree, that is, a symphony.

Kokkonen's predilection for Sibelius's Fourth Symphony can be seen in his First String Quartet, from the 1950s, which does have an affinity to the Sibelian intensity of feeling; however, the Kokkonen work fails to create the sense of excitement at the anticipation of the unexpected that is Sibelius's forte. Kokkonen concedes that his *Music for String Orchestra* in four movements (1957) does have a Sibelian element that is attributable to the Finnish environment rather than any direct musical influence.

Kokkonen's Third Symphony dates from 1967, and thus it could be considered, for many reasons, representative of the mature composer. It won recognition in the form of a prize from the Nordic Council. According to the composer, the basic idea of the work came from a strong personal experience in nature, but he emphasized that from there on the work is absolute music. How does the composer interpret "the basic idea" in his music? He uses a short harp introduction somewhat reminiscent of the opening upward motif of Sibelius's Seventh Symphony in that the motion is in small steps instead of the large leaps typical of romantic composers. The harp tones are sustained in the winds anchored over an E major triad in the trombones. Something of a layering of chords is suggested by the basic idea. In addition to the E major chord, the harmonically important chords included the E-flat major and D major chords, and the fundamentals of these chords, E-flat, E, D, are the cornerstone of the work, which can be seen from the conclusion of the first movement as well as from the close of the finale.[8]

The first movement, *Andante sostenuto*, has a secondary theme based partly on the introductory harp theme with an important new added element, a rising fifth step. Traditionally this implies association with nature and it is reminiscent of Sibelius's use of the same step in the finale of the Fourth Symphony (solo oboe, p. 44, 6th bar after cue D). It seems to indicate expansion after the small steps of the opening theme. Towards the end of the work, a descending fourth step becomes significant in the "winding down" process, obviously signaling the closing of a circle of thought. It is tempting to think of the use of the processes of opening and closing as an adaptation of the technique used by Sibelius in his Fifth Symphony in the famous "Thor's hammer" theme.

We might recall that the second, fourth, and fifth steps, common in Finnish folk music, are the cornerstones of Sibelius's idiom and often contrasted with triadic thinking. Thus the basics of Kokkonen's thematic material, the hint of the layering of the triads on the one hand, and themes built from second, fourth, and fifth steps on the other, reflect the basic conflict in most works by Sibelius. Although no real tonic-dominant relationships exist in Kokkonen's Third Symphony, the basic conflict is, as is usual in Sibelius, suggested in the thematic material.

Freer in his use of tonalities than Sibelius, Kokkonen, nevertheless, frequently puts emphasis on a given chord, often a major triad, which stands out against the chromatic background. Frequently the crucial chord is carried by the brass, and the effect is solemn and majestic, suggesting a mystic feeling associated with nature – or perhaps a religious experience – as in many works by Sibelius.

These structurally important chords also assume a major role in sonority and tone color in a way that reflects Sibelius's use of polyphony, in particular in his Sixth Symphony. As in Sibelius's works, in Kokkonen's textures the intervals are important from the linear point of view as well as from the harmonic, and both the linear and harmonic effects reflect the influence of folk music and church music, in particular of the chorale.

The balance between emphasis on linearity and verticality in Kokkonen's Third Symphony has structural implications in a manner reminiscent of Sibelius's Sixth Symphony, in which the musical process starts from a short ascending motif and, after a rich polyphonic web, ends in a thinning-out process in which only one fundamental tone remains. The Sibelian practice of both the thematic and harmonic material creating a logical structure seems to be reflected in Kokkonen's frequent use of an adagio as the finale of a work, which, according to the composer, corresponds better to his idea of organic growth than the traditional sonata structure does. Even the rapid forward motion of the two fast scherzo-like movements of Kokkonen's Third Symphony contribute more clearly to the feeling of growth than, say, Shostakovich's fast movements.

Although Kokkonen emphasizes the fact that he considers Bach the greatest genius and Mozart almost equal to him, this thinking is not really in conflict with his idea of organic growth in composition, because he considers Bach's two-part inventions the basis of all composition just as a seed is basic to growth. As a token of his admiration, Kokkonen constructed his *Sinfonia da camera*, a work for twelve solo strings written by request for the Lucerne Festival Strings, on the motif B-A-C-H. In this the tonal centers that occurred every now and then in Kokkonen's earlier works have disappeared and are replaced by a polyphonic twelve-tone fabric.

Kokkonen's Cello Concerto (1969) is closely connected with three personalities: the Finnish cellist Arto Noras, for whom the work was written; Alvar Aalto, to whom the work is dedicated as the first composition written in the composer's new home designed by Aalto; and the composer's mother, who passed away the same year. Kokkonen emphasizes that the dedication to Aalto is more than anything a token of gratitude to a fellow member of the Finnish Academy for their interesting discussions on music and architecture and about the connection, "deeper and richer than what can be expressed in words,"[9] between the two art forms.

As representative works among Kokkonen's solo instrumental pieces, mention could be made of his Five Bagatelles for Piano (1969), the composer's instrument. They are by no means bagatelles in the usual sense but rather difficult works, which bring to mind both Debussy and Bartók. An important part of Kokkonen's career has been his role as professor of composition at the Sibelius Academy. Among his students were Einojuhani Rautavaara and Aulis Sallinen. Rautavaara (b. 1928), a gifted composer and at the present time professor of composition at the Sibelius Academy, is even more markedly individualistic than Kokkonen. The differences in the most prominent personalities in Finnish music today, which are reflected in their music, are rooted in their character: where Kokkonen is a calm and deliberate member of numerous committees, Rautavaara has managed to ruffle quite a few egos with his caustic remarks on the Finnish radio as a commentator on the works of young Finnish composers. Although Rautavaara belongs to a family prominent in Finnish music, he did not study the discipline as a child. At the age of seventeen, he suddenly decided to become a composer and made such fast progress with his youthful works that he was recommended by Sibelius himself for a scholarship and studies at Tanglewood with Aaron Copland and at the Juilliard School of Music.

Rautavaara's first breakthrough came in 1953, when he won an American competition with his *A Requiem in Our Time*, much of whose character is derived from its scoring for brass and percussion. As the title implies, it is a modern work, harsh and unsentimental; its associations are not those of a traditional requiem and, like many of the composer's works, show the influence of his teacher Aarre Merikanto in his probing and experimentation. This can be deduced from the titles of many of Rautavaara's works, which reveal a mind preoccupied with introspection and intellectual speculation, as of such orchestral works as *Regular Sets of Elements in Semiregular* (1971), the self-analytical *A Portrait of the Artist at a Certain Moment* (1972), and *To Grow, Develop, Change* (1974).

An indication of the mercurial changes in Rautavaara's inspiration is the work, *Angel of Dusk*, a concerto for double bass and orchestra, a haunting, funereal piece composed in memory of Olga Koussevitzky, whose conductor-husband was also a double bass virtuoso. An inspiration somewhat reminiscent of Sibelius is manifest in a number of more recent works by Rautavaara, such as *Angels and Visitations*, an orchestral work from 1978. A clear affinity to Sibelius's appreciation of the mysteries of nature permeates the atmosphere of Rautavaara's *Cantus arcticus*, a work composed for the graduation ceremonies of the first doctoral candidates at the University of Oulu. The composer characterized the piece as "a concerto for birds and orchestra," into which sounds of arctic birds are incorporated partly by the instruments and partly in the form of electronic tapes. The choice of the titles of the three movements, "The Ant," "Melancholy," "The Swans Are Migrating," seems to contain definite echoes of Sibelius's interest in nature.   However, the techniques used are reminiscent of

Messiaen with a more realistic approach to bird song than the mere hint in a Sibelian work like *Nightride and Sunrise*. Certain Tchaikovskyan-Sibelian echoes are present also in the introductory part of the work, and the composer himself has encouraged the flute soloist playing the introduction to think of "autumn and Tchaikovsky."[10]

Restless experimentation is characteristic of Rautavaara to the extent that his countryman and fellow-composer Heininen stated that his style has gone from neo-Ravelism in the First Quartet and some other early works to dodecaphony and serialism.[11] Heininen prefers Rautavaara's Second Piano Concerto, whose style he characterizes as "beautiful, practical modernism," to his more experimental works, such as *Ithaka*, a piano work, or such representatives of his fling with electronic music as *The Sirens*.

Rautavaara's career could best be described as a circle. He began in the early 1950s with a strong interest in the folk music of the province of Ostrobothnia, the area whose music inspired also Kuula, Madetoja, Nordgren, and Panula, while at the same time studying the music of Prokofiev and Stravinsky. Besides studying in the United States, Rautavaara was also a pupil of Vladimir Vogel, under whose influence he employed the twelve-tone method in such works as his Second String Quartet and the opera, *The Mine*. In the Third Symphony, which is still serialist, there is, however, a certain tonal background implied. In Rautavaara's later works the return to tonality is carried out even more fully while it is often contrasted with atonality; in other words, the circle is completed.

Restless experimentation is characteristic also of Usko Meriläinen's output. The composer, who was born in 1930, attracted attention in the 1950s with a type of modernized classicism distinguished by propulsive motor movement in his *Partita* and First Piano Concerto, probably under the influence of his childhood idol Stravinsky. The chromaticism of the latter work led to dodecaphony in the First Piano Sonata and the Chamber Concerto for Violin and Strings after his studies in Darmstadt, which, together with his additional studies with Vladimir Vogel, helped him to refine his serial technique and facilitated the logical control of his musical ideas, a claim also made by Rautavaara. Meriläinen feels that dodecaphony taught him how to make the logical sequence of the musical material work, even if the nature of his basic ideas keeps changing during the course of his career. Thus the Second Symphony, while still characterized by chromatic intervals like the First Piano Concerto, is full of small details, which vary quickly in rhythm and tone color. The composer himself has referred to the technique as "the metamorphoses of characters,"[12] the "characters" being short, multidimensional ideas that are the basis of his non-dodecaphonic, athematic music. Meriläinen's restless experimenting includes the novel techniques of his Fourth Piano Concerto, as well as electronic music. His Second String Quartet, subtitled *Kyma*, has attracted attention.

Like Meriläinen, Jouko Linjama (b. 1934) was an avant-gardist in the 1950s. Then he discovered pre-Baroque music and its architectonic quality, from whose rigors he moved to monody with scant triadic accompaniment. Linjama, a pupil of Aarre Merikanto and Kokkonen and a scholarship student in Cologne, where he attended seminars conducted by Stockhausen, became a polyphonist and a church musician. He rejected dodecaphony and became convinced that polyphony was the most important form of composition. However, as a result of his studies, he approached polyphony with a desire to apply it on many different levels, such as polytonality, the use of different tempi simultaneously, and even the development of a type of multilayered canon of rhythmic motifs. It is as if he used Sibelius's Sixth Symphony as his starting-point and were determined to expand its means to comprise the techniques of another era. In his "modernization" trend he even went as far as to minimize the importance of melody, using in his symphony several madrigals simultaneously in a type of polyform. Those of his works whose affiliation to church music is closest, such as his *Magnificat* for organ, bring Messiaen to mind.

Erkki Salmenhaara (b. 1941) began also as an experimenter. After studies with Kokkonen, he continued his studies in Vienna with György Ligeti about whom he wrote his doctoral dissertation. From the early avant-garde period under the influence of Ligeti up to the late 1960s, Salmenhaara switched to neoromanticism. His orchestral work *Le bateau ivre* combines his earlier structural principles with emphasis on the thematic material, with three triads as the cornerstones of the motivic ideas. He started to use small ensembles, as in his *Sinfonietta for Strings*, whose language is purely diatonic. His style went through simplification, a kind of peeling-off process, and from impulsive use of rhythm to neoharmonics in the miniature orchestral suite entitled *Adagietto*. Indicative of the new direction is also his *Poem* for cello and string orchestra (1975), which shows clearly that the composer has abandoned his earlier love of dodecaphonism. In fact, Salmenhaara's recent motto, "harmony is the theme,"[13] is oddly reminiscent of Grieg's principle.

The 1959 première of Paavo Heininen's (b. 1938) First Symphony branded him the *enfant terrible* of Finnish music. His studies included courses in composition in Helsinki with Aarre Merikanto and Kokkonen and abroad in Cologne and New York. Exposed to Bernd Alois Zimmermann's and Vincent Persichetti's ideas, Heininen was ready to absorb influences from all sorts of sources, instrumental and electronic music, jazz, and pop music. However, in his view, neither Lutoslawski's nor Ligeti's concept of form nor serialism's way of creating order out of the musical material is suitable for his purposes to express his fantasy world in music. His aim is to create configurations of individual tone points, in which not only the rhythmic, dynamic, melodic, harmonic, coloristic, and spatial properties but also their mutual balance vary from one point to another.

However, in spite of Heininen's highly original ideas, his compositions are not necessarily a reflection of his theories; and, for example, in his *Adagio, Concerto per orchestra in forma di variazioni* (1963), many have seen a homage to Mahler. The variation principle assumes a form of metamorphoses of the material in the Third Symphony (Opus 20), on which Heininen worked from 1969 to 1977. Indicative of the composer's wide interests are his references to Joseph Conrad, Lawrence Durrell, and Herman Hesse, with which Heininen illustrated the work. As might be expected from a highly volatile artist, there is a Finnish side to the composer as well; he based a short symphonic poem on a Finnish folk song entitled "Laakson ruusu" (A Rose in the valley).

Some observers have seen influence of Shostakovich in the musical expressions of Kalevi Aho and Pehr Henrik Nordgren. Aho (b. 1949) studied with Rautavaara and later in Germany with Boris Blacher. Aho's method of composition is characterized by a polyphonic approach, which, in his view, was prompted by his childhood desire to compose melodies on the violin, and emphasis on melody has remained a focal point in his works. He considers himself a tonal composer, but only in a loose sense. Typical of his style are polyphonic voices occurring at different intervals, often at seconds.

As a representative piece by Aho we might mention his Third String Quartet (1971), in which emphasis is on linearity and clarity of form. The eight-movement work is shaped like an arch in which the final movement is almost a parody of the first, the second has an affinity with the seventh movement, and so on. The arch shape is also reflected in the fact that the work opens on a simple introduction, culminating in the richly dissonant and intricate middle movements after which the musical language becomes simplified again.

As in the case of Aho, a youthful interest in the violin resulted in a clear preference for linearity in the works of Pehr Henrik Nordgren (b. 1944). However, Nordgren refused to study the instrument systematically and for this reason was rejected for admission to the Sibelius Academy, although he did study music theory at the University of Helsinki and also composition as Kokkonen's private pupil. Nordgren wrote his dissertation on Shostakovich's orchestral techniques, but, strangely enough, this did not result in any massive influence in his music. Nordgren's musical language has shown changes from combinations of triads and ponderous clusters to emphasis on a given tone. Although Aho began with classical clarity, which he enriched with new ideas, and Nordgren as an experimenter in fusing influences of Baroque music into a type of chaotic expressionism, both composers are, in principle, opposed to avant-gardism. Nordgren's works, characterized by a great deal of attention to the properties of each instrument, include the use of traditional Japanese instruments in his *Autumnal Concerto*, while the chief foreign influence in Aho's music is Viennese. An essential facet of Nordgren's idiom is the impact of *pelimannimusiikki*, the instrumental folk music of Finland.

A search for a personal voice in composition in the case of Leif Segerstam (b. 1944) has been hampered by the diversity of his musical activity. He is a capable violinist and pianist, who showed interest in composition as early as the age of five. During his studies at the Sibelius Academy he was equally fascinated by the violin, conducting, and composition. At the Juilliard School of Music he was awarded a diploma in conducting while he was also studying composition with Vincent Persichetti and Hal Overton. Since then, numerous conducting engagements, both on a semi-permanent and visiting basis, have prevented Segerstam from devoting as much time to composition as he would have liked.

Conducting works of various composers and in vastly different styles — Segerstam has acquired fame also as an opera conductor — has resulted in a pull of varied forces in his creative work. Basically, he is a product of the Viennese school, with a definite penchant for expressionism and, in particular, for Alban Berg. In the 1970s he was set on the development of a style he characterizes as "freely pulsatory."[14] In the compositional process his aim is to choose his material according to his mental images as if he were playing an instrument. The images that are transferred to paper are so loosely delineated that much of the interpretation is left to the soloist's or conductor's discretion, as can be seen from the fact that he likes to omit the barline and even dynamic markings. According to Segerstam, his final goal in composition is a musical kaleidoscope created by a group of musicians on a highly improvisational basis in a manner that would reflect the gathering of birds in a flock. However, the composer admits that his method of composition, not dependent on notation, is not realizable in the near future. The titles and genres of Segerstam's compositions mirror his diverse interests: *Pandora*, a ballet for orchestra (1967), Violin Concerto (1967), *Six Songs of Experience* (1971), *A NNNOOOOOWW*, for wind quintet (1973), seven string quartets (1962-1975), and so on.

While there is influence of André Jolivet and Elliott Carter in the music of Jouni Kaipainen (b. 1956), a pupil of Sallinen and Heininen, his experimentation has never been as extreme as Segerstam's. Kaipainen's *Trois morceaux de l'aube* for cello and piano won first prize in the UNESCO International competition in 1981.

Deep involvement in electronic music has been characteristic of Magnus Lindberg (b. 1928), a pupil of Osmo Lindeman, who has been credited with the introduction of electronic composition in Finland. For his *Action-Situation-Signification* (1982) Lindberg drew a "Klang map" of nature's basic elements, fire, water, and so on, with the aid of Elias Canetti's *Masse und Macht*, and in his *Linea d'ombra* (1981) he uses materials like metal and wood for production of sounds. In *Action-Situation-Signification* every element has its own identity, with the sea being portrayed by repeated cycles and fire by irregular motion. While the direction and intensity of the wind keep changing constantly, rain is characterized by monotonous repetition. "Fire" and "Water" are the most important movements of the composition.

Lindberg, who studied in Darmstadt and in Paris with Vinko Globokar, attracted international attention with his orchestral work *Kraft*, which was commissioned by the Helsinki Music Festival committee in 1985. The work received the International Rostrum of Composers' recognition in 1986, the Nordic Council music prize in 1987, and the Koussevitzky prize in 1988. Lindberg's idea was to reverse the traditional concept of musical composition starting from a simple beginning and developing into something more complicated. In *Kraft* (Power), the musical material is treated as a mass of sound, not as individual notes, and the most powerful chords of the work consist of seventy-two voices. In the Finlandia label recording of the composition by the avant-garde Toimii Ensemble under the direction of Esa-Pekka Salonen, all sorts of junkyard objects are used as percussion "instruments." The harsh sounds produced are held together by rhythm to the point that certain rhythmic sequences even evoke Baroque music.

As in the Lindberg work, electronic sound production is used by Kaija Saariaho (b. 1952) in her *Verblendungen*. Her experimentation includes requiring instrumentalists to talk as well as combine sustained electronic dissonances with enormous outbursts on the percussion in a style that appears to be characterized by an artificial seeking of effect. Electronic music has been incorporated into film scores by Kari Rydman, whose quartets displaying influence of a variety of styles have attracted attention.

Side by side with experimentation in various internationally inspired styles and methods, there has also been in Finnish music the tendency to rely on domestic models and on inspiration derived from Finland's past. Whether the latter trend is conscious or unconscious is a matter of dispute, and such prominent personalities in Finnish music of today as Kokkonen and Aulis Sallinen claim these influences to be environmental rather than the result of a conscious effort.

Sallinen (b. 1935), who began his career with chamber music like his teacher Kokkonen, declared his independence from his other teacher of composition, Aarre Merikanto, by using at first a serial technique. He modified it later adopting use of free tonality and neoclassical influences reminiscent of Hindemith, Prokofiev, and Shostakovich. In his early chamber music work, *Elegy for Sebastian Knight* (Opus 10; 1964), he shows the tendency towards expansion of the twelve-tone system to include tonal elements. Some of the ideas in this work the composer used later for a larger composition entitled *Metamorphoses* for piano and chamber orchestra. Likewise, in his *Quattro per Quattro*, (Opus 12; 1964-65), there is evident a desire to return to the old, even to the extent of using the triad which, as the composer pointed out, had to be "rediscovered" in the 1960s.[15]

A feature of Sallinen's style, which he is quick to point out, is a pastiche-like treatment of a given motif, its variation with styles of older periods. This type of use of the variation method is in keeping with the composer's personality, because it allows him to be facetious, less serious than Sibelius. Behind this thinking we can detect a kinship with Nielsen, whom Sallinen admires very much and who, in his view, was "at least as good a composer as our Sibelius."[16]

This pastiche-like variation method is very much in evidence in Sallinen's Third Quartet, Opus 19 (1969), subtitled *Aspects of Peltoniemi Hintrik's Funeral March*. The subtitle refers to a *pelimanni* tune, a popular Finnish instrumental theme, that Sallinen had used earlier in a short piece and now uses as the basis of his Quartet. The composer was asked by the Swedish School

Board to give demonstration classes in several schools and he used the Quartet for that purpose. On those occasions Sallinen played the viola part, "which was the reason why I had to write that part in an easy style," as the composer stated.[17]

A remarkable feature of the Third Quartet is the use of the fiddle tune to conjure up the harmonium-like effect of the music of Finnish religious meetings at the turn of the century. This is accomplished by the first violin and the cello playing the melody two octaves apart without vibrato with bowing that is not quite identical. However, after this portentous beginning the work slides into various styles that appear to be reminiscences of Bartók and, towards the end of the work, of the *Allegretto* of Sibelius's *Voces intimae*. The composition seems to conclude with a recollection of *Rakastava*. Thus the overall impression of the Quartet is that it is too disparate and derivative, lacking the stylistic unity of, say, *Voces intimae*. However, the Sallinen work is typical of the composer in that the Sibelian seriousness is tempered by a slightly humorous touch, although derived from a "funeral march." Indicative of Sallinen's mercurial change form the somewhat lighthearted parody of the Third String Quartet to extreme seriousness is his Fourth Quartet with its "strange, contemplative stillness."[18]

If Kokkonen is particularly fond of Sibelius's Fourth Symphony, it is easy to see why Sallinen's favorites are the master's last three symphonies. Sallinen's First Symphony, a prize winner in a contest on the occasion of the inauguration of the new Finlandia Concert Hall in Helsinki, was perhaps intended to be both a homage to Sibelius and a declaration of independence. The one-movement Symphony opens on an F-sharp minor chord followed by a short motif and its insistent repetition in a manner that brings Sibelius to mind (see Example 54). Although the short motif seems to be of vital importance, it is not brought back until towards the end of the work (p. 47), and even then its return is not sustained. Perhaps this could be interpreted as Sallinen's way of expressing his independence of Sibelius, whose insistent presence in the beginning is brought back only as a fleeting remembrance towards the end of the symphony.

The work ends in the F-sharp minor chord, with which it opened, and contains tonal themes and motifs. The scoring is generally sparse despite a variety of orchestral instruments, ranging from the strings and harp to two flutes, three oboes and three clarinets, to bassoons, horns, trumpets, trombones, timpani and percussion instruments. A conflict between the short

Symphony No. 1

AULIS SALLINEN

Example 54 Reproduced by permission of Novello and Company Limited.

rhythmic motif of the opening of the First Symphony and the stepwise progressions and clusters dominating the middle section of the work also seems to contain echoes of Sibelius's method, as does the main principle of the Second Symphony, which he called first *Symphonic Dialogue* for percussion and orchestra. The "dialogue" is carried out by two main motifs, a falling one and a fanfare.

In the Third Symphony Sallinen abandons the one-movement form in favor of three movements. Continuity is created with the second movement, a *chaconne*, growing out of the first. The Finnish conductor Okko Kamu characterized the work as Sallinen's "sea symphony" because of its element of surprise reflecting a constantly changing ocean. Undoubtedly, some Sibelian undercurrents can be felt in Sallinen's portrayal of the sea.

A reflection of Sibelius's statement of his being "a slave" to his themes is seen in Sallinen's view of the origin of his Fourth Symphony (1978). According to the composer, he intended it to be a joyous work but, instead, it turned out to be created by an attempt to be optimistic; we might recall the opposite course from the initial statement by Sibelius about his Sixth Symphony to the final product. A desire to conquer a fear of impending doom is embodied in the subtitle of the second movement of the Sallinen work, "Dona nobis pacem." The speculative mood of the Fourth Symphony is carried over to the Fifth, which was premiered at the Kennedy Center in Washington, D.C., in 1985, with Mstislav Rostropovich conducting. A desire to make sense out of the puzzle of life seems to be the driving force behind the shifting and juxtaposing of short, pregnant motifs, whose growth process spreads over five movements. Although the pastiche-like element is present in the Fifth Symphony in the spooky clowning of the waltz in the first movement and of the march in the finale, one gets the feeling that Sallinen has reached maturity with a style that is related also to his Fifth Quartet and Chamber Music III. It is characterized by a variation technique in which short motifs, "mosaics," as the composer called them in the Fifth Quartet, are used to create phrases with the imitative method. In essence, it is an individual version of Sibelius's variation method.

No matter how emphatically Sallinen claimed that Sibelius was "past history," the fact that both he and Kokkonen usually build a work around a core motif or theme is in itself a reflection of Sibelius's approach to composition. When we add that these basic motifs in Sallinen's, as well as in Kokkonen's, music are loaded with dynamic potential for growth despite the fact that they appear to be nothing but curt little ideas, we cannot help but think of Sibelius's symphonies which, starting with the Second, are constructed on the same principle. Another Sibelian element of Sallinen's work is his frequent use of pedal points and melodies of long notes in his ominous-sounding passages, which contribute to the Nordic mood of desolation and menace. Sibelian echoes are found also in Sallinen's contrast between the brooding atmosphere of winter contrasted with the exhilaration of spring, as expressed, for example, in Sallinen's Cello Concerto (1976) in the elegiac melancholy of the first section and the joy of spring in the finale.

Sallinen's interplay of different instruments is also reminiscent of Sibelius, although, naturally, with a more contemporary emphasis on the percussion and with strange and at the same time somber and lyrical effects with bells in Sallinen's works. However, the feeling the listener gets from Sallinen's compositions is that in the long run modern techniques mean less to the composer than the dramatic tension conveyed by linear progressions of melody. In short, Sallinen is at heart a romantic, as was Sibelius, and a romantic's inspiration depends largely on dramatic tension.

Tension is evident already in Sallinen's first large-scale orchestral work, *Mauermusik* (1962), which was inspired by fatal shots at an escapee at the Berlin Wall. Indicative of the composer's early period of experimentation is the fact that the work includes some aleatory passages. Although Sallinen's dramatic talent is expressed in all his compositions from orchestral to small ensemble works, it is of course particularly evident in his operas, which we shall discuss in the next chapter.

All prominent Finnish composers of today have shown keen interest in chamber music, the level of which they have raised from that prevalent at the turn of the century. Although the earlier small ensemble tradition was strong in Finland, it had assumed a semi-popular character due to a growing demand for easy pieces for amateur groups. This "restaurant music" was a curious mixture of influences of Finnish and Scandinavian folk song, the Viennese waltz, and other popular and semi-popular concert music of the period. The sentimental tunes of Lehár, Kalmán and Millöcker operettas were played at all fashionable establishments. In many cases they were even performed by German musicians like Karl Ganszauge whose orchestra played at many popular spas and restaurants in and around Helsinki in the 1840s.

Recordings of popular pieces were at first produced in Germany where Finnish entertainers traveled to produce popular hits. After the founding of the Finnish Broadcasting Company in 1926, strains of German operettas and records by native popular composers and singers started to compete with one another. After the First World War, jazz spread to Scandinavia, and with it the saxophone. However, the somewhat misguided efforts of the Nordic interpreters of jazz failed to gain the popularity of native Finnish singers like Georg Malmsten. He had received a solid musical training in the Navy Band, and this "Sibelius of the suburbs," as he was nicknamed, is credited with the fact that popular music in Finland remained closely tied to the continental tradition of light music. Only after the Second World War did lively contact with musicians of the United States bring genuine jazz to Finland. The Pori Jazz Festival has become one of the most prestigious events in this field in Europe, if not in the world. The trend in Finland clearly has been towards the breaking down of the barrier between jazz and concert music. This is discernible in the works of Heikki Sarmanto, a composer and jazz pianist, whose composition *Opuscule* won a prize at the 1960 Minneapolis Festival.

A curious fusion of genuine Finnish kantele music and continental popular music came into existence in the 1960s and it has proved vital indeed. It has received a strong boost from the Kaustinen Folk Music Festival, where kantele players and fiddlers get together to play genuine Finnish folk tunes on the kantele, as well as later folk-style music and dance music including *purppuris*, polkas, and other dances popular in the eighteenth and nineteenth centuries. An indication of the mixed character of the popular folk tradition is the inclusion of the accordion, which appeared in Finland in the 1880s replacing to a large extent the fiddle, popular since the seventeenth century.

The resurgence of interest in Finland in kantele music has been largely due to the efforts of Marjatta and Martti Pokela, who have managed to create a veritable renaissance in folk ballads. The Pokelas' use of the enlarged kantele and their studiedly understated dramatic renderings of the lyrics have given new life to this type of folk song. It is due to their efforts that old kantele tunes and songs with kantele accompaniment, if not the genuine runo songs have sustained both academic and popular interest. There is now a chair in kantele-playing in the Sibelius Academy.

On the other hand, in adherence to cosmopolitan trends, the guitar, the flute, and the saxophone have become important concert instruments in Finland. We might recall that Sibelius's father used the guitar to accompany his songs, but playing the instrument was only a hobby for him and it remained so for his countrymen until after the Second World War. Although Per-Olof Johnson, professor of music at Lund, introduced the classical guitar in Scandinavia, the instrument was still a hobby for Ivan Putilin after the Second World War. He earned his living by playing the double bass in the Finnish Radio Symphony Orchestra while teaching classical guitar to many young Finns. In 1968 a chair in the instrument was established in the Sibelius Academy, and many of the ranking composers of the country have written pieces for the guitar, as well as for other lesser known instruments.

The first classical guitar composition in Finland was written by Erik Bergman, who composed his Suite for Guitar in 1949 for the Swiss guitarist Hermann Leeb. Since then, two young Finnish guitarists, Seppo Siirala and Jukka Savijoki, have inspired many composers to write works for the instrument. Bergman continued his interest in the guitar with *Dialogue* for flute and guitar, and in the flute with a concerto subtitled "Birds in the Morning." Rautavaara expressed his interest in the guitar with *Monologues of the Unicorn* and *Serenades of the Unicorn* and Heininen with his solo guitar piece entitled "...touching...," a masterful and difficult work.

Among the young Finnish experimenters is Jukka Tiensuu (b. 1948), a proponent of "new music" who is very much interested in tone colors, as can be seen from his works, which include *M* for cembalo and strings and *Sinistro* for guitar and two accordions. Mikko Heiniö wrote *Champignons à l'herméneutique* for flute and guitar and Esa-Pekka Salonen, *Goodbye* for violin and guitar. The saxophone has also become an accepted concert instrument in Finland, as shown by the popularity of Paavo Heininen's Saxophone Concerto, a nostalgic work for the instrument, and of performers like the saxophonist Pekka Savijoki, brother of the guitarist Jukka Savijoki.

Despite the variety of new music that Finland has produced, the post-Sibelian composers of the country have had to fight the preconceived notion of most foreigners of the transfer of the nationalistic tradition to the younger composers. However, when some Finnish composers between the two World Wars wrote works based on the nationalistic tradition established by Sibelius, it was due to the changed political situation that the enthusiasm and the sense of national pride characteristic of Sibelius's works inspired by the *Kalevala* or the *Kanteletar* was no longer there. International influences compete strongly with the impact of folk music in Madetoja's and Klami's orchestral works and they are dominant in the output of Aarre Merikanto. Sibelius's influence on the development of Finnish music cannot be considered anything but crucial nevertheless.

After the Second World War, even the composers for whom the nationalistic tradition had lost its significance were influenced, perhaps subconsciously, by many Sibelian principles. We can detect the impact of Sibelius's germ motif technique particularly in Kokkonen's use of short motifs in the construction of musical forms. Likewise, Sallinen's love of monothematicism based on metamorphoses of a given theme could be considered another adaptation of the Sibelian technique. A step towards an even more abstract employment of the principle could be seen in Bergman's emphasis on certain intervallic figures or Heininen's method of creation of *gestalter*, musical configurations put together of basic units, a principle which the composer himself characterized as "an expansion of the concept of the interval"[19] with emphasis on the relationship of one multidimensional characteristic point to another. However, in reality Heininen's *gestalter* often concentrate on melody and harmony as a consequence of the shock he received at the realization that orchestras refused to play some of his avant-garde works.

Individual views of the magnitude of Sibelius's impact on younger Finnish composers may differ, but his influence certainly cannot be denied. As a matter of fact, Heininen claims that post-Sibelian music in Finland follows two main lines: one derives from the master's Fourth Symphony and *Tapiola* and the other from his Fifth, Sixth, and Seventh Symphonies.[20] In his view, during the period between the two World Wars, Aarre Merikanto represented the former school and Madetoja the latter. However, Heininen maintains that the division can still be applied to many composers, and he juxtaposes Erik Bergman as a representative of the former group and Joonas Kokkonen of the latter and, likewise, Usko Meriläinen and Einojuhani Rautavaara, himself and Sallinen and even Jukka Tiensuu and Kalevi Aho among the younger composers. Heininen does admit that the grouping is by no means clear, since any composer's style varies from one creative period to another and, to a certain extent, even from one work to another. It is interesting to observe, nevertheless, that with the composers who followed chronologically closest to Sibelius, Merikanto and Madetoja, the distinction is clear indeed. The further away we come from Sibelius's era, the more blurred the distinction based on Heininen's criteria seems to become.

We can talk about "new music" in Finland with the première of Einar Englund's First Symphony and of Erik Bergman's *Burla*. In both works modality no longer has the role it had in Sibelius's idiom, and often it yields to serially organized chromaticism. Although the common trend in composition during this century has been the abandonment of tonality, there are features in this area in the works of all Finnish post-Sibelian composers that bring to mind the master's "democratic" view of tonality, particularly in the Seventh Symphony and *Tapiola*. Likewise, echoes of the

Sibelian emphasis on rhythm, especially in his choral works, can be detected in most younger Finnish composers. Foreign observers have usually attributed these influences to Stravinsky in the case of Englund and to Shostakovich and Karl Orff as far as Sallinen is concerned.

Influence of church music, which was an important facet of Sibelius's idiom, is still evident in the musical expression of the present-day Finnish composers, and we shall return to this issue in the next chapter. Related to the influence of church music is the Sibelian orchestral sound, an area in which the younger Finnish composers have reacted to Sibelius's impact either positively or negatively: some have imitated him while others have made an effort to get as far away from him as possible.

In some composers there has been an almost defiant desire to turn their backs to the native tradition by experimentation with new instruments and techniques. A Finnish composer could hardly get further away from native music than Jukka Linkola, who began his career with interest in Afro-American music. His recent composition Crossings (1984) for tenor saxophone and symphony orchestra is, according to the composer, a journey through a musical landscape that includes Stravinsky and modern music up to Lutoslawski, as well as jazz, both old and new. Extremes of experimentation are evident also in Magnus Lindberg's latest works, such as Sculpture II (1981) for orchestra and Zona (1983) for cello and instrumental ensemble. In the former work, Lindberg's technique involves musical happenings on various levels to the extent that the work requires two conductors. As a result of a few years' stay in Japan, Pehr-Henrik Nordgren often includes in the interpretation of his exotic inspiration genuine Japanese instruments, such as the koto, as in his Quartet and Autumnal Concerto, although the basics of his idiom are Nordic. Even a composer like Einar Englund, who has in general been labeled as a somewhat "dry" academic type, experimented with a rumba in the finale of his Concerto for Twelve Cellos (1981). The instrumental technique of the work even calls for the performers to tap the body of the instrument.

We might mention that Sibelius never approved of experimentation for its own sake, including the introduction of new instruments, unless there was a valid reason for it. In his view, composers would do well to learn thoroughly the potentials of the standard instruments rather than engage in experimenting with new ones. He set a good example with the hauntingly beautiful English horn obbligato in "The Swan of Tuonela," and very few connoisseurs recognize the fact that Sibelius's "Nocturne" for *Belshazzar's Feast* was in 1906 the first important work composed in Finland for solo flute. For this reason, one of Finland's foremost flutists today, Mikael Helasvuo, considers "no less a figure than our great symphonist. . . the father of Finnish music for the flute."[21] He deems the "Nocturne," as well as the "Oaktree" of Sibelius's *The Tempest*, "even if small in form,"..."great in musical substance." We might point out that the flute also plays an important role in Sibelius's incidental music for Strindberg's *Swanwhite* as well as in the Fourth Symphony, and the piccolo in the sunrise section of *Nightride and Sunrise*.

However, Helasvuo's statement about Sibelius as the father of Finnish music for the flute has to be qualified somewhat. The Finnish-born composer Bernhard Henrik Crusell had written an early nineteenth-century work, Quartet in D Major for Flute and Strings (Opus 8), but since Crusell's musical activity was carried on outside Finland in adherence to the continental tradition of the period, Helasvuo feels that, as far as genuinely Finnish music for the instrument is concerned, Sibelius was a pioneer.

Sibelius's pupil Toivo Kuula must have valued highly his teacher's prowess in flute writing, since he composed several Sibelian-style flute solos for his stage works. However, the instrument did not have much of a following in Finland and, except for Heino Kaski's amateurish Sonata for Flute and Piano of 1937, practically no works were composed for the instrument in Finland until the 1960s, when the influence of the Darmstadt school on young Finnish composers was strong.

Henrik Otto Donner's Three Pieces for Flute and Piano (1962) are composed in the spirit of the Darmstadt school in a terse, aphoristic style. Influences received from the same school are discerned also in Paavo Heininen's *Discantus I* for alto flute (1965). The work manages to express so much tension and so many conflicts in the writing for the solo instrument that it has become a Finnish "classic" for flutists anxious to meet the challenges presented by it.

Avant-garde works for the instrument have also been composed by the Austrian-born resident of Finland, Herman Rechberger, as well as by Esa-Pekka Salonen. The latter's *Yta I* (Surface I) for alto flute is a nervous work and difficult to play because of its employment of the rarely used highest registers of the instrument. Helasvuo feels that the forte of the work may lie in its dramatic power.

Despite the late start of music for the flute in Finland, recent interest in the instrument has been manifest also in the classical repertory. In 1972 Tauno Marttinen composed the first flute concerto written in Finland, and the second was composed by Rautavaara. The latter work is in four movements, with one movement dedicated to each instrument of the family ranging from the piccolo to the bass flute.

International influences on recent Finnish music are infinitely more varied, due to easy travel, than the continental influences on Sibelius and his contemporaries. However, the impact of German music has remained strong in the form of the avant-garde school of Darmstadt and influence of composers who lectured there, in particular Varèse, Messiaen, and Cage, can be detected in the works of many Finnish composers. Webern's influence is seen in the Finnish students of Ligeti and Lutoslawski, while the American impact on Finnish music has been considerable after numerous Finns had studied with prominent teacher-composers ranging from Copland to Babbitt.

Because of some influence of Sibelius in Shostakovich's music, naturally it is difficult to determine how much of the influence in Sallinen, and others, that foreign critics in particular ascribe to Shostakovich, or even to Stravinsky or Prokofiev, could actually be attributed to a modern approach to Sibelius and the native Finnish influences in his idiom. As in the case of Sibelius, Finnish folk poetry still plays an important role as a source of inspiration for most Finnish composers and Sallinen, Nordgren, Panula, and others, have incorporated influence of *pelimannimusiikki*, instrumental folk music, into their works.

Since vocal music is by its very nature tied more intimately to the spoken word than instrumental music, it stands to reason that, as far as Finland is concerned, it was with works like *Kullervo* and *Luonnotar*, as well as with many choral works, that much of Sibelius's pioneering work was carried out. Therefore, it is not at all surprising that post-Sibelian Finnish music has come into its own particularly in the field of opera, an area in which Sibelius did not excel but for which he prepared the ground for future generations of composers.

STAGE AND VOCAL MUSIC IN FINLAND

Credit for the introduction of opera into Scandinavia belongs to the Danes. A small opera house, the first in Scandinavia, was established near the Charlottenburg Palace for an operatic performance (in German) in honor of the birthday of King Christian V in 1689. The house burned down, but in 1722 a new opera house was built to which Reinhard Keiser brought his opera company from Hamburg and composed his *Ulysses* specifically for the Danish stage.

Performances were given also by visiting Italian opera companies, but soon the Danes opposed this mass importation of foreign opera. They found a vigorous spokesman in the Norwegian-born eighteenth-century dramatist Ludvig Holberg (we should bear in mind that we are speaking about the Dano-Norwegian kingdom at that time). He was also quite a competent musician and his comedies often included musical interludes. His spoof of Keiser's opera entitled *Kilderrejsen* centers on a heroine who, unable to speak, must express herself only in trills. Despite this protest, the operatic repertories continued to consist of Italian, German, and French operas, although Giuseppe Sarti, the court music director whose father had worked for the first Danish opera house, made concessions to the natives by adapting the operatic style of his native Italy to Danish comedies.

In Sweden, the development of opera was basically the same as in Denmark, although with the difference that French opera tended to dominate in Sweden over Italian, thanks to the interests of the Swedish Royal Court. King Adolf Fredrik and Queen

Lovisa Ulrika also invited Francesco Uttini, who performed several operas by Gluck. For the inauguration of a new opera house in 1773, Uttini added Swedish recitatives to several operas based on Metastasio's libretti. Soon another court theater was built on the island of Drottningholm near Stockholm. It is still used for performances with its original machinery for stage settings in place.

In 1782 King Gustav III, who maintained the Drottningholm theater in an even more lively state of activity than his predecessors, opened yet another theater intended to serve as a training stage for actors and singers in the Swedish language, which was to be given preference over French and Italian. Since the King also established Kungliga Musikaliska Akademin (later the Stockholm Conservatory), native training of musicians became possible, and soon Stockholm attracted gifted young musicians from Finland as well.

For the inauguration of the new opera house, Johann Gottlieb Naumann (1741-1801) was brought from Dresden, and four years after his arrival in Sweden he produced *Gustav Vasa*, the first Swedish opera on a national topic, to a libretto by the Swedish poet J. H. Kellgren, reportedly on the basis of a sketch supplied by King Gustav III.

Closely tied to the beginning of opera in Denmark was ballet-opera whose initiation is to be accredited to Auguste Bournonville. He established the Royal Danish Ballet in 1760 and engaged the most prominent Danish composers of the period, J. P. E. Hartmann and his son-in-law Niels Gade, to collaborate on a score. This was followed by several ballet scores based on Norse mythology or historical topics like Oehlenschläger's dramas of *Olaf den Hellige* (Saint Olav) and *Haakon Jarl*. Inspired by Hartmann, Edvard Grieg started work on an opera based on the legendary figure of Olav Tryggvason, which, unfortunately, he never finished. However, the incomplete form was produced on stage in 1908. As is known, Grieg's incidental music for Ibsen's *Peer Gynt*, composed in 1874-75, has been a tremendous popular success. After Grieg, Halvorsen, Svendsen, and Sinding carried on the tradition of incidental music for stage plays.

Norway and Finland, the more far-off and poorer countries, were slower in developing an operatic tradition than Denmark and Sweden. However, following the example of historian Anders Fryxell, who in 1824 had used the Swedish folk song "Värmlandsvisa" in his folk play *Värmlandsflicka* (The Girl of Värmland), the Norwegian musician Waldemar Thrane introduced a Norwegian tune into a stage production four years later, which may have influenced Grieg's "Solveig's Song" from *Peer Gynt*. It is natural that Fryxell's democratic view of history and art — with its emphasis on the conflict between the nobility and the common people — was eagerly embraced in Norway and Finland, the Nordic countries in which the far-off presence of the Royal Courts of Copenhagen and Stockholm was not particularly influential. When Norway declared its independence from Sweden in 1905, the Norwegian Royal House was established on a truly democratic basis, but Finland became a republic after its independence in 1917. Thus the political situation in the two countries was favorable to a democratic view of art and music.

The novels on Finno-Swedish history written in Finland in Swedish by Zacharias Topelius Jr. echo Fryxell's democratic views. We might recall that it was on a libretto by Topelius that Pacius based his first opera in Finland, *King Charles's Hunt*, in 1852. Its impact on the tradition of semi-popular music in the country was enormous, and people used to sing tunes from it as if they were folk songs.

As mentioned above, Sibelius did not object to the historical topic of the opera, but he did not approve of Pacius's Italianate German score. Sibelius was keenly aware of the lack of genuine Finnish opera, and was determined to fill the gap by the creation of the first Finnish grand opera based on the *Kalevala*. As we know, the boat foundered, and the composer rescued the wreckage in his *Lemminkäinen* suite. Obviously the only Finnish stage tradition at the time, that of the popular *laulunäytelmä* (play with song), did not provide Sibelius with a basis to build on. Despite his considerable feeling for drama and for native Finnish recitative, Sibelius was forced to admit that he was no Mussorgsky or Wagner, and his only attempt at opera after *The Building of the Boat*, his *Jungfrun i tornet* (The Maid in the Tower), does not qualify as the first truly Finnish opera, despite a few vocal numbers, albeit in Swedish, somewhat reminiscent of Finnish folk songs.

Jungfrun i tornet, composed in 1896 to a poor libretto by Rafael Herzberg, more of a translator than writer, does not show Sibelius in his best light. The score points to influences of Italian opera and of Gounod, and at times to the *verismo* style, which is ironic in view of Sibelius's criticism of Pacius's opera as imitation of German and Italian opera.

Sibelius's *Jungfrun i tornet* is in the traditional operatic style of arias, duets, orchestral interludes, and so on, and the composer seems to have been determined to avoid any suggestion of Wagner's influence by rejecting the idea of leitmotifs, except for the repetition of the love motif. The score does not indicate any typically Sibelian development of themes either. Something of the atmosphere of the overture and of the climax that we could call Finnish is due to superficial techniques only, somewhat in the manner of Rimsky-Korsakov's use of Russian folk material in early operas, such as *May Night* and the *Snow Maiden*. Likewise, there is no sign of Wagnerian *Sprechgesang* in Sibelius's opera. The unity of text and melody is not up to par with the Sibelian standards in his solo and choral songs, perhaps due in part to the miserable libretto.

However, Sibelius did contribute to the stage music tradition in Finland in an important way with his incidental music for tableaux, including *Karelia* and the *Scènes historiques*, as well as with ambitious scores of incidental music for stage plays. The original suite of incidental music for Adolf Paul's play *King Christian II* clearly derives from Sibelius's cosmopolitan side. It dates from 1898 and was one of his early popular successes. Even today many consider the well-known "Elegy," nostalgic in the Scandinavian style, among his best popular pieces. "Fool's Song of the Spider" has remained the Finns' favorite, but Sibelius did not include it in the suite, to which he added the following summer three numbers, "Nocturne," "Serenade," and "Ballade." While the original suite derives from the cosmopolitan Sibelius, the later additions reveal more specific Finnish influence, for example, in the repetitions in the theme of the "Nocturne."

Two sets of Sibelius's incidental music for stage plays made successful suites: one for Sibelius's brother-in-law Arvid Järnefelt's play *Kuolema* (The Death), written in Finnish and premiered in 1903, the other for Sibelius's friend Hjalmar Procopé's Swedish-language play *Belshazzar's Feast* in 1906. *Kuolema* is the Finnish answer to Strindberg's *Drömspelet* (The Dream Play) in that both works are indicative of the interests of the Scandinavian intellectuals at the time in their speculation on the phenomena of dreams and reality. The well-known "Valse triste," to whose tunes the aging matron relives a ball scene from her youth, reflects the dream-like atmosphere. As is known, it became a huge popular success. Sibelius scored it originally for strings only and later for small orchestra.

If Järnefelt's play reflects the common Scandinavian interests at the time, Procopé's work does so equally clearly in the region's fascination with the exotic. This found in Sibelius's score a somewhat grotesque expression in the "Oriental Procession" and a considerably more convincing one in "Khadra's Dance," although the latter does bring to mind "Anitra's Dance" from Grieg's *Peer Gynt*. Sibelius's dance includes a short reminiscence of his "Valse triste." Many observers feel that Sibelius succeeds best with "Solitude," which is closer to his métier, as is "Night Music," but it would be difficult to detect anything oriental about the two last-mentioned pieces.   The Helsinki critics did not think much of Procopé's play.   After the première with Sibelius's incidental music, a Helsinki paper printed a cartoon of Sibelius carrying Procopé on his shoulders.   However, internationally, the *Belshazzar* Suite has been at least as successful as the incidental music for *Kuolema*, except for "Valse triste," of course.

Sibelius's interest in Strindberg found another manifestation in 1908, when the Swedish writer's fairy-tale *Svanhvite* (Swanwhite) was produced in Helsinki, and Sibelius was asked to write incidental music for the performance. Originally Strindberg wanted to compose music for the play himself, but nothing ever came of this plan. Sibelius was unusually enthusiastic about this request, and it is ironical that none of the pieces of the suite has matched the popularity of his best known incidental pieces, although they are musically competent creations bearing the stamp of the mature master of his craft. The story of *Svanhvite* is a traditional fairy-tale, unusual for Strindberg, of Swanwhite, who has been promised as a child to be the wife of a king whose spokesman, a young prince, falls in love with her. The young prince is drowned, Swanwhite brings him back to life and true love prevails at the end. Sibelius's score is in harmony with the fairy-tale atmosphere in such parts of the suite as "Listen, the Robin Sings," with the flute carrying the melody while "The Prince Alone" expresses depth of feeling comparable to Sibelius's best incidental pieces.

In 1905, Sibelius's friend Bertel Gripenberg's translation of Maeterlinck's *Pelléas et Mélisande* was produced in the Swedish Theater in Helsinki with Sibelius's incidental music. Of the suite many consider the "Pastorale" the best piece with its transparent coloring reminiscent of northern summer nights and their elegiac atmosphere, which is characteristic also of the "Death of Mélisande." Sibelius's incidental music for the Maeterlinck play is good in rendering the ominous mood, but it moves along somewhat heavily, as does Schoenberg's treatment of the same topic, unlike Debussy's and Fauré's, which catch the elusiveness that is the forte of the play.

Sibelius's contribution to the Danish stage came with a commission by the Royal Theater of Copenhagen for incidental music for Shakespeare's *The Tempest*, Opus 109. It is the most successful of Sibelius's suites of incidental music and the last major work of his career. The master of orchestration is evident in one of the most impressive descriptions of a storm ever written, while "Intrada," "Berceuse," and "Miranda" are elegiac in the Scandinavian spirit. The "Oaktree" displays Finnish influence most clearly with its insistent *ostinato* symbolizing the unyielding quality of the tree.

While individual pieces of different suites of Sibelius's incidental music have been popular successes, there are some scores that are virtually forgotten. These include two ambitious suites: music for Hofmannsthal's play *Jedermann*, Opus 83, and for Poul Knudsen's pantomime *Scaramouche*, Opus 71. Neither score shows the composer at his most typical, and in particular in the latter some influence of Richard Strauss seems to lurk in the background. It is easy to be critical of this part of Sibelius's output, but we have to remember that in most instances they were the result of commissions the composer could not turn down, for financial reasons. If hasty workmanship is too often evident in these works, we have to realize that even the technical aspects of scoring and copying without any help took away time from works the composer considered more serious.

Thanks to Bournonville, the spreading of the operatic tradition in Scandinavia was closely tied to dance or ballet. For this type of expression, the suite of incidental music provided ample opportunity for variety and color, as it did for theater performances with song and dance included. Sibelius's music for *The Tempest* and *Scaramouche* are indicative of this Scandinavian style of stage production of mixed genres.

While popular plays often include folk dances, classical ballet arrived in Finland even much later than opera with the establishment of the National Ballet of Finland in 1921. From its beginnings, the classical ballet in Finland has been characterized by the duality that is typical of the country's culture in general. Russian influence has been prevalent in the technique in the pose of the dancers, the powerful, big jumps and the emotional interpretation, while choreography has been modeled largely on the Western tradition. Since classical ballet is of recent origin in Finland, the first ballet scores date from the period between the two World Wars, and we shall return to them in connection with individual composers.

Although Sibelius was not able to create a native tradition of opera, without his suites of incidental music and his impact on the creation of Finnish recitative, his pupil Leevi Madetoja would not have been able to compose truly Finnish operas. While Sibelius rejected the idea of fusion of influences of Finnish popular music into an operatic idiom, Madetoja relied heavily on the tradition of popular "opera" called in Finnish *laulunäytelmä*, borrowed from Sweden, where it was known as *sångspel*. They were short plays, usually by unknown authors, on folk-like topics into which musical interludes — sometimes even folk dances — were incorporated.   They were not of high artistic merit, but their popular appeal was comparable to that of today's musicals. This was the tradition on which Oskar Merikanto relied heavily for the score of his 1899 opera *Pohjan neiti* (The Maid of Pohja, i.e. Pohjola), the first composed to a Finnish libretto. As the title indicates, Merikanto was inspired by the spirit of nationalism, but his score relies more on the popular rather than the runo song tradition.

The next step away from the popular *laulunäytelmä* came with Madetoja's folk opera *Pohjalaisia* (Ostrobothnians) in 1922. In this work the impact of the genuine folk song of Madetoja's native province of Ostrobothnia is so strong that many considered it Finland's national opera. *Pohjalaisia* is based on a drama by Artturi Järviluoma, which premiered in 1914. At that time it was a particularly appropriate symbol of the political situation in its description of a conflict between a freedom-loving peasant and an autocratic sheriff, thus setting up the view of history familiar from works reflecting Fryxell's ideas. The story of *Pohjalaisia* is worthy of mention because of the fact that, basically, it is the story that recurs in Sallinen's operas. In the dramatic climax the peasant breaks the sheriff's whip, the sheriff pulls out his revolver and shoots the peasant who manages to stab the sheriff before dying in the arms of his beloved. Naturally, by the time of the première of Madetoja's opera, in 1924, the story must have lost much of its poignancy, since Finland was by then a free nation.

Madetoja composed another opera in the folk-inspired spirit, although *Juha* is more lyrical in nature than *Pohjalaisia*. *Juha* is based on a libretto drawn from Juhani Aho's novel by the same title, a work whose operatic possibilities had fascinated Sibelius. The famous Finnish opera singer Aino Ackté, to whom Sibelius dedicated his *Luonnotar*, wrote a libretto in 1912 based on Juhani Aho's novel *Juha* and she wanted Sibelius to compose a score based on it. The composer was intrigued by the idea, but at the time he was so deeply involved in his large symphonic works that he put off the plan. It was left to Aarre Merikanto to use the libretto by Ackté for his opera *Juha*. Merikanto worked on the score in 1919 and 1920, but it was turned down by the Finnish Opera. The composer reworked the score, but it was turned down a second time, and it was finally performed at Lahti in 1963. In 1967, ten years after the composer's death, the opera was performed at the Finnish Opera.

The Swedish critic Gunnar Sjöqvist sees influence of Puccini and Richard Strauss in Merikanto's *Juha*, as well as similarities to Janacék and Alban Berg, but he concludes that in 1920 Merikanto could not have been familiar with the music of the two last-mentioned composers.   Nowadays Merikanto's *Juha* is considered musically the most significant of the early Finnish operas.

While in Madetoja's operas the popular *laulunäytelmä* still plays an important role, in Aarre Merikanto's *Juha* international influences dominate.   Thus it was left to two of Merikanto's pupils, Kokkonen and Sallinen, to fuse the native and foreign influences into a genuinely Finnish operatic idiom.   This would not have been possible without the great interest the Finns have always had in vocal music, in choral song in particular, and without Sibelius's pioneering work in the area.

As we might recall, the old Finnish vocal tradition of runos considered the lyrics more important than the music, and a person could take credit for being a good runo-singer, if he was able to memorize a large number of lyrics.   Since the other early tradition of music in Finland, that of religious music, was originally closely linked with the continental tradition, the discrepancy between the imported hymns, liturgy, and so on, and the translation of texts mostly from German or Swedish into Finnish dulled the Finns' feeling for the supremacy of the word typical of the runo song. The pre-Sibelian tradition of easy lieder came into existence under the influence of the German-Scandinavian lied from the pens of Pacius, Crusell, and Collan.   It became extremely popular and a veritable wealth of easy lieder, which fused influences of the late type folk song, was written by composers like Ilmari Hannikainen, Oskari Merikanto, and Yrjö Kilpinen (1892-1959), the latter having composed over eight hundred songs.

The position of this type of song was so firmly established in Finland that when Sibelius introduced genuine Finnish recitative in his *Kullervo* and later in *Luonnotar* and strict observance of the Finnish lyrics in such choral works as *Venematka*, *Saarella palaa*, and in numerous cantatas (*Tulen synty*, *Oma maa*, and so on), even the Finns' original reaction was one of slight confusion at the unexpected.

The tradition of the through-composed song established by Sibelius continued in the works of his pupil Leevi Madetoja, who contributed to the wealth of Finnish choral songs.   Many of them have remained in the standard repertory.   Characteristic of Madetoja's vocal idiom are short phrases in constant repetition in the style of genuine Finnish folk songs.   The impact of the vocal tradition can be seen even in Madetoja's "Little Romance" for piano (cf.Example 51 above).

Toivo Kuula wrote a number of solo songs for his wife Alma Kuula, a competent interpreter of her husband's lieder.   His songs are permeated much more deeply by the spirit of Finnish folk songs than are Sibelius's lieder, which by and large remained tied to the continental tradition. In Kuula's songs, the dark foreboding spirit of the Ostrobothnian folk song is often reminiscent of Mussorgsky's songs, as in a specimen like "Sinikan laulu" (Sinikka's Song), dedicated to the composer's little daughter.

Thanks to Bournonville and the native tradition of the *laulunäytelmä*, which often incorporated folk dances, the beginning of Finnish ballet music is tied to opera as well as to incidental music for stage plays. Although Tauno Pylkkänen (b. 1918) is known in Finland chiefly for his ballets and opera *Sudenmorsian* (The Wolf's Bride), for which he won an international competition organized by the Italian radio in 1950, the specifically Finnish character of this opera is not strong despite its folk atmosphere. Much more obviously in the nationalistic tradition are the sources of inspiration of Ahti Sonninen (b. 1914), many of whose works are based on the *Kalevala*. Indicative of the Finns developing an interest in the ballet is Sonninen's *Pessi ja Illusia*. Its fairy-tale atmosphere based on a story by the modern writer Yrjö Kokko relies heavily on Finnish folklore, but Sonninen's musical idiom is basically international, inherited from his teachers Selim Palmgren and Aarre Merikanto.

When Einar Englund composed in the late 1950s a ballet score entitled *Odysseus*, Finland obviously was not yet ready for a native tradition in the field, because the work failed to gain the kind of recognition that was given to Englund's other works. The effort of creating a Finnish tradition of ballet during the period between the two World Wars did not, however, have as much of an impact on the creation of native Finnish opera as did the tradition of vocal music.

Erik Bergman, one of Finland's most prominent composers after the Second World War, has contributed a great deal to the Finns' favorite genre, the choral song. His works include *Nox* and *Aton*, for chorus, soloists, and orchestra, and *The Birds* for men's chorus and percussion. Their varied topics indicate interests ranging from Egyptology in *Aton* to Messiaen-style ornithological concerns with a more Nordic flavor in *The Birds*.

Among Bergman's most ambitious works are his monumental *Mass for Chorus and Organ* and in particular *Noah*, Opus 78, for soloists, chorus, and orchestra. The latter is in one movement with the text consisting of about twenty Hebrew words, which remind the listener of the world being threatened by the Deluge and of its rescue. Whether the work contains a hint at the possibility of a nuclear holocaust is an open question. The Bergman work is both powerful and colorful and it is considered by many to be among the most important choral works in Finland.

Particularly impressive is the beautiful song of praise "Elohin, Adonai, Jahve" as the climax.

A humorous approach to vocal composition is in evidence in Bergman's *Vier Galgenlieder* for baritone solo and chorus, with piano accompaniment. They are based on lyrics by the Munich-born poet Christian Morgenstern. Bergman's use of *Sprechgesang* has suggested to many a reflection of Karl Orff's technique. Choral works with visual implications and thus with a natural affinity to ballet are represented by Bergman's *Samothrake*, *Arctica*, and an *a cappella* choral suite, *Lapponia*. The last-mentioned work derived its inspiration from *juoigos*-songs and was choreographed by Birgit Cullberg, as was *Arctica*. The choice of the text for a vocal setting has been important for Bergman, and it stands to reason that he could easily relate to poems written by his wife Solveig von Schoulz. These include the text for Bergman's choral setting *The Birds*, mentioned above.

The choice of the text for a vocal setting was of primary importance also for another Finnish-Swedish composer, Bengt Johansson (b. 1914), as can be seen from the inspiration he derived from Ezra Pound for his vocal work *Tomb at Akr Caar*. Perhaps as a result of his employment as the sound editor at the Finnish Radio Corporation, Johansson likes to concentrate in his compositions on harmony and a type of group polyphony rather than on melody. Characteristic of his harmony is his emphasis on relationships in seconds, which, as he stated, he has always used instinctively, most likely a result of his familiarity with Finnish folk music. In his *Requiem* Johansson had a chance to adapt his use of polyphony to an orchestral work as well.

Johansson represents the favorite Nordic line of composition, the vocal tradition, kept alive by numerous choral societies in each Scandinavian country. The typical pieces representative of the genre are not particularly innovative, except for some inclusion of influence of folk music of each country, but they have always been well received by audiences and most composers have yielded easily to this instant gratification. On the other hand, a much clearer adherence to nationalistic thinking is in evidence in the origins of the Finnish tradition of grand opera.

The two creators of genuine Finnish grand opera, Kokkonen and Sallinen, approach the genre from the nationalistic point of view, as well as from the Finnish tradition of vocal music. The nationalistic thinking, which is the core of their first operas, is basically the view they inherited from Fryxell's concept of history through Madetoja's operas. In Kokkonen's *The Last Temptations* the moral conflict of the work derives from religion, which, in turn, has nationalistic as well as social implications. In Sallinen's

Horseman and *The Red Line* the basic conflict is nationalistic, social and humanitarian.

In Kokkonen's output religious speculation has been a central issue, but he is by no means a church composer. His *Missa a cappella* and his *Requiem* for soprano and baritone solos, chorus and orchestra to a Latin text bring to mind works like Debussy's *Martyrdom of St. Sebastian* and Stravinsky's *Symphony of Psalms*, although the strongest influence seems to be that of Messiaen. The *Requiem* is a beautiful work and deeply felt, as one might expect, for it is dedicated to the memory of the composer's wife Maija Kokkonen. The finale, entitled "Lux aeterna," reflects the optimism of the composer's organ piece with the same title.

Although Kokkonen's all-pervasive interest in religion obviously led him to the topic of his grand opera, *The Last Temptations*, it is not a biblical opera in the style of Raitio's works but it is rather an opera on moral issues, even if the approach is that of a person heavily trained in religion. Perhaps because of the fact that instruction in religion has played an important role in Finnish schools, the Kokkonen opera is a work with which the Finns can easily identify, and it played for full houses for several years, an unprecedented event in Finland.

The protagonist of *The Last Temptations* is a historical figure: a Lutheran evangelical preacher by the name of Paavo Ruotsalainen, who died in 1852 after creating a fundamentalist religious movement, which continued to have followers even after his death. As the title implies, the opera centers on the moral and psychological conflict between Ruotsalainen's simple belief in the Bible as the only authority and his human weaknesses of addiction to aquavit, attraction to women, and desire for recognition from the religious establishment of Finland.

The opening scene depicts Ruotsalainen's death, and the story of his struggles unfolds in the form of flash-backs divided into two acts and fourteen scenes. The libretto is by the composer's cousin Lauri Kokkonen. In keeping with the composer's personality, the work concentrates on the simple preacher's metaphysical speculation rather than on action. The spirit of the opera is somber and with its lack of dramatic power it is difficult to see a bright international future for the work. A clumsy English translation does not help either and, naturally, one of the chief assets of Kokkonen's writing, his sensitivity to the Finnish language in his melodic line, is largely lost to foreign audiences as is the beauty of a repeated use of a genuine sectarian tune. However, Kokkonen's expertise in orchestral scoring is bound to arouse admiration in any audience.

Sallinen's love of the Finnish tradition of vocal music is seen from his *Songs for the Sea: In the Style of Folk Songs* and two children's songs, "The Winter Is Harsh" and "The First Snow" for children's chorus. Indicative of the composer's love of the choral medium is also his *Song around a Song*. However, Sallinen is less serious about his respect for the Finnish vocal tradition than most Finnish composers, and his humorous approach is manifest in the fact that Car! Michael Bellman's "Old Man Noah" is an important element in the metamorphoses of the last-mentioned work.

An important work emanating from Sallinen's nationalistic thinking is *The Iron Age*, originally composed for Finnish television as a celebration of the 150th anniversary of the first publication of the *Kalevala*. The composer made out of the original music an orchestral suite, which also includes a chorus, a children's chorus, and soprano soloists. The music is more primitive than Sibelius's works based on the *Kalevala*. In short, it represents a more modern approach to the national epic. However, some of the typical features of Sibelius's vocal works, such as his respect of the *Kalevala* text, are also characteristic of Sallinen's work.

Thus Sallinen's approach to opera adheres more clearly than Kokkonen's to the nationalistic vocal tradition established by Sibelius. However, Sallinen has obviously more dramatic talent than his teacher Kokkonen, and the pupil's operas, barring language difficulties, could have vaster possibilities on the international scene than Kokkonen's.

Sallinen's first successful opera *Ratsumies* (The Horseman) premiered at the Savonlinna Festival in 1975. This three-act opera is based on a libretto by Paavo Haavikko after his play by the same title. The story centers around topics that were to also fascinate Sallinen in his later operas. The work is basically about power in different manifestations: a struggle for power between human beings, between man and woman (Strindbergian implications?). In the third act the power play shifts from individuals to groups of people.

The struggle for power is manifest at first in action that takes place in Russia and then in Finland at the time of its union with Sweden. The idea of Finland as a battlefield between Sweden and Russia is a variation of the basic motif of human drama, of man as a hapless victim of his circumstances. The drama of cruelty between the sexes, as expressed by the Merchant in act I, contains almost eerie echoes of Strindberg:[1]

At a market you can buy anything
But not a heart for a woman.

The pessimistic view of life as a battle between the sexes is summarized in the following lines of act II:

> There's no point in listening when a man speaks,
> All you can do is wait for what he never says.
> No river is as swift as life;
> It is evening by the time you've crossed it.

Strong influence of folk poetry can be seen in the fact that this speculation often assumes the form of riddles, occasionally with a strange surreal effect as in the Merchant's statement in act I:

> I am only sad because there can be
> No happier man than I am.

Influence of Finnish folklore can be seen in the ease with which man communicates with nature in the belief that oftentimes nature is more sympathetic than a fellow man, as in the statement about the Horseman (act II):

> He can speak the language of horses.
> The horses heed, when he speaks to them.

Disillusioned with man, the Horseman has renounced all involvement with society. At the end of the opera, he is persuaded to lead an uprising, which fails. Obviously this implies that man's attempts to guide his destiny are futile. The philosophy of the work is expressed in the metaphor that life is like a river on which man is carried along by the current.

Is the basic message of the opera true not only on the level of individuals but also on the national level? Is it the opera's way of saying that the struggle of a small country is hopeless, because it is dependent on outside forces, on the power play between mightier ones? It is natural that this topic fascinated both the librettist and the composer in post-World War II Finland, and, despite a feeling of elemental power also reflected in the music, the opera is, in the final analysis, pessimistic. The concluding scene, almost surreal, with the sheriff worrying about the payment for partly rat-eaten candles lit in honor of those fallen in battle, confirms the philosophy that raw power does not help man, who is helpless against the turns of fate. This is also the subject of *The Red Line*, which premiered in 1978.

Like *The Horseman*, *The Red Line* is a historical opera. It is about the events of 1907 in Finland against the background of the period. Thus it is also a descendant of Madetoja's *Pohjalaisia* and more contemporary in spirit than *The Horseman*. The score, with occasional touches of Puccini, is less harsh than that of *The Horseman*. Many observers have seen in *The Red Line* an affinity with Janacék's *Jenufa*, although Sallinen's opera brings out the historical milieu better than the Janacék work. In *The Red Line* we are not dealing with the problems of individuals but with human drama in which some people are caught as pawns of social and moral change. The "red line" of the voting ballot and on the protagonist's neck, after he was mutilated by a bear, symbolizes both universal suffrage and the price the individual pays for progress.

The story of *The Red Line* is based on a libretto drawn from a historical novel by the same title by Ilmari Kianto, considered one of the early successful Finnish writers to describe peasant life. The events unfold in a way that has implications on three levels: personal, political, and universal. On the first level it is a story of a peasant, Topi, who comes home in the opening scene with a bundle of lamb's wool and a bell, the remains of a sheep killed by a bear. His wife cries out: "In the forest sleeps a bear stuffed with meat. In the home, the children are hungry as wolf cubs." In the end, the children die of starvation and Topi is killed offstage by a bear.

The story is also political and connected with the struggle in 1905 between Finland and Russia and its political aftermath culminating in the bitter election campaign of 1906 between the Conservatives and the Social Democrats. Most importantly, *The Red Line* is a story of peasants struggling against hostile forces. The bear, which also appears in *The Horseman*, is used in both operas with dual symbolism: man trying to survive in harsh natural circumstances and the Finns trying to survive the political and social upheavals of their neighbor Russia. We might recall that man caught in the power of a political system represented by a sheriff was the topic of Madetoja's opera *Pohjalaisia*, which, in turn, represents Fryxell's democratic view of history.

While in *The Red Line* Topi sees the Social Democratic Party providing a solution to his problems, his wife Riika is more skeptical of the agitator's lure of a better life for peasants through social change. Her traditional way of thinking is manifest in her reaction to Topi's report of a Socialist Party meeting where the speakers were the tailor and "the shoemaker's woman." "Wasn't the cantor there either?" she asks her husband. For her, a meeting could not be legitimate, if the Church was not represented at least by the cantor. Obviously Topi also has pangs of conscience about attending the meeting, and he keeps having nightmares —

prophetic ones, as it turns out — about his children dying of starvation.   In one of those dreams he is scolded by the vicar to whom he reports the deaths: "The Lord helps those who truly believe in Him and pray to Him, but you have not been to church for quite a while."   In the final analysis, is it the Church or is it God who is punishing those who voted for the Socialist Party and drew the red line? Even if Riika considers Topi being mauled to death by a bear a form of God's punishment, she cannot become resigned to the impending death of another child and prays to the Lord to punish her and her husband, not the children.

The conflict between the conservative thinking represented by the ministers of the Church and the radical thinking expressed by the agitator of the Socialist Party and his followers is interpreted quite masterfully in Sallinen's music.   In the scene of Topi's nightmare, both dramatically and musically one of the most effective in the opera, the irony of Topi's plight is manifest in the mock authoritarian style of singing by the vicar, poignantly supported by lashes of a whip in the orchestra. The crowd scenes of the party meetings, on the other hand, are carried by propulsive rhythms somewhat reminiscent of such Russian composers as Shostakovich.   In fact, the sense of realism in Sallinen's crowd scenes also echoes Mussorgsky's expert handling of scenes with Russian peasants, and the frequent use of bells in Sallinen's scores fortifies the impression of Mussorgsky's influence, although we might recall that Sibelius had used the instrument effectively in *Tulen synty* (The Origin of Fire).   A particularly dramatic crowd scene in *The Red Line* is that of the chorus of act II, scene 6 representing the Church in the traditional choral style while the agitator and his supporters answer in a mockingly militaristic style: "Certainly it is your turn to fall ... singing your old hymns."

However, no matter how effective and lively Sallinen's crowd scenes might be, there is a somber mood about *The Horseman*, and *The Red Line* ends in a mood of hopelessness and despair stated in Riika's reference to a ski track leading nowhere, thus echoing the mood of Gripenberg's poem "Ett ensamt skidspår" (A Lonely Ski Track), which intrigued Sibelius at the time he was working on *Tapiola*.

Another similarity in the vocal idioms of Mussorgsky, Sibelius and Sallinen can be seen in their observance of the requirements of the language, which certainly will pose problems for foreign performers of Sallinen's operas. Although *The Horseman* does not draw heavily from the influence of folk music, *The Red Line* includes two important scenes based on folk songs: one in which the Pedlar sings the "Ballad of Vestmanviiki" and the other which features a folk tune, a lullaby to a dead child "Tuuti lasta Tuonelahan" (Sleep, my child, in Tuonela). The Finnish love of proverbs and riddles evident in the ballad is rendered nicely in Sallinen's score.

Despite the fact that *The Horseman* and *The Red Line* are definitely Finnish operas, they do appeal to basic human emotions as well. Are they universally valid? We could answer this by stating that *Boris Godunov* certainly is Russian, but it is one of those rare works with the undefinable spark that transcends national boundaries despite strong nationalistic influence. Only the future will show whether the Sallinen operas have transcended those boundaries. In the meantime, Sallinen must have been aware of the limitations of an opera composed to a Finnish libretto. After *The Red Line* he got together with his librettist Paavo Haavikko, and they worked together on an opera, *The King Goes Forth to France*, for which an English-language libretto is provided. It premiered at the Savonlinna Opera Festival in 1984.

The libretto centers on a political satire set in England after the onset of a new ice age. The King and his troops march across the Channel to France at some point in the future, although the expedition is reminiscent of that of King Edward 600 years earlier. After several battles, the King enjoys the attention of four women, all of them anxious to be crowned queen.

The fanciful story was originally written by Haavikko for a Finnish radio play, although the libretto fused into the play elements suggested by the composer. As with Sallinen's earlier operas, the story can be interpreted on many levels, although it is, above all, an updated version of a morality play with, paradoxically, no relationship to any given period. It is an allegorical commentary on human weaknesses, a spoof in which the basic message is, nevertheless, just as serious as in Sallinen's first two operas. The King, too, is caught in the vicissitudes of fate just as the protagonists of *The Horseman* and *The Red Line* are.

Thus the basic thinking in the Sallinen operas is the same despite the change of milieu in *The King Goes Forth to France*. Has the composer adjusted his musical thinking to suit the change in the environment? Sallinen's approach is more direct, in a way more simple than in his earlier operas. This is manifest, for example, in the profuse use of repetition in a manner reminiscent of that of early Finnish music. Obviously this is not easy for foreign audiences to appreciate. It is not surprising that Bernard Holland referred to Sallinen's idiom as "a kind of persistent secularized plainsong that becomes tedious indeed."[2] Holland characterized the style as having "open references to Weill and

Orff." However, we might recall that in his choral songs Sibelius had already used a technique that relied heavily on repetition and exploitation of monotonous rhythms, influenced by the runo song which pointed to Orff's choral technique.

If there are direct echoes of Sibelius's choral style in Sallinen's writing, it is not to say that the idioms are identical. On the contrary, where Sibelius's approach to choral writing is chiefly through polyphony, Sallinen's primary emphasis on rhythm makes comparisons of his style to Orff's and Shostakovich's partly justified. In short, despite definite influence of Sibelius's vocal writing, Sallinen is a contemporary composer, who does not shy away from the present-day approach to rhythm and key relationships.

An interesting vignette in *The King Goes Forth to France* is an orchestral episode incorporated into the third act of the opera. It has been performed as an independent work (for example, by Rostropovich in Washington, D.C., in 1982) entitled *Shadows*. It is, indeed, a shadow-play reflecting the contents of the opera.

Sallinen's Finnish operas were a success in establishing a new operatic tradition in Finland. Was the composer over-ambitious in his desire for further conquests with his *King*? Perhaps Sallinen himself supplied the answer with an entry in his diary (June 16, 1982): "It's always worthwhile to write an opera. If it's a success, I'm happy; if it isn't, somebody else is happy."[3]

Like most composers in Finland, Rautavaara has contributed a large number of vocal works to Finnish concerts: solo songs, obviously inspired by his wife Maaria Eira, as well as choral works. His *Children's Mass* was occasioned by the prominence of many youth choruses in Finland, such as the Tapiola Choir, while his *Vigilia* was written at the request of the Russian Orthodox Church of Helsinki. The latter represents a modern approach to Byzantine music, an interest also evident in Rautavaara's piano piece *The Icons*. Although the *Lorca Suite*, a set of four songs, is obviously of Spanish inspiration, the musical idiom can hardly be characterized as Spanish-influenced, except for the somewhat strange *malagueña* as the finale.

In the 1970s Rautavaara composed two choral operas based on the *Kalevala*. In these works the chorus may assume the role of one of the dramatis personae, of a commentator in the style of Greek drama or of players of different instruments. *Runo 42* is a description of Finland around the year 800 and *Marjatta, matala neiti* (Marjatta, the insignificant girl), is based on the *Kalevala* legend of the Virgin Mary. The work is for three solo voices and a small instrumental group with a prominent solo flute.

Despite Rautavaara's great interest in the vocal genre, his satirical opera *Apollo contra Marsyas* (1970) failed to gain popularity, maybe because of the composer's approach, with which the audiences failed to identify.   The same reason may have doomed Rautavaara's opera *The Mine*, despite the fact that it is considered an important work.   Its libretto was influenced by Rilke, one of the composer's favorite writers.

Perhaps a brighter future is in store for the composer's recent opera entitled *Thomas*.   It was written at the request of Jorma Hynninen, who performed the title role at the première, also the 150th anniversary celebration of the *Kalevala* at the Finnish city of Joensuu.   In the opera Rautavaara combines his interest in the nationalistic topic with an approach that reflects both native and cosmopolitan influences.   The protagonist of the opera, Bishop Thomas Anglicus, came to Finland in 1220 claiming to have a papal letter that would authorize him to lead an excursion against heretical Novgorod and to create a church state between East and West.   The Livonian noblemen were ordered to take part in a crusade led by Thomas.   It ended in a defeat at the Neva River, where Thomas's army was destroyed by Alexander Nevsky. Thomas managed to escape to Turku.   A few years later he was, by his own request, relieved of his episcopal duties.   Suffering from guilt for having acquiesced to the torture murder of a man and, "misled by Satan," for falsifying a papal brief, he died a broken man at the Dominican monastery at Visby on the island of Gotland.   Rautavaara's opera is important musically in that the conflict between the Christian and the peasant cultures is reflected in the musical language as a conflict between influences of primitive folk music and church music.   Rautavaara uses different tonal systems: diatonic, modal, twelve-tone, and atonal, side by side, one often generating another.   Thus the principle of regeneration in the musical language symbolizes the cultural rebirth, the topic of the work, with the pagan culture generating the Christian.   Therefore, the significance of Rautavaara's *Thomas* is in the fusion of native and foreign elements, which, in his works, have tended to exist as separate entities.

Kalevi Aho's *Avain* (The Key) derives from international influences, and it could be classified as a work of philosophical and psychological speculation.   Even more markedly international is Paavo Heininen's opera *The Silk Drum* (1984), which is of Japanese inspiration.

The Finnish nationalistic tradition has continued strong, however, and the *Kalevala* has inspired many recent composers to write works in which one can detect the influence of the old vocal tradition.   The "heroic age" of Finland is represented, for example, in Tauno Marttinen's orchestral song *Kokko, ilman lintu* (Kokko, the Bird of the Air), even if the musical language is far from that of the runo song.   In fact, Marttinen's work incorporates an eleven-note series into a composition based on the world of the *Kalevala*.

If the *Kalevala* runos were created by the people, a curious form of creative participation by a community is still carried on in the small Ostrobothnian town of Ilmajoki.   The *Jokiooppera* (The River Opera) is enacted by about three hundred people, mostly local residents, including school children.   Although the work is called an "opera," it is more of an action piece, "a living open-air museum."[4]   The work is composed by the conductor-composer Jorma Panula, himself an Ostrobothnian, to a libretto by the director of the performance, Tapio Parkkinen.   The feeling the audience receives is not that of watching an opera but rather of witnessing a slice of life being enacted in a natural setting.

The action takes place around 1900 and it includes work at the sawmill, the arrival of a small steamboat, and so on.   Basically, the work is about life, love and hatred, honesty and dishonesty.   The sense of realism created by the action and the setting is enhanced by the music, which incorporates the influence of the folk music of the region in an idiom that to a foreigner sounds somewhat like that of Orff.   Judging from the strong local input on every level of the "opera," one would expect the results to be somewhat in the style of folk opera, appealing only to provincial tastes.   However, the sense of real life that emanates from the production has fascinated many non-Finnish viewers as well.

Although Panula has also composed a more traditional-style nationalistic opera entitled *Jaakko Ilkka*, based on the life of the hero of the same name, it is with his *River Opera* that the composer has created a virtually new genre.   Another completely new direction in the use of folk material and participation by the audience is Panula's *Peltomiehen rukous* (A Farmer's Prayer), which some observers have characterized as a church opera.   Indeed, this 45-minute work has been performed in churches around Finland.   As in the *River Opera*, the main strength of *A Farmer's Prayer* is the feeling that the work is by people and for people.   In keeping with this spirit, the farmer's role has been sung at various performances by the untrained voices of real-life farmers, not by trained singers.

The work is interesting in that it seeks to maintain the old hymn-folk-song tradition, the impact of which was considerable on such composers as Sibelius and Madetoja, on a level that would be appealing to any audience.   While most Finnish composers' output still includes vocal works that could be used for church occasions, the approach is too cerebral for laymen in such works as Bergman's *Sela*, a setting for chorus and baritone of a retranslation of one of the Psalms by Martin Buber, with its symbiosis of speech and music in difficult rhythmic patterns. Panula, on the other hand, respects the old tradition of sacred music while seeking to bring it even closer to ordinary people than the church music of composers like Sulo Salonen and Bengt Johansson. Salonen's choral motets from the 1930s clearly indicate a return to Baroque music, and his *Missa a cappella* (1957) with its refined counterpoint has been highly appreciated in Finland. Bengt Johansson's *Mass* and *Stabat mater* explore polyphonic writing, which has more recently intrigued Jouko Linjama in an even more modern approach in his simultaneous use of several madrigals in a type of polyform.

Although Finnish opera has recently acquired world-wide attention, we have to realize that without the pioneering work of Sibelius in the field of choral music and in the creation of genuine Finnish recitative, the achievements of Kokkonen, Sallinen, and others would hardly have been possible. The influence of Sibelius's choral technique can readily be heard, for example, in Kokkonen's and Sallinen's works in the genre, although naturally with the influences of another era. This has inevitably led to the comparison of their method to that of Karl Orff or of Alban Berg. However, based on our perusal of the influence of the Finnish language and of the runo song on Sibelius's idiom, we can understand the impact of native influences on the post-Sibelian composers.

Without Sibelius's input, Finnish opera probably would still heavily rely on foreign models as it did in the days of Pacius. Even later, Wagner's influence was so strong in Selim Palmgren's historical opera *Daniel Hjort* (1910) that Finnish choral master Heikki Klemetti characterized it as "half-Wagnerian."[5]   Erkki Melartin's opera *Aino* (1907), based on the *Kalevala*, employed twenty-one leitmotifs.

However, echoes of French impressionistic music can also be detected in Palmgren's *Daniel Hjort* in such a feature as the use of the whole-tone scale. Some French influence, perhaps that of Darius Milhaud or of Debussy's *Pelléas et Mélisande*, can be seen in a recent opera like Salmenhaara's *Portugalin nainen* (The Portuguese Woman) from 1972, based on a short story by Robert Musil.

Unfortunately, the operatic style Aarre Merikanto developed in his *Juha* could not have any immediate impact on the evolution of Finnish opera since the work was not performed until 1963, after the composer's death. In 1922, when Merikanto tried to get the opera performed, Finland was not yet ready for his innovative style into which he incorporated influence of Richard Strauss in the orchestral sound and of Janacék in the vocal.

However, there is one dimension that younger Finnish composers have added to the Sibelian tradition: that of humor. As early as 1937 Armas Launis, the folk-song specialist, composed a comic opera entitled *Karjalainen taikahuivi* (The Karelian Magic Scarf) based on his own libretto; however, the work has never been performed. On the other hand, Lauri Saikkola's Finnish-style *opera buffa Mestarin nuuskarasia* (The Master's Snuffbox) was presented on the Finnish radio in 1973. We might add that several operas by Finnish composers have been shown on television, a few even abroad.

A comic opera, perhaps more of a musical, is Rautavaara's *Apollo contra Marsyas* (1970), a satire that transfers the antique tale of Marsyas challenging Apollo to a musical contest to the present day in a musical collage consisting of influence of Viennese classicism, dodecaphony, jazz, and other types of pop music. Collage is also very much in evidence in the humorous operas of Ilkka Kuusisto, whose *Miehen kylkiluu* (Adam's Rib) contrasts the influence of folk music of the province of Savo with imitation of turn-of-the-century salon music.

With Finland's recovery form the economically destitute and somewhat spiritually confused period following the Second World War, there has been a greater variety of music composed and performed in the country than ever before. The Sibelius Academy has broadened its curriculum, and regional music centers have reached levels of achievement Sibelius would have never dared to dream of. Numerous summer festivals of music have been organized around the country and, thanks to such competent vocal performers as Jorma Hynninen, Matti Salminen, the late Martti Talvela, Tom Krause, and numerous others, as well as prominent conductors like Okko Kamu, Paavo Berglund, Esa-Pekka Salonen, Jukka-Pekka Saraste, Jorma Panula, Leif Segerstam, and Paavo Pohjola the level of performances has attracted even international audiences. One of the most successful of these festivals by international standards has been the Savonlinna Opera Festival, something which would have been unthinkable when Sibelius was beginning his career as a composer.

CONCLUSION

Inspired by the spirit of the nationalistic movement, Sibelius was perspicacious enough to realize during his student year in Vienna that Finnish folk poetry and folk song could serve as a source of revitalization of the romantic tradition of music. That he took Finnish folk poetry more seriously than his followers is seen, symbolically, in the fact that the books he took along to Vienna included the *Kalevala*, whereas Klami, a generation later, had to resort to the well-stocked shelves of the Sorbonne library in order to be able to work on his *Kalevala* suite. The difference in the two composers' approaches to Finnish folk poetry is evident in the runo-style melodies in Sibelius' *Kullervo* on the one hand, and in Klami's predominantly impressionistic idiom with the spirit of the *Kalevala* manifest in the general atmosphere, on the other.

If Madetoja followed in Sibelius's footsteps, Aarre Merikanto declared his independence of the master by initiating the trend towards worship of foreign idols, his linear counterpoint based on intellectual inspiration having been compared to Paul Hindemith's. However, Merikanto's closest follower, Einar Englund, also was influenced by Stravinsky and by Shostakovich's virtuosic pianism.

Something of the extroverted side of Sibelius's compositions recognizable in Klami's works, especially in his association with nature, contrasts with Kokkonen's works, as the latter took the introverted side of Sibelius as his starting point. It is by no means an accident that Kokkonen, with his feeling for construction of phrases and their employment in well-built structures, is the most respected post-Sibelian symphonist in Finland. There is also a vague sense of an emotional connection with nature in Kokkonen's works, but the sense of intimacy with the phenomenal world, which is characteristic of Sibelius, is absent in Kokkonen.

On the other hand, the down-to-earth side of Sibelius is a strong presence in Sallinen's oeuvre to the extent that he could even construct a string quartet on a high-spirited fiddle tune. Sibelian echoes can also be discerned in Sallinen's love of short germs in the construction of musical structures, in which the serious element is often contrasted with the lyrical, as in Sibelius, or even with the humorous. A spiritual heir to the Nordic seriousness of Sibelius is Usko Meriläinen, whom the English seem to admire greatly, while Erik Bergman's inspiration includes a type of "crystallized nationalism," as Seppo Nummi characterized the Nordic side of Bergman.

Is nationalism in the Sibelian sense dead as a force in Finnish music? Certainly not, although, due to political changes, its manifestations are different from those of Sibelius's time. Practically every composer's output still includes works based either on Finnish folk poetry or on folk song inspiration. Even Erik Bergman, despite his predominantly international interests, composed in 1984 *Lemminkäinen*, whose vocal line reveals influence of East Karelian laments. It could be added that interest in folk music is continuing and numerous folk music festivals still draw large audiences every summer.

Although religion interwoven with nationalism has ceased to be a force in the daily lives of the Finnish people, its cultural significance is still vital, as can be seen from the fact that almost every composer's oeuvre includes some religious works. At least one hymn by Sibelius is included in the Hymn Book of the Finnish Church and, more recently, compositions like Sallinen's *Chorali* adhere to the Sibelian concept of church music. While Kokkonen's *Requiem* and *Lux aeterna* represent traditional church music, his opera *The Last Temptations* is concerned with religion as a moral force. Rautavaara's opera *Thomas* approaches religion from the ethical point of view while Panula's church opera, *A Farmer's Prayer*, seeks to reconcile church music with folk music. International influences are incorporated into religious compositions by Rautavaara in his *Icons* and *Vigilia*, while Tauno Marttinen's *The Shaman* and *Dalai Lama* reflect recent interest in exotic religions.

Even though it appeared for a while as if Sibelius's immediate impact on Finnish music were paralyzing, after a period of recuperation from the effects of the Second World War the country's music scene is more lively than ever, in particular in the field of opera. Approximately twenty new Finnish operas have been composed and produced in the nineteen seventies and eighties.

There seems to be a healthy respect for the past, as is evidenced by the Second Symphony of the young Finnish composer, Eero Hämeenniemi.   The work premiered at the Helsinki Music Festival of 1988 and it indicates a return to turn-of-the-century romanticism in a three-part structure with cheerful outer movements and a long, melancholy middle movement.

On the other hand, the avant-garde Toimii Ensemble presented at the festival under the direction of Esa-Pekka Salonen a new work, *Hommage à Dr. T.*, by Magnus Lindberg.   It is a group effort in which both musical instruments and electronic devices are used to produce a swell of sound in which the conductor indicated divisions by means of loud strikes of a gong. The same group also carried out an effort to which the originator, Kaija Saariaho, had given the poetic title *Petals*, although it was difficult for the audience to connect the title with the activities of the group, which included a percussion ensemble, a cellist producing the most unusual sounds of his instrument, and a clarinetist who played other instruments as well.   The effort was supported by an expert in electronic sound production and guided by Salonen.

An important boost in Finland's musical life will be provided by the new opera house, whose inauguration is scheduled for the early 1990s.   Both Sallinen and Bergman have been invited to write operas for the occasion.   The latter, now in his seventies, has chosen a folk tale from Småland, Sweden, for the topic of his first opera, *Det sjungande trädet* (The Singing Tree), while Sallinen is working on a score based on Aleksis Kivi's play *Kullervo*.   Thus, Sallinen will inaugurate the new opera house with a work on the same Kalevalaic hero on whom Sibelius based his first major work.

NOTES

INTRODUCTION

1. "Finnish Opera at Santa Fe," Music Notes, *New York Times*, July 20, 1986, section 2, p. 21.
2. The term Scandinavia, as used in this study, includes Finland, since the country belongs culturally to the Scandinavian domain, although geographically the term Fenno-Scandia is used. The names of provinces and towns in Finland will be given in Finnish, with the Swedish name in parentheses upon first occurrence.
3. Ernest Newman, *More Essays from the World of Music* (1958), p. 113.
4. Santeri Levas, *Sibelius: a Personal Portrait* (1972), p. 89.
5. Levas, p. 90.
6. Bengt de Törne, *Sibelius: A Close-Up* (1938), p. 15.
7. Simon Parmet, *The Symphonies of Sibelius* (1955), p. xii.
8. Newman, p. 128.

CHAPTER 1: THE HISTORICAL PERSPECTIVE

1. Erik Tawaststjerna, *Sibelius* II (1986), p. 145.
2. Eino Jutikkala and Kauko Pirinen, *A History of Finland* (1974), p. 19: "Finland is mentioned along with Estonia (*Findia* and *Hestia*) in a list of Swedish provinces drawn up for the Pope as early as 1120," for purposes of missionary work.
3. All these castles are still in existence. The Castle of Turku was badly damaged during World War II, when the Soviets bombed Turku because of its shipyards. The castle has been restored and it is now an attractive museum.

4. Voltaire, *Oeuvres historiques*, p. 57, mentions "des liqueurs fortes et des vins." While the Swedish population of Finland consumed more brandy and wine, the Finns fell easily into excesses in their consumption of home-brewed beer (called *olut*, *sahti*, or *kalja*) or of illegally distilled aquavit, often called *korpikuusen kyyneleet* (tears of a spruce in the deep woods).

5. A song of the Finnish folk epic, the *Kalevala*, is sometimes called *virsi* and more often *runo*. The latter should not be confused with Scandinavian *rune*, although both terms are ultimately of the same origin. In order to keep the distinction, the songs of the *Kalevala* will be referred to as runos rather then runes, although the latter is used frequently in English-language works in reference to the poems of the *Kalevala*. For the reader's convenience, only the number of the runo will be indicated. In accordance with Agricola's use, Sibelius referred to composing as "forging," for example, in the following statement about the Fourth Symphony: "Took a ten-kilometre walk while composing, forged the musical metalwork and fashioned sonorities of silver." (Tawaststjerna II, p. 139)

6. When quarrels arose between Johan and his brother Erik, the latter sent Swedish soldiers to take over the Castle of Turku. Some thirty Finnish noblemen remained faithful to Johan and were executed. Johan and his wife Katarina Jagellonica were imprisoned in the Castle of Gripsholm in Sweden. In an attack of madness Erik freed them and the noblemen revolted, deposed Erik, and set up Johan on the throne. Erik was imprisoned in the Castle of Turku.

7. Jutikkala and Pirinen, p. 123.

8. Jutikkala and Pirinen, p. 207.

CHAPTER 2: PRE-SIBELIAN MUSIC OF FINLAND

1. Robert Austerlitz, "Text and Melody in Mansi Songs," *Current Musicology* (Spring 1966), p. 40: "In Mansi culture verse is by nature a correlate of music; all poetry is always (or almost always) sung."

2. Lajos Lesznai, *Bartók* (1973), p. 50.

3. P. Járdányi, "Bartók und die Ordnung der Volkslieder," in *Bericht über die zweite internationale musikwissenschaftliche Konferenz Liszt-Bartók*, p. 436.

4. A. O. Väisänen, *Untersuchungen über die ob-ugrischen Melodien* (1939), p. 60.

5. Otto Andersson, *Studier i musik och folklore* I (1964), p. 353.

6. Andersson I, p. 360.

7. Theodor Hundt, *Bartóks Satztechnique in den Klavierwerken* (1971), p. 22 refers to the parlando-rubato and the dance-like rhythms of the older Hungarian folk melodies.

8. Hundt, p. 24 refers to the ambitus of Hungarian folk melodies and p. 25 of Slovak folk melodies, based on Bartók's observations.

9. Väisänen, *Untersuchungen*, p. 94.

10. Andersson I, p. 57.

11. Ernst Tanzberger, *Jean Sibelius* (1962), p. 170.

12. A. O. Väisänen, *Suomen kansan sävelmiä*, viides jakso, Kantele-ja jouhikkosävelmiä (1928), p. 1x.

13. Carl Engel, *An Introduction to the Study of National Music* (1866; 1976), p. 59.

14. Väisänen, *Untersuchungen*, p. 73.

15. Väisänen, *Untersuchungen*, p. 85.

16. Lesznai, *Bartók*, p. 50.

17. John Horton, *Scandinavian Music: A Short History* (1963), p. 18.

18. Leea Virtanen, *Kalevalainen laulutapa Karjalassa* (1968), p. 42.

19. Horton, p. 18.

20. Veikko Helasvuo, *Sibelius and the Music of Finland* (1952), p. 8.

21. Paavo Helistö, *Music in Finland* (1980), p. 23.

22. Hundt, p. 22ff.

23. Andersson I, p. 50.

24. Andersson I, p. 67.

25. The Estonian national anthem "Mu isamaa" (My Fatherland) uses the same tune by Pacius and a free rendering of the Runeberg poem into Estonian.

26. Erik Tawaststjerna, *Sibelius* I (1976), p. 47.

27. Helasvuo, p. 11.

28. Edward J. Dent, *Ferruccio Busoni* (1974), p. 77.

29. Dent, *Busoni*, p. 77.

30. Dent, *Busoni*, p. 79.

31. Martti Similä, *Sibeliana* (1945), p. 46.

32. *Finländskt herrgårdsliv*, p. 545.

33. James Rhea Massengale, *The Musical-Poetic Method of Carl Michael Bellman*, p. 18.

34. Massengale, p. 34. Bellman's popularity and the influence of King Gustav III's court with its emphasis on French culture (the King founded the Swedish Academy in 1786 based on the French model) marks the high point of the impact of French culture in Scandinavia, but this influence reached Finland only as a weak ground swell despite the fact that later romanticism (*nyromantiken*) made Bellman a veritable cult figure in Sweden.

CHAPTER 3: SIBELIUS AND FINNISH NATIONALISM

1. Eino Jutikkala and Kauko Pirinen, *A History of Finland* (1974), p. 216: "Public opinion had begun to demand a more varied education for citizens, and the Rev. Uno Cygnaeus came out with a bold proposition: the schools should operate apart from a supervision of the Church, though on a Christian basis. In 1865, the municipalities and rural communes were granted the right to found State-subsidized elementary schools."

2. This practice was taken over from Sweden. Regarding Sweden, Carl Allan Moberg states in *Från kyrko- och hovmusik till offentlig konsert* (1970), p. 13: "Sedan gammalt intog musiken en fast plats på skolschemat..." (For a long time music has had a firm place in the school curriculum.)

3. Caution is urged in the use of Swedish and Finnish titles of Sibelius's songs because of numerous errors that have been perpetuated from one list to another.

4. The title occurs in most listings as "The Ferryman's Brides," but "The Rapids-Shooter's Brides" corresponds more accurately to the Finnish title of "Koskenlaskijan morsiamet." The Finnish National Opera Company performed the work in New York in 1983.

5. Hjalmar Alving, *Svensk litteraturhistoria* (1952), p. 288.

6. Karl Ekman, *Jean Sibelius: His Life and Personality* (1945), p. 84.

7. Jouko Hautala, *Suomalainen kansanrunoudentutkimus* (1959), p. 36.

8. Hautala, p. 105.

9. Hautala, p. 110.

10. Nils-Erik Ringbom, *Jean Sibelius: A Master and His Work* (1977), p. 26.

11. Hautala, p. 162.

12. Veikko Helasvuo, *Sibelius and the Music of Finland* (1952), p. 17.

13. Erik Tawaststjerna, *Sibelius* I (1976), p. 138.

14. Tawaststjerna I, p. 153.

15. Otto Andersson, *Studier i musik och folklore* II (1969), pp. 198-200, discusses the similarity between the story of the *Kalevala* about Väinämöinen's boat trip and that of the Novgorod legend in *Sadko* (the *goosli* of *Sadko* is similar to the kantele). In reworking his ideas of the boat trip into the *Lemminkäinen* music, Sibelius was influenced by Liszt, whose *Ce qu'on entend sur la montagne* had an impact on Rimsky-Korsakov's *Sadko*.

16. Hautala, p. 271.

17. Ringbom, p. 45.

18. Since the poetry of the *Kalevala* is largely untranslatable, the writer's prose translations are aimed at conveying the meaning of the original Finnish.

19. Ringbom, p. 48.

20. James Rhea Massengale, *The Musical-Poetic Method of Carl Michael Bellman* (1979), p. 80.

21. Ringbom, p. 51.

22. Harold Truscott, *The Symphony* 2 (1977), p. 97.

23. The translations of the passages of the *Kanteletar* are the writer's.

24. Erik Tawaststjerna, "Sibelius sena dirigentdebut i Stockholm," *Musikrevy* 39, no. 2 (1984), p. 72.

25. Otto Andersson, *Studier i musik och folklore* I (1964), p. 113.

26. Gregory L. Lucente demonstrates in *The Narrative of Realism and Myth* (1981) the relatedness and inseparability of realism and myth rather than the incompatibility suggested by many.

CHAPTER 4: THE PATRIOT

1. Eino Jutikkala and Kauko Pirinen, *A History of Finland* (1974), p. 188.

2. Wendy Hall, *Green Gold and Granite* (1953), p. 128.

3. Jutikkala and Pirinen, p. 222.

4. Jutikkala and Pirinen, p. 179.

5. Harold E. Johnson, *Jean Sibelius* (1959), pp. 57-58.

6. When Nicholas II ascended the throne, the Finns expected him to respect the special status of Finland, but when it became clear that as Czar he would not honor the commitment, they became anxious about their future.

7. Jutikkala and Pirinen, p 231.

8. See further in Chapter 9 the discussion of Aulis Sallinen's opera *The Red Line*, which is based on the events of this period.

9. *Vapautettu kuningatar* and *Tulen synty* were presented by the Boston Symphony Orchestra at a concert on December 31, 1937.

10. Karl Ekman, *Jean Sibelius: His Life and Personality* (1945), p. 237.

11. Jutikkala and Pirinen, p. 253.

12. Ekman, p. 244.

13. Ekman, p. 251.

CHAPTER 5:   THE COMPOSER IN SEARCH OF HIS OWN VOICE

1. Patrick Carnegy, *Faust as Musician* (1973), p. 73.

2. It was in the program notes for this concert that the name change took place, obviously prompted by Sibelius's discovery of his late uncle's visiting cards and not by Strindberg's *Fröken Julie* from 1888, in which one of the main characters is called Jean.

3. Alec Harman and Wilfrid Mellers, *Man and His Music* (1962), p. 929.

4. Eric Walter White, *Stravinsky: The Composer and His Works* (1966), p. 506, refers to the entry in the composer's diary of September 10, 1961. Stravinsky was invited to Helsinki to receive the Wihuri Foundation Sibelius Prize in 1963 and he offered an arrangement of Sibelius's *Canzonetta* as a token of gratitude.

5. Arnold Schoenberg, *Style and Idea* (1975), p. 311.

6. Schoenberg, p. 312.

7. Bela Bartók, *Béla Bartók: Essays* (1976), p. 8.

8. Erik Tawaststjerna, *Sibelius* I (1976), p. 76.

9. Karl Ekman, *Jean Sibelius: His Life and Personality* (1945), p. 116.

10. The topic makes one recall Bartók's discourse from 1921 entitled "Vom Einfluss der Bauernmusik auf die Musik unserer Zeit."

11. Robert Layton, *Sibelius* (1965), p. 112.

12. Statement by Wagner quoted by Jack M. Stein, *Richard Wagner: the Synthesis of the Arts* (1960), p. 39.

13. Donald Jay Grout, *A History of Western Music* (1980), pp. 666-67.

14. Richard Wagner, *Wagner on Music and Drama* (1964), p. 203 ff.

15. Zoltán Kodály, *The Selected Writings of Zoltán Kodály* (1974), p. 12.

16. Nors S. Josephson points out in "Die Skizzen zu Sibelius' 4. Symphonie (1909-1911)," *Musikforschung* 40, no. 1 (1987), pp. 38-49, that even in the case of the Fourth Symphony, in many respects the composer's least Finnish symphony, Sibelius's first sketches are characterized by a fairly traditional structuring of his musical ideas, by symmetrical phrasing and numerous repetitions, which are features that point to a stronger infuence of Finnish folk music than in the final version.

17. Ernst Tanzberger, *Jean Sibelius* (1962), pp. 213-14 for a discussion of *Luonnotar*.

18. Edward Garden, "Sibelius and Balakirev" in *Slavonic and Western Music: Essays for Gerald Abraham* (1985), p. 218.

19. London Symphony Orchestra, RCA DM 394-4/12859-A.
20. James Anderson Winn, *Unsuspected Eloquence* (1981), p. 283.
21. Lionel Pike, *Beethoven, Sibelius and the 'Profound Logic'* (1978), p. 21ff.
22. Walter Frisch, *Brahms and the Principle of Developing Variation* (1984), p. 9.
23. Tawaststjerna I, p. 77.
24. Claude Debussy, *Debussy, Letters* (1987), p. 42.
25. Schoenberg, p. 164.
26. Schoenberg, p. 163.

CHAPTER 6: THE WATERSHED AND ITS AFTERMATH

1. Erik Tawaststjerna, "Sibelius vid tiden för fjärde symfonins tillkomst", *Musikrevy* 30 no. 3 (1975), p. 118 (the double exclamation point is Sibelius's).
2. Lionel Pike, *Beethoven, Sibelius and the 'Profound Logic'* (1978), p. 100.
3. William C. Hill, "Some Aspects of Form in the Symphonies of Sibelius," *Music Review* 10 (1949), p. 165ff.
4. Robert Simpson, "Sibelius, Nielsen, and the Symphonic Problem" in *Carl Nielsen, Symphonist* (1979), p. 206.
5. Simpson, p. 206.
6. Simpson, p. 201.
7. Béla Bartók, *Béla Bartók: Essays*, (1976) p. 338: "One point, in particular, I must again stress: our peasant music, naturally, is invariably tonal, if not always in the same sense that the inflexible major and minor system is tonal."
8. Pike, p. 171ff.
9. Pike, p. 59ff.
10. Simpson, p. 195.
11. Elliott Antokoletz, *The Music of Béla Bartók* (1984), p. 78.
12. Tawaststjerna, "Sibelius vid tiden för fjärde symfonins tillkomst," p. 118.
13. Otto Andersson, *Studier i musik och folklore* I (1964), p. 103.
14. Karl Ekman, *Jean Sibelius: His Life and Personality* (1945), p. 264.
15. Erik Tawaststjerna, *Sibelius* II (1986), p. 262.
16. Ekman, p. 255.
17. Christopher Ballantine, *Twentieth Century Symphony* (1983), p. 113.
18. Pike, p. 130ff.
19. Simpson, p. 207.
20. Simpson, p. 211.

21. Pike, p. 130.

22. Ekman, p. 255.

23. Erik Tawaststjerna, "Sibelius sena dirigentdebut i Stockholm," *Musikrevy* 39 (1984), no. 2, p. 75.

24. Harold Truscott, *The Symphony*, 2 (1977), p. 96.

25. Pike, p. 190ff.

26. Pike, p. 139.

27. Ilkka Oramo, "Vom Einfluss der Volksmusik auf die Kunstmusik: Ein unbekannter Aufsatz von Sibelius aus dem Jahre 1896," *Musikforschung* 36, no. 4 (1983), Supplement, p. 442.

28. Pike, p. 203ff.

29. Simpson, p. 217.

30. V. V. Yastrebtsev, *Reminiscences of Rimsky-Korsakov* (1985), p. 29.

31. Yastrebtsev. p. 420.

32. Donald Jay Grout, *A History of Western Music* (1980), p. 673.

33. Zoltán Kodály, *The Selected Writings of Zoltán Kodály* (1974), p. 95.

34. Richard Norton, *Tonality in Western Culture* (1984), p. 133.

CHAPTER 7: THE SIBELIAN LEGACY

1. Bengt de Törne, *Sibelius: A Close-Up* (1938), p. 16.

2. Erik Tawaststjerna, *Sibelius* II (1986), p. 67.

3. Tawaststjerna II, p. 82.

4. Ilkka Oramo, "Vom Einfluss der Volksmusik auf die Kunstmusik: Ein unbekannter Aufsatz von Sibelius aus dem Jahre 1896", *Musikforschung* 36, no. 4 (1983), Supplement, p. 442.

5. Donald Jay Grout, *A History of Western Music* (1980), p. 664.

6. Karl Ekman, *Jean Sibelius: His Life and Personality* (1945), p. 265.

7. The contrasts in the work are rendered splendidly in recordings by such Russian-trained violinists as Oistrach, Gideon Kramer, and Boris Belkin.

8. Wilfrid Mellers, "Sibelius and 'the Modern Mind,'" *Music Survey* 1, no. 6 (1949), p. 182.

9. W. F. Kirby, "Introduction" to his English translation of the *Kalevala* (1923-25), p. ix.

10. Marc Vignal, *Jean Sibelius* (1965), p. 157.

11. Burnett James, *The Music of Jean Sibelius* (1983), p. 112.

12. Erik Tawaststjerna, "Sibelius sena dirigentdebut i Stockholm," *Musikrevy* 39, no. 2 (1984), p. 74.

13. Another Finnish architect whose designs have attracted attention even abroad is Viljo Rewell.

14. Robert Simpson, "Sibelius, Nielsen, and the Symphonic Problem" in *Carl Nielsen, Symphonist* (1979), p. 217.

15. Lionel Pike, *Beethoven, Sibelius and the 'Profound Logic'*, (1978), p. 114.

16. Michael McMullin, "Sibelius: An Essay on his Significance," *The Music Review* 46 (1985), p. 199, states that for an explanation of "the silence of Järvenpää" we have to look for a philosophical one connected with Sibelius's relationship to art and the historical situation in which the composer found himself.

17. Andrew Saint's review of Demetri Porphyrios, *Sources of Modern Eclecticism, Studies on Alvar Aalto*, Academy Editions, in the *Times (London) Literary Supplement*, October 8, 1982, p. 1095.

18. *See* Anthony Savile, *The Test of Time: An Essay in Philosophical Aesthetics* (1982); and a review of the same work in the *Times (London) Literary Supplement*, February 8, 1983 by Kendall L. Walton.

CHAPTER 8: POST-SIBELIAN INSTRUMENTAL MUSIC

1. Paul Juon, a Moscow-born German composer, admitted that one of his three violin concertos is modeled on the Sibelius Concerto, and Sibelius felt that works like Heinrich Zöllner's Third Symphony and Julius Weismann's Piano Concerto showed the influence of his works.

2. David Cox, "Ralph Vaughan Williams" in *Symphony* 2, p. 121.

3. John Horton, *Scandinavian Music: A Short History* (1963), p. 150.

4. Erik Tawaststjerna, *Sibelius* II (1986), p. 133.

5. Paavo Heininen, "Ett (alltför) öppet brev till vänner," *Musikrevy* 39, no. 2 (1984), p. 41.

6. Heininen, p. 40. Seppo Nummi, on the other hand, feels that in the early 1950s Englund was influenced by Prokofiev (*Musica Fennica* (1985), 2d ed., p. 84). However, in my view Sibelius's influence on Englund is stronger than is generally believed, and his Fourth Symphony twice quotes a passage from *Tapiola* despite the fact that Englund dedicated the work to the memory of Shostakovich and even used in it a scale of alternate whole tones and semitones, which had occurred in works by both Rimsky-Korsakov and Shostakovich.

7. Gunnar Sjöqvist, "Joonas Kokkonen: Symfoniker vid sidan av moderiktningar," *Musikrevy* 39, no. 2 (1984), p. 51.

8. Erkki Salmenhaara, "Joonas Kokkonen, en klassiker med romantisk tendens," *Musikrevy* 28, no. 2 (1973), p. 74.

9. Sjöqvist, "Joonas Kokkonen," p. 52.
10. Gunnar Sjöqvist, "Finn Finland med musik," *Musikrevy* 38, no. 1 (1983), p. 28.
11. Heininen, p. 41.
12. Heininen, p. 42.
13. Gunnar Sjöqvist, "Möte med finländsk tonsättare: Erkki Salmenhaara," *Musikrevy* 42, no. 2 (1987), p. 95.
14. Jarmo Sermilä, "Biografier över sexton nutida finska tonsättare," *Musikrevy* 30, no. 3 (1975), p. 138.
15. Gunnar Sjöqvist, "Aulis Sallinen," *Musikrevy* 39, no. 2. (1984), p. 55.
16. Sjöqvist, "Aulis Sallinen," p. 56.
17. Sjöqvist, "Aulis Sallinen," p. 56.
18. Robert Henderson, "Aulis Sallinen: Singing of Man," *The Musical Times* 128, no. 1730 (April 1987), p. 191.
19. Sermilä, p. 129.
20. Heininen, p. 39.
21. Mikael Helasvuo, "Om finländskt flöjtmusik," *Musikrevy* 39, no. 2 (1984), p. 65.

CHAPTER 9: STAGE AND VOCAL MUSIC IN FINLAND

1. The translations of the quotes of the libretti of Sallinen's operas are the writer's.
2. Bernard Holland in the *New York Times*, August 11, 1986.
3. Tiina-Maija Lehtonen and Pekka Hako, *Kuninkaasta kuninkaaseen* (1987), p. 248.
4. Bert Wechsler, "Finland Revisited: Summer Music and Dance on a Nationwide Level," *Music Journal* 42, no. 3 (Fall 1985), p. 8.
5. Lehtonen and Hako, p. 69.

BIBLIOGRAPHY

GENERAL SOURCES

Alving, Hjalmar. *Svensk litteraturhistoria*, 3d ed. by Gudmar Hasselberg. Stockholm: Bonniers, 1952.

Ansermet, Ernest. *Les Fondements de la musique dans la conscience humaine*. Neuchâtel, Suisse: Editions de la Baconnière. 1961.

Antokoletz, Elliott. *The Music of Béla Bartók: A Study of Tonality and Progression in Twentieth-Century Music*. Berkeley: University of California Press, 1984.

Asaf'yev, Boris. *A Book about Stravinsky*. Translated by Richard F. French. Ann Arbor, Mich.: University of Michigan Press, 1982.

Ballantine, Christopher. *Twentieth Century Symphony*. London: Dennis Dobson, 1983.

Bartha, Dénes. "On Beethoven's Thematic Structure," in *The Creative World of Beethoven*. Edited by Paul Henry Lang. New York: W. W. Norton Co., 1971, pp. 257-76.

Bartók, Béla. *Béla Bartók: Essays*. Selected and edited by Benjamin Suchoff. New York: St. Martin's Press, 1976.

Bellman, Carl Michael. *Carl Michael Bellmans skrifter*, standard-upplaga utgiven av Bellmansällskapet. Stockholm: Bonniers, 1927.

Boyd, Malcolm. *Palestrina's Style*. London: Oxford University Press, 1973.

Bright, William. "Language and Music: Areas for Cooperation," *Ethnomusicology* 7 (1963), p. 27ff.

Calvocoressi, M. D. *Mussorgsky*. Completed and revised by Gerald Abraham. London: Dent & Sons Ltd., rev. ed., 1974.

Carnegy, Patrick. *Faust as Musician: A Study of Thomas Mann's Novel "Doctor Faustus."* London: Chatto & Windus, 1973.

Cox, David. "Ralph Vaughan Williams (1872-1958)" in *Symphony 2.* Edited by Robert Simpson. London: Penguin Books, 1977, pp. 114-127.

Dahlhaus, Karl. *Realism in Nineteenth-Century Music.* Translated by Mary Whittall. Cambridge: Cambridge University Press, 1985.

Debussy, Claude. *Debussy's Letters.* Selected and edited by François Lesure and Roger Nichols, translated by Roger Nichols. Cambridge, Mass.: Harvard University Press, 1987.

Dent, Edward J. *Ferruccio Busoni.* London: Eulenburg Books, 1974.

Druskin, Mikhail. *Igor Stravinsky: His Life, Works, and Views.* Translated by Martin Cooper. Cambridge: Cambridge University Press, 1983.

Engel, Carl. *An Introduction to the Study of National Music*, reprinted from the 1866 ed. New York: AMS Press, Inc., 1976.

von Fischer, Kurt. *Griegs Harmonik und die nordländische Folklore.* Bern: Berner Veröffentlichungen zur Musikforschung, Heft 12, 1938.

Frisch, Walter. *Brahms and the Principle of Developing Variation.* Berkeley: University of California Press, 1984.

Gray, Cecil. *A Survey of Contemporary Music*, 2d. ed. London: Oxford University Press, 1927.

_____. *Predicaments: or Music and the Future.* London: Oxford University Press, 1936.

Grout, Donald Jay. *A History of Western Music*, 3d ed. with Claude V. Palisca. New York: W. W. Norton & Co., 1980.

Harman, Alec and Wilfrid Mellers. *Man and His Music.* New York: Oxford University Press, 1962.

Horton, John. *Scandinavian Music: A Short History.* London: Faber & Faber, 1963.

Hundt, Theodor. *Bartóks Satztechnik in den Klavierwerken.* Kölner Beiträge zur Musikforschung. Regensburg: Gustav Bosse Verlag, 1971.

Járdányi, P. "Bartók und die Ordnung der Volkslieder," in *Bericht über die zweite internationale musikwissenschaftliche Konferenz Liszt-Bartók.* Budapest: Akadémiai Kiadó, 1961 (1963).

Jonas, Oswald. *Introduction to the Theory of Heinrich Schenker.* Translated and edited by John Rothgelb. New York: Longman, 1982.

Kodály, Zoltán. *The Selected Writings of Zoltán Kodály.* Edited by Ferenc Bonis, translated by Lili Halapy and Fred. Macnicol. London: Boosey & Hawkes, 1974.

Kramer, Lawrence. *Music and Poetry: The Nineteenth Century and After.* Berkeley: University of California Press, 1984.

Kroó, G. "Monothematik und Dramaturgie in Bartóks Bühnenwerken," in *Bericht über die zweite internationale musikwissenschaftliche Konferenz Liszt-Bartók.* Budapest: Akadémiai Kiadó, 1961 (1963).

Lang, Henry. *Music in Western Civilization.* New York: W. W. Norton & Co., 1941.

Lerdahl, Fred and Ray Jackendorf. *A Generative Theory of Tonal Music.* Cambridge, Mass.: MIT Press, 1983.

Lesznai, Lajos. "Realistische Ausdrucksmittel in der Musik Bartóks," in *Bericht über die zweite internationale musikwissenschaftliche Konferenz Liszt-Bartók.* Budapest: Akadémiai Kiadó, 1961 (1963).

_____. *Bartók.* The Master Musicians Series. London: J. M. Dent & Sons, Ltd., 1973.

Lévi-Strauss, Claude. *Structural Anthropology.* Translated by Claire Jacobson and Brooke Grundfest Schoepf. New York: Basic Books, Inc., 1963.

Lucente, Gregory L. *The Narrative of Realism and Myth.* Baltimore: The Johns Hopkins University Press, 1981.

Mann, Thomas. *Doktor Faustus: Stockholmer Gesamtausgabe der Werke von Thomas Mann.* Frankfurt am Main: S. Fischer, 1954.

Massengale, James Rhea. *The Musical-Poetic Method of Carl Michael Bellman.* Uppsala: Acta Universitatis Upsaliensis, Studia musicologica Upsaliensia, Nova series 6, 1979.

Mellers, Wilfred. *Romanticism and the 20th Century: Man and His Music.* Fair Lawn, New Jersey: Essential Library of Books, 1957.

Menhennet, Alan. *The Romantic Movement.* London: Croom Helm, 1981.

Meyer, Leonard B. *Emotion and Meaning in Music.* Chicago: University of Chicago Press, 1956.

Moberg, Carl Allan. *Från kyrko- och hovmusik till offentlig konsert: Studier i Stormaktstidens svenska musikhistoria.* Uppsala: Uppsala Universitets Årsskrift 1942, no. 5, 1970.

Nemmers, Erwin Esser. *Twenty Centuries of Catholic Church Music.* Milwaukee: Bruce Publishing Co., 1949.

Nettl, Bruno. *Folk and Traditional Music of the Western Continents.* Englewood Cliffs, N.J.: Prentice-Hall, Inc., 1973.

Newman, Ernest. *More Essays from the World of Music.* New York: Coward-MacCann, Inc., 1958.

Norton, Richard. *Tonality in Western Culture: A Critical and Historical Perspective.* University Park, Pa.: Pennsylvania State University Press, 1984.

Savile, Anthony. *The Test of Time: An Essay in Philosophical Aesthetics.* Oxford: Clarendon Press, 1982.

Schelderup-Ebbe, Dag. *Edvard Grieg 1858-1867: with a special reference to the evolution of his harmonic style.* London: Allen & Unwin, 1964.

Schoenberg, Arnold. *Style and Idea: Selected Writings of Arnold Schoenberg.* Edited by Leonard Stein. Translated by Leo Black. Berkeley: University of California Press, 1975.

Simpson, Robert, editor. *The Symphony 2: Elgar to the Present Day.* London: Penguin Books, 1977.

de Staël, Madame. *Choix de lettres (1776-1817),* présenté et commenté par Georges Solovieff. Paris: Editions Klincksieck, 1970.

Stein, Jack M. *Richard Wagner: The Synthesis of the Arts.* Detroit: Wayne State University Press, 1960.

Stravinsky, Igor. *Chronicle of My Life.* London: Gollancz, 1936.

_____. *Dialogues and Diary.* Garden City, N.Y.: Doubleday and Co., Inc., 1963.

_____. *Poetics of Music, in the Form of Six Lessons.* Translated by Arthur Knödel and Ingolf Dahl, preface by George Seferis. Cambridge, Mass.: Harvard University Press, 1970.

_____ and Robert Craft. *Expositions and Developments.* Garden City, N.Y.: Doubleday and Co., Inc., 1962.

Tarasti, Eero. *Myth and Music: A Semiotic Approach to the Aesthetics of Myth and Music, especially that of Wagner, Sibelius and Stravinsky.* The Hague: Mouton Publishers, 1979.

Vaughan Williams, Ralph. *National Music.* London: Oxford University Press, 1935.

Vlad, Roman. *Stravinsky.* Translated by Frederick Fuller. 3d ed. London: Oxford University Press, 1978.

Voltaire. *Oeuvres historiques.* Bibliothèque de la Pléiade. Paris: Librairie Gallimard, 1957.

Wagner, Richard. *Wagner on Music and Drama: A Compendium of Richard Wagner's Prose Works,* selected and arranged with an introduction by Albert Goldman and Evert Sprinchorn. Translated by H. Ashton Ellis. New York: E. P. Dutton, Inc., 1964.

Weber, Max. *The Rational and Social Foundations of Music.* Translated and edited by Don Martindale, Johanna Riedel, and Gertrude Neuwirth. Urbana: University of Illinois Press, 1958.

White, Eric Walter. *Stravinsky: The Composer and His Works.* Berkeley: University of California Press, 1966.

Winn, James Anderson. *Unsuspected Eloquence: A History of the Relations between Poetry and Music.* New Haven: Yale University Press, 1981.

Yastrebtsev, V. V. *Reminiscences of Rimsky-Korsakov.* Edited and translated by Florence Jonas. Foreword by Gerald Abraham. New York: Columbia University Press, 1985.

Yoell, John H. *The Nordic Sound: Explorations into the Music of Denmark, Norway, Sweden.* Foreword by Antal Dorati. Boston: Crescendo Publishing Co., 1974.

WORKS ON FINLAND, FINNISH AND FINNO-URGRIC STUDIES

Andersson, Otto. *Studier i musik och folklore.* Helsinki: Suomalaisen Kirjallisuuden Seura, vol. I, 1964; vol. II, 1969.

Austerlitz, Robert. "Text and Melody in Mansi Songs," *Current Musicology* (Spring 1966), pp. 37-57.

Hall, Wendy. *Green Gold and Granite: A Background for Finland.* London: Max Parrish, 1953.

Hautala, Jouko. *Suomalainen kansanrunoudentutkimus.* Helsinki: Suomalaisen Kirjallisuuden Seura, 1954.

Jutikkala, Eino and Kauko Pirinen. *A History of Finland,* rev. ed. Translated by Paul Sjöblom. New York: Praeger Publishers, 1974.

Kiparsky, Paul. "Metrics and Morphophonemics in the Kalevala," *Studies Presented to Professor Roman Jakobson by His Students.* Cambridge, Mass.: Slavica Publishers, Inc., 1968.

Kirby, W. F., trans. *Kalevala.* London: J. M. Dent & Sons, Ltd.; New York: E. P. Dutton & Co., vols. I-II, 1923-25.

Lönnqvist, Bo, editor. *Finländskt herrgårdsliv: En etnografisk studie över Karsby gård i Tenala ca. 1800-1970.* Helsingfors: Svenska litteratursällskapet i Finland, 1978.

Lönnroth, Elias, editor. *Kalevala.* Helsinki: Suomalaisen Kirjallisuuden Seura, 1935.

_____, editor. *Kanteletar elikkä Suomen kansan vanhoja lauluja ja virsiä.* Helsinki: Suomalaisen Kirjallisuuden Seura, 5th ed., 1906.

Sadeniemi, Matti. *Die Metrik des Kalevala-Verses*. Translated by Iris Walden-Hollo. Helsinki: Suomalainen Tiedeakatemia, 1951.

STUDIES ON FINNISH MUSIC

Abraham, Gerald, editor. *The Music of Sibelius* (symposium). New York: W. W. Norton & Co., 1947.

Andersson, Otto. *Studier i musik och folklore*. Helsinki: Suomalaisen Kirjallisuuden Seura, vol. I, 1964; vol. II, 1969.

Borg, Kim. "Jean Sibelius und die Finnen," *Österreichische Musikzeitschrift* 12 (1957), pp. 386-89.

Cherniavsky, David. "The Use of Germ Motives by Sibelius," *Music and Letters* 23, no. 1, January 1942.

Ekman, Karl. *Jean Sibelius: His Life and Personality*. Translated by Edward Birse, foreword by Ernest Newman. New York: Tudor Publishing Co., 1945.

Furuhjelm, Erik. *Jean Sibelius: Hans tondiktning och drag ur hans liv*. Borgå: Holger Schildt, 1916.

Garden, Edward. "Sibelius and Balakirev" in *Slavonic and Western Music: Essays for Gerald Abraham*. Edited by Malcolm H. Brown and Roland J. Wiley. Ann Arbor: University of Michigan Press, 1985, pp. 215-28.

Gray, Cecil. *Sibelius, the Symphonies*. Freeport, N.Y.: Books for the Libraries Press, 1970; reprint of London: Oxford University Press, 1935.

_____. *Sibelius*. Westport, Conn.: Hyperion Press, Inc., 1979; reprint of London: Oxford University Press, 1931.

Gregory, Robin. "Sibelius and the *Kalevala*," *Monthly Musical Record* (March-April), 1951.

Hannikainen, Ilmari. *Sibelius and the Development of Finnish Music*, preface by Toivo Haapanen. Translated by Aulis Nopsanen. London: Hinrichsen Edition, 1948.

Heininen, Paavo. "Ett (alltför) öppet brev till vänner," *Musikrevy* 39, no. 2 (1984), pp. 39-46.

Helasvuo, Mikael. "Om finländskt flöjtmusik," *Musikrevy* 39, no. 2 (1984), pp. 65-66.

Helasvuo, Veikko. *Sibelius and the Music of Finland*. Translated by Paul Sjöblom. Helsinki: Otava, 1952.

Helistö, Paavo. *Music in Finland*. Huhmari, Finland: Finnish-American Cultural Institute, 1980.

Henderson, Robert. "Aulis Sallinen: Singing of Man," *The Musical Times* 128, no. 1730 (April 1987), pp. 189-91.

Hill, William C. "Some Aspects of Form in the Symphonies of Sibelius," *Music Review* 10 (1949), pp. 165-82.

James, Burnett. *The Music of Jean Sibelius.* East Brunswick, N.J.: Associated University Presses, Inc., 1983.

Johnson, Harold E. *Jean Sibelius.* New York: Alfred Knopf, 1959.

Josephson, Nors S. "Die Skizzen zu Sibelius' 4. Symphonie (1909-1911)," *Musikforschung* 40, no. 1, (1987), pp. 38-49.

Karila, Tauno. *Vesimaisemat Jean Sibeliuksen, Oskar Merikannon ja Yrjö Kilpisen yksinlaulujen melodiikassa* (Seascapes in the Lieder of Jean Sibelius, Oskar Merikanto and Yrjö Kilpinen). Helsinki: Sanoma Oy, 1954.

Krohn, Ilmari, editor. *Suomen kansan sävelmiä: toinen jakso, laulusävelmiä.* Helsinki: Suomalaisen Kirjallisuuden Seura, vol. 3 (1932); vol. 4 (1933).

Launis, Armas, editor. *Suomen kansan sävelmiä: neljäs jakso, Runosävelmiä, Inkerin runosävelmät.* Helsinki: Suomalaisen Kirjallisuuden Seura, 1930.

Layton, Robert. *Sibelius.* The Master Musicians Series. London: Dent & Sons, Ltd.; New York: Farrar, Straus and Giroux Inc., 1965.

Lehtonen, Tiina-Maija, and Pekka Hako. *Kuninkaasta kuninkaaseen: Suomalaisen oopperan tarina.* Porvoo-Helsinki: Werner Söderström Oy., 1987.

Levas, Santeri. *Sibelius, a Personal Portrait.* Translated by Percy M. Young. London: Dent & Sons Ltd, 1972.

Maeckelmann, Michael. "Jean Sibelius: 'Tapiola,' Tondichtung, Op. 112," *Neue Zeitschrift für Musik* no. 5 (May 1986), pp. 32-36.

Mäkinen, Timo, and Seppo Nummi. *Musica Fennica.* Translated by Kingsley Hart. Helsinki: Otava, 1965; 2d ed., 1985.

McMullin Michael. "Sibelius: An Essay on His Significance," *The Music Review* 46 (1985), pp. 199-211.

Mellers, Wilfrid. "Sibelius and 'the Modern Mind,'" *Music Survey* 1, no. 6 (1949).

Nummi, Seppo. "Den finländska musikens Janus-ansikten," *Musikrevy* 30, no. 3 (1975), pp. 97-100.

Oramo, Illka. "Vom Einfluss der Volksmusik auf die Kunstmusik: Ein unbekannter Aufsatz von Sibelius aus dem Jahre 1896," *Musikforschung* 36, no. 4 (1983), supplement, pp. 440-44.

Parmet, Simon. *Sibelius symfonier.* Translated as *The Symphonies of Sibelius.* Helsingfors, 1955; London, 1959.

Pike, Lionel. *Beethoven, Sibelius, and the 'Profound Logic': Studies in Symphonic Analysis.* Foreword by Robert Simpson. London: University of London, Athlone Press, 1978.

Richards, Denby. *The Music of Finland.* London: Hugh Evelyn, 1968.

Ringbom, Nils-Erik.   *Jean Sibelius: A Master and His Work.*
Translated by C. I. de Courcy. Westport, Conn.: Greenwood
Press, 1977.

Roiha, Eino.   *Die Symphonien von Jean Sibelius.*   Jyväskylä, 1941.

Rosas, John.   *Otryckta kammarmusikverk av Jean Sibelius.*   Åbo:
Åbo Akademi, 1961.

Salmenhaara, Erkki.   "Joonas Kokkonen, en klassiker med
romantisk tendens," *Musikrevy* 28, no. 2 (1973), pp. 72-76.

Savijoki, Jukka.   "Något om det klassiska gitarrspelets historia i
Finland," *Musikrevy* 39, no. 2 (1984), pp. 68-69.

Sermilä, Jarmo.   "Biografier över sexton nutida finska tonsättare,"
Musikrevy 30, no. 3 (1975), pp. 127-39.

Similä, Martti.   *Sibeliana.* Helsinki: Otava, 1945.

Simpson, Robert.   "Sibelius, Nielsen, and the Symphonic Problem,"
in *Carl Nielsen, Symphonist.* New York: Taplinger, 1979.

Sjöqvist, Gunnar.   "Finn Finland med musik," *Musikrevy* 38, no. 1
(1983), pp. 28-29.

_____.   "Finland: musikspelens förlovade land," *Musikrevy* 38, no.
1 (1983), pp. 22-27.

_____.   "Joonas Kokkonen: Symfoniker vid sidan av
moderiktningar," *Musikrevy* 39, no. 2 (1984), pp. 50-52.

_____.   "Aulis Sallinen," *Musikrevy* 39, no. 2 (1984), pp. 54-56.

_____.   "Möte med finländsk tonsättare: Erkki Salmenhaara,"
Musikrevy 42, no. 2 (1987), pp. 95-96.

Tanzberger, Ernst.   *Jean Sibelius*, eine Monographie. Wiesbaden:
Breitkopf & Haertel, 1962.

Tarasti, Eero.   *Myth and Music: A Semiotic Approach to the
Aesthetics of Myth and Music, especially that of Wagner,
Sibelius and Stravinsky.* The Hague: Mouton Publishers,
1979.

Tawaststjerna, Erik.   *Ton och tolkning: Sibelius studier.*
Helsingfors: Holger Schildt, 1957.

_____.   *Sibeliuksen pianoteokset säveltäjän kehityskuvan
kuvastajina.* Helsinki: Otava, 1960.

_____.   "Sibelius vid tiden för fjärde symfonins tillkomst,"
Musikrevy 30, no. 3 (1975), pp. 116-119.

_____.   *Sibelius*, vol. 1 (1865-1905). Translated by Robert Layton.
London: Faber & Faber, 1976.

_____.   "Sibelius sena dirigentdebut i Stockholm," *Musikrevy* 39,
no. 2 (1984), pp. 72-75.

_____.   *Sibelius*, vol. 2 (1904-1914). Translated by Robert Layton.
Berkeley: University of California Press, 1986.

de Törne, Bengt.   *Sibelius: A Close-Up.* Boston: Houghton-
Mifflin Co., 1938.

Tovey, Donald Francis. "Analyses of Sibelius's Seventh Symphony
    and *Tapiola*," *Essays in Musical Analysis* vol. 6.   London:
    Oxford University Press, 1939.
_____.   "Analyses of Sibelius's Third and Fifth Symphonies,"
    Essays in Musical Analysis, vol. 2, 12th ed. London: Oxford
    University Press, 1972.
Truscott, Harold. "Jean Sibelius" in *Symphony 2:   Elgar to the
    Present Day*. Edited by Robert Simpson. London: Penguin
    Books, 1977, pp. 80-103.
Väisänen, A. O., editor. *Suoman kansan sävelmiä: viides jakso,
    Kantele-ja   jouhikkosävelmiä.*   Helsinki: Suomalaisen
    Kirjallisuuden Seura, 1928.

_____. *Untersuchungen über die ob-ugrischen Melodien.* Helsinki:
    Suomalaisen Kirjallisuuden Seura, 1939.
Vignal, Marc. *Jean Sibelius*. Paris: Editions Seghers, 1965.
Virtanen, Leea.   *Kalevalainen laulutapa Karjalassa.*   Helsinki:
    Suomalaisen Kirjallisuuden Seura, 1968.
Wechsler, Bert. "Finland Revisited: Summer Music and Dance on
    a Nationwide Level," *Music Journal* 42, no. 3 (Fall 1985), pp.
    5-9.
Wood, Ralph W. "Sibelius's Use of Percussion," *Music and Letters*
    23, no. 1 (January 1942), pp. 6-33.

DISCOGRAPHY

INFORMATION ON SCANDINAVIAN AND OTHER RARE LABELS:

CAP: Caprice (distributed by International Book & Record)
Con: Connaisseur Musik, Bluebell; Karlsruhe
DACO: Danacord (distributed by Qualiton Imports)
FA: Finlandia (distributed by International Book & Record)
FENO: Fennica nova
FUGA (a Finnish label)
GDL: Levytuottajat
H: Hyperion (distributed by Harmonia mundi)
KK: Konserttikeskus
LR: Love Records
ODE: Ondine (represented by Caprice)
PEA: Ponsi
PROP: Proprius
S: Scandia
SA: Record Series of the Sibelius Academy
SF: Finnlevy
SM: Da Camera Magna
TA: Tactus

For further information on the Scandinavian labels, inquire at: Polygram Special Imports, 810 Seventh Ave., New York, N.Y. 10019.

Aho, Kalevi (b. 1949)
Quintet, for bassoon and string quartet. FA 340.
Quintet, for oboe and string quartet. FA 320.
Sonata, for piano. FA 332.
String Quartet No. 3. FAD (digital) 348.
Symphony No. 4. SFX 44.

Bergman, Erik (b. 1911)
Aspects, for piano. EMI 5E063-34484.
Aubade for Orchestra, Op. 48 (1958). FA 314.
Bim Bam Bum, for tenor, ensemble, and chorus, Op. 80 (1976).
CHAN 8478 DDD.
Colori ed improvvisazioni, for orchestra, Op. 72 (1973). FA
330.
Concertino da camera. LR 28 LP, EMI 228.
Concerto for Violin and Orchestra. BIS CD 326.
Energien, for harpsichord, Op. 66 (1970). BIS 68.
Exsultate, for organ. EMI 5E063-34484.
Fåglarna (The Birds), for chorus and baritone. RCA YSVL 1-
559; Philips 839705; CHAN 8478 DDD.
Hathor Suite, for soprano, baritone, ensemble, and chorus, Op.
70 (1971). CHAN 8478 DDD.
Lapponia, for chorus. EMI HMV 9C063-38214.
Missa in honorem Sancti Henrici. EMI HMV 9C063-38214.
Noah, for baritone, chorus, and orchestra, Op. 78 (1976). FA
330.
Nox, for baritone, chorus, and ensemble. EMI 5E063-34484;
CHAN 8478 DDD.
Vier Galgenlieder, for chorus. EMI 5E063-34484.

Byström, Thomas (1772-1839)
Air russe variée, for piano. FA 336.
Sonata in B-Flat for Violin and Piano. FA 322.

Collan, Karl (1828-71)
Songs to texts by Topelius and Runeberg. SFX 59 stereo.

Crusell, Bernhard Henrik (1775-1838)
Concerto No. 1 in E-Flat for Clarinet and Orchestra. Hyperion
A-66055, also CD; BIS CD 345.
Concerto No. 2 in F Minor for Clarinet and Orchestra. ASV
DCA 559; BIS CD 345.
Concerto No. 3 in B-Flat for Clarinet and Orchestra. Hyperion
CDA 66055; BIS CD 345.

Divertimento for Oboe and String Quartet, Op. 9.   Hyperion A-66143; FA 320.

Introduction and Variations on a Swedish Air, Op. 12. Hyperion CDA 66022; ASV CDDCA 585 DDD.

Quartet No. 1 for Clarinet and Strings in E-Flat, Op. 2. BIS 51 LP.

Quartet No. 3 for Clarinet and Strings in D Major. BIS 51 LP.

Quartet for Flute and Strings in D Major, Op. 8. DACO 204.

Quintet for Clarinet and Strings, Op. 4.   ORFE S 141 861, also available on cassette.

Sinfonia Concertante in B, Op. 3, for clarinet, horn, bassoon, and orchestra. EMI 157-30762/66 (5 LP); DC CAP 1144.

Englund, Einar (b. 1916)

Arioso interrotto, for violin. SALP 1.

Concerto No. 1 for Piano and Orchestra.   EMI HMV 5E63-34471; SALP 2.

Concerto for Violin and Orchestra.   FAD 335; FACD 343 AAD/DDD.

Epinikia, for orchestra. SFX 34.

Introduzione e capriccio, for violin and piano. RCA PL 40058.

Introduzione e toccata, for piano.   EMI HMV 5E063-34283; SALP 1.

Passacaglia for organ. FA 308.

Piano Music (complete) BIS 277 CD.

Sonata No. 1 for Cello and Piano. FAD 335.

Symphony No. 1 (1946). FA 304.

Symphony No. 2. SFX 34.

Symphony No. 4 for Strings and Percussion (1976). FA 329.

Hannikainen, Ilmari (1892-1955)

Piano Pieces. FA 341.

Heininen, Paavo (b. 1938)

Adagio for String Orchestra. Philips 802 854 LY; SM 91022.

The Autumns, for chorus. FENO 1.

Concerto No. 3 for Piano and Orchestra. SALP 2.

Discantus I, for flute. Cipango/Asia Rec. CC 5002; SALP 1.

Maiandros, for piano (electro-acoustic). FENO 5.

...poesia squillante ed incandescente..., for piano. TA 8010.

Sonatina della primavera, for piano. KKLP 174.

Touching, for guitar. BIS 207 LP.

Heiniö, Mikko (b. 1948)

Framtidens skugga, for soprano and brass ensemble.   FUGA
    3043.
Landet som icke är, for women's chorus and piano.   FUGA
    3043.
Notturno di fiordo, for flute and harp.   TA 8103.

Johansson, Bengt (b. 1914)

Cum essem parvulus, for chorus.   EMI Columbia 5E062-34670.
Missa a quattro voci, for chorus.   RCA Victor LSP 10340.
Pater noster, for chorus.   SFLP 8502.
Three Chansons for Baritone and Piano (based on Ezra Pound).
    SFX 12.
The Tomb of Akr Caar.   Philips 839 705 LY.
Triptych and Three Classical Madrigals, for chorus.   SFX 14.
Vesper, for chorus.   EMI HMV 5E063-34517.

Jokinen, Erkki (b. 1941)

String Quartet No. 1.   FUGA 3023.
String Quartet No. 2.   TA 8002.

Kaipainen, Jouni (b. 1956)

Sonatina per pianoforte.   SAOLP 1.
Trois morceaux de l'aube, for cello and piano.   FUGA 3023.

Kantele Music

Performed by Martti Pokela, Eeva-Leena Pokela-Sariola, Matti
    Kontio.   Electra FFM 205 (stereo).
Kanteleduo.   EMI 9C062-38413.

Kaski, Heino (1885-1957)

Piano Music, selections.   FA 333.

Kilpinen, Yrjö (1892-1959)

Lieder 1, lyrics by Morgenstern, Bo Bergman, etc.   SM 90017.
Lieder 2, lyrics by Hesse, Morgenstern, Lagerkvist, and the
    Kanteletar.   SM 90018.
Lieder 3, lyrics by Blomberg, Morgenstern, Österling, and the
    Kanteletar.   SM 90019.
Lieder.   FA 803.
Sonata in F for Cello and Piano, Op. 90.   Vox Cum Laude
    MCD 10050 DDD.
Songs about Love I, Op. 60.   BIS 43 LP.
Songs about Love II, Op. 61.   BIS 43 LP.
Songs about Death, Op. 62.   BIS 43 LP.

Klami, Uuno (1900-1961)

Concerto for Violin and Orchestra (1942). FA 334.
Fantaisie Tscherémisse, for cello and orchestra. FA 302.
Kalevala Suite (1933, rev. 1943). FA 302.
Sea Pictures, for orchestra (1928-30). FA 334.

Kokkonen, Joonas (b. 1921)

Concerto for Cello and Orchestra (1969). FA 310.
Duo, for violin and piano. SALP 1.
"*...durch einen Spiegel...*" (1977). FA 323.
Five Bagatelles for Piano.   EMI HMV 5E063 34483; MHS
    (Musical Heritage Society) 3401; TA 60001-4.
Illat (Evenings), song cycle (1955) BIS 89.
The Last Temptations, opera. FA 104; DG 2740 190, 3 LP.
Laudate Domini, for chorus. Philips 839705 LY.
Lux aeterna, for organ (1974). FA 308.
Missa a cappella. EMI HMV 5E063-34483.
Music for String Orchestra (1956-57). FA 329; Fennica 558.
Paavo's Hymn from *The Last Temptations*. FA 327.
Piano Quintet. EMI HMV 5E063-34330.
Piano Trio. LRLP 203.
Requiem, in memoriam Maija Kokkonen (1981). FAD 353.
Sinfonia da camera (1961-62). FA 323; SM 91022.
Sonata for Cello and Piano. FA 335 (digital); FUGA 3012.
Sonatina for piano. SFX 45/MHS 3596; TA 60001-4.
String Quartet No. 1. EMI HMV 5E063 34444.
String Quartet No. 2. Philips 802855 LY.
String Quartet No. 3. FUGA 3012.
Symphony No. 2 (1961). BIS 189 LP.
Symphony No. 3 (1967). FA 311; EMI CSDS 1086.
Symphony No. 4 (1971). BIS 189 LP.
Wind Quintet. BIS 11.

Kuula, Toivo (1883-1918)

Choral Works, for mixed chorus. FA 306.
Lampaan polska (A Sheep's Polka), for piano. FA 347.
Meren virsi (Hymn of the Sea), for mixed chorus (1909). FA
    306.
Songs for Male Choir (complete), Op. 4, 27a, 27b, 28, 34. FA
    203 (2 disks).
Three Pieces, Op. 3b, for piano. FA 347.
Trio in A Major for Piano, Violin, and Cello (1908). BIS 56.

Kuusisto, Ilkka (b. 1935)

Suomalainen vieraanvaraisuus (Finnish Hospitality), song cycle based on recipes from a book by H. Vuorenjuuri (1970). BIS 89; SFX 12.

Kuusisto, Taneli (b. 1905)

Fantasia "Ramus virens olivarum," for organ, Op. 55, 1.   FA 308.

Interludio, for organ, Op. 18, 1. SS (Sound Star) 0162.

Pastorale for Organ, Op. 18, 2. FA 325.

Lindberg, Magnus (b. 1958)

Action-Situation-Significance. FA 372 CD.

Kraft. FA 372 CD.

Three Pieces for Waldhorn, Violin, Viola, and Cello. SAOLP 1.

Lindeman, Osmo (b. 1929)

Ritual (electronic music). FENO 5.

Spectacle (electronic music). SALP 1.

Linjama, Jouko (b. 1934)

Consolation pour l'orgue. PROP 7847.

Missa cum jubilo per organo LOFV 77/1-2.

Missa de angelis per coro e quintetto a fiato. FENO 1.

Partita-Sonata "Veni Creator Spiritus," for organ (1967).   FA 325.

Lithander, Fredrik (1777-1823)

Variations on a Theme by Haydn, for piano. FA 336.

Madetoja, Leevi (1887-1947)

20 Choral Works, Op. 13, 23, 28, 30, 50, 56, 57, 66, 72, 82. FACD 006 AAD.

De profundis for chorus Op. 56 (1925). FA 908.

Huvinäytelmäalkusoitto (Comedy Overture), Op. 53 (1923). FA 307.

Juha, opera. ODE 712-14.

Kullervo, symphonic poem, Op. 15 (1913). FA 103.

Okon Fuoko, suite, Op. 58 (1930). FA 103.

Pohjalaisia (Ostrobothnians), opera, SFX 22-24.

Songs. BIS 89.

Symphony No. 1, Op. 29 (1916). FA 103.

Symphony No. 2, Op. 35 (1918). FA 103.

Symphony No. 3, Op. 55 (1926). FA 307, FA 103.

Marttinen, Tauno (b. 1912)
Delta, for clarinet and piano. PEA 10 LP.
Ilmatar, Virgin of Air, for piccolo. BIS 100 LP.
Rembrandt, for cello and piano. SFX 37.
Septemalia, for 7 double basses. TA 8002.

Merikanto, Aarre (1893-1958)
Concerto for violin, Clarinet, Horn, and String Sextet.   ODE
    703.
Concerto No. 2 for Piano and Orchestra. EMI 063-36024.
Concert Piece for Cello and Orchestra. EMI 063-36024.
Fantasy for Orchestra (1923). FACD 349 DDD.
Juha, opera. SFX 1-2-3 stereo.
Largo misterioso, from *Ten Pieces for Orchestra* (1930). FACD
    349 DDD.
Notturno, for orchestra (1929). FACD 349 DDD.
Pan (1924) for orchestra. FACD 349 DDD.
Prelude and Fugue in E Minor, for organ. FA 325.
Symphonic Study (1928) (revised by Paavo Heininen).   FACD
    349 DDD.

Merikanto, Oskar (1868-1924)
From the World of Children, for piano, Op. 31. BIS 198.
Passacaglia, for organ, Op. 80. FA 308; Pape OD 18.
Piano Miniatures. SI (Signum) 005.
Piano Music, selections. FA 904.
Songs. FA 344.

Meriläinen, Usko (b. 1930)
Concerto for Double Bass and Percussion (1973). FA 339.
Concerto No. 1 for Piano and Orchestra (1955).   Philips 802
    854.
Concerto No. 2 for Piano and Orchestra (1969). FA 305.
Sonata No. 2 for Piano. Philips 802 855.
Sonatas Nos. 3 and 4 for Piano. EMI 063-35064.
Symphony No. 3 (1971). FA 305.
Tre notturni per piano. EMI 063-35064.

Nordgren, Pehr-Henrik (b. 1944)
Butterflies, for guitar. BIS 207 LP.
Concerto No. 1 for Cello and String Orchestra, Op. 50.   FACD
    310 DDD.
Concerto for Strings, Op. 54. FACD 350 DDD.
Concerto No. 2 for Violin and Orchestra (1977).   BIS CD
    500326.

Concerto No. 3 for Violin and Orchestra, Op. 53. FAD 343; FACD 343 DDD/AAD.

Kwaidon Ballads, for piano. Toshiba LF-91027 and LF 91037.

Spelmansporträtt (The Portrait of a Fiddler), for string orchestra. TA 7910.

String Quartets Nos. 4 and 5. ODE 712-13.

Symphony for Strings. TA 8111.

Pacius, Fredrik (1809-1891)
Songs. FA 902.

Palmgren, Selim (1878-1951)
Concerto No. 2 for Piano ("The River"). EMI 063-34471.

Piae cantiones
Performed by Vantaanjoki Choir. FUGA 3051.

Piae cantiones and *Codex potatorum*, performed by vocal ensemble Poor Knights and instrumental ensemble Sonores antiqui. FUGA 3032.

Pylkkänen, Tauno (b. 1918)
Kuoleman joutsen (The Swan of Death), song cycle, Op. 21 (1954). BIS 89.

Raitio, Pentti (b. 1930)
Nocturne for Violin and Piano. FUGA 3023.

Raitio, Väinö (b. 1891-1945)
Umbra beata, for organ. FA 325.

Rautavaara, Einojuhani (b. 1928)
Angel of Dusk, Concerto for Double Bass and Orchestra (1980). FA 339.

Ave Maria, for chorus. SFX 58.

Cantus arcticus, for orchestra and tape, Op. 62 (1972). FA 328.

Children's Mass, for children's chorus. FUGA 3046; BIS 94.

Choral Music to Texts by Bo Setterlind. Philips 839 705 LY.

Cycle for Chorus to Poems by Lorca (1973). FA 327, FUGA 3046, SFX 52.

Divertimento for Chamber Orchestra. SFX 52.

Elämän kirja (The Book of Life) for chorus. SFX 58.

The Icons, for piano. SFX 45.

Ludus verbalis, for chorus. BIS 4.

Marjatta, matala neiti (Marjatta, the Insignificant Maid), for chorus. BIS 132.

Monologues of the Unicorn and *Serenades of the Unicorn*, for guitar. BIS 207 LP.
Pelimannit (The Fiddlers), Six Pieces for Piano, Op. 1. FA 347.
Pelimannit (The Fiddlers), for String Orchestra. BIS 19.
Playgrounds for Angels, for brass ensemble (1981). CHAN 8490 DDD.
A Requiem in Our Time, for Brass and Percussion, Op. 3 (1953). FA 313; Decca SXL 6433.
Sonata, for Flute and Guitar. BIS 30 LP.
Sonata No. 2, for Piano. SFX 45.
Sonetto for Clarinet and Piano, Op. 53. BIS 62 LP.
String Quartet No. 1. EMI HMV 5E 063-34444.
String Quartet No. 3. Philips 802 855.
String Quartet No. 4. BIS 66.
Tarantará, for Trumpet. SOMA 781.
Thomas, opera. ODE 702-04.
Three Shakespeare Sonnets, for baritone and piano. BIS 88.
Two Preludes and Fugues for Cello and Piano. Da camera 93710; EMI HMV 5E061-34017.
Variétude, for violin. SFLP 8569.
Vigilia, for chorus. EMI HMV 5E063-34516.

Rechberger, Herman (b. 1947)
Consort Music, for recorders and orchestra. TA 8103.
Cordamix (electronic music). FENO 5.
Himojen puutarha (The Garden of Passions), for orchestra. FUGA 3022.
Il fa-to-re, for recorder. FUGA 3022.
The King's Hunt, for waldhorn. PAN 005 LP.
Quotations, for soprano. FUGA 3022.
Rotazioni, for violin. FUGA 3022.
...Szene am, for bass clarinet and piano. FUGA 3022.

Saariaho, Kaija (b. 1952)
Jardin secret (electronic music) (1984-85). BIS 307 LP.
Laconisme de l'aile, for solo flute (1982). BIS 307 LP.
... sah den Vöglen, for soprano, flute, oboe, cello, prepared piano, and tape (1981). BIS 307 LP.

Sallinen, Aulis (b. 1935)
Cadenze per violino solo. BIS 18 LP; SALP 1; SLP (Scandia) 575.
Chaconne, for Organ. BIS 12 LP.

Chamber Music I, for String Orchestra, Op. 38 (1975). FA 328; BIS 46 LP.

Chamber Music II for Alto Flute and Strings. Op. 41. BIS 64.

Chorali, for wind, percussion, harp, and celesta. BIS 41 LP.

Concerto for Cello and Orchestra, Op. 44. FA CD 346.

Elegy for Sebastian Knight. SM 93710; BIS 64 LP; SLP 575.

Lauluja mereltä (Songs from the Sea), for chorus. FA 327.

Mauermusik (1962), for orchestra. FA 312.

Neljä laulua unesta (Four Dream Songs), Song Cycle (1973). BIS 89.

Notturno, for Piano. EMI 5E063-34283.

Punainen viiva (The Red Line), opera (1977-78). FA 102, 3 disks.

Quattro per quattro, for oboe (flute), violin, cello, and cembalo. BIS 64.

Ratsumies (The Horseman), opera (1973-74). FA 101, 3 disks.

Shadows, Prelude for Orchestra, Op. 52 (1982). FA DC 346.

Sonata for Solo Cello. SLP 575.

String Quartet No. 3 ("Some Aspects of Peltoniemi Hintrik's Funeral March") (1969). BIS 64; EMI 5E063-34330; Elektra/Nonesuch 79111-2 DDD.

String Quartet No. 3, arranged for string orchestra (1981). FA 328.

String Quartet No. 4. SLP 575.

Suite grammaticale, for Children's Chorus and Chamber Orchestra. EMI 5E062-34670.

Symphony No. 1. BIS 41 LP.

Symphony No. 2, Symphonic Dialogue for Percussion and Orchestra. CAP 1073.

Symphony No. 3. BIS 41 LP.

Symphony No. 4, Op. 49 (1979). SCL 6431 Decca; FA CD 346.

Two Children's Songs, for Chorus. SF 8549 LP.

Salmenhaara, Erkki (b. 1941)

The Face of the Moon, for chorus. BIS 4 LP; Philips 839705 LY.

Lamento, for string orchestra. TA 8111.

Prelude-Interlude-Postlude, for Organ. FA 325.

Prelude, Pop Tune, and Fugue for Solo Flute. BIS 150 LP.

Sonatas Nos. 1 and 2, for Piano. EMI 5E063-35065.

Three Japanese Songs. BIS 88 LP.

Wind Quintet. BIS 24 LP.

Salonen, Esa-Pekka (b. 1958)

Aubades, for Flute and Orchestra. TA 8109.

Horn Music I, for Waldhorn and Piano. SAOLP 1.
Horn Music II, for 6 Waldhorns, Percussion, and Tape. PAN
    005 LP.

Segerstam, Leif (b. 1944)
  A Last Melodioso (1976/85), Poem for Violin and Orchestra.
      BIS 500326 CD.
  A NNNNOOOOWWW, for wind quintet. BIS 11 LP.
  Concerto No. 1 "Concerto serioso", for violin and orchestra.
      BIS 84; BIS CD 326.
  Divertimento, for String Orchestra (1962). BIS 19.
  Moments Kept Remaining, for clarinet, violin, and piano. DGG
      0666 937.
  Patria, for orchestra. BIS 84.
  Poem, for violin and piano. BIS 18 LP.
  Rituals in F, for two pianos. BIS 20.
  Seven Questions to Infinity, for piano. EMI 5E063-34283.
  Six Songs of Experience, for soprano and orchestra. BIS 83.
  Skizzen aus Pandora, for orchestra. BIS 84.
  String Quartet No. 2. EMI HMV 5E063-35038.
  String Quartet No. 6 (1974). BIS 20.
  String Quartet No. 7 (1975). BIS 39.
  String Quartet No. 8. SFX 54.
  Three Leaves of Grass, song cycle based on Walt Whitman.
      Philips 802 855.
  Three Moments of Parting, for violin and piano. BIS 39.

Sermilä, Jarmo (b. 1939)
  Contemplation I, for trumpet. TA 8002.
  Cornologia for 24 Waldhorns. PAN 005 LP.
  Monody for Waldhorn and Percussion. LRLP 57; MGE 21.

Sibelius, Jean (1865-1957)
  [For basic listings, see any recent Schwann catalogue.]

ADDENDA:

  The Complete Orchestral Music (Gothenburg Sym. Orch.,
      Neeme Järvi). BIS LP 221, 222, 228, 237, 252, etc.
  Symphonies 1-7 (Vienna Phil. Orch., Maazel). Decca 635 709
      DX, 3 LP.
  Symphonies 1-7 (+ *Kullervo*) (Bournemouth Sym. Orch.,
      Berglund). EMI SLS 5129.
  Symphonies 1, 2, 3 (+ *The Bard*, *En Saga*) (Finnish Radio Sym.
      Orch., Kamu). DG 2720 067.

Symphonies 4, 5, 6, 7 (+ *The Swan of Tuonela*, *Finlandia*, *Valse triste*) (Berlin Phil. Orch., Karajan). DG 2720 067.

OTHER ORCHESTRAL WORKS:

Alla marcia. EMI 037-146 175-1.

The Bard, Op. 64. CHAN 1027/8 LP; CHAN 8395/6 CD.

Berceuse, Op. 79, 6. TIS MEN 160 004 2 CD.

Canzonetta, Op. 62, 1. FA 354; BIS 292; Starek (Patmos-Schwann) 2053.

Concerto in D Minor for Violin and Orchestra, Op. 47. DG 2530 552; FSM PCD 7434; TEL 843 241, also CD; EMI HMV ASD 3199.

The Dryad, Op. 45 (1909). CHAN 1027/8 C, 2 LP; CHAN 8395/6 2 CD.

En Saga, Op. 9. CHAN 8395/6 CD; CHAN 1027/8 LP; EMI 555-769017-2; Ariola 201 992-250; Decca 643596 AD.

Finlandia, Op. 26. CHAN 1027/8 2 LP; CHAN 8395/6 2 CD; EMI 555-769017-2; EMI 567-747484, 2 CD; Decca 411933-2 ZK, CD; TEL 843241 ZK; Ariola 201992-250; Decca 648 193 DM 2 LP.

Four Legends (the *Lemminkäinen Suite*), Op. 22. DG 2530 656 1 MS.

Humoresques, for Violin and Orchestra, Op. 87, 1-2; Op. 89, 1-4. Philips 420308-1; Starek (Patmos-Schwann) 1604; Decca 643596 AD; Ariola 201992-250, 200054-250.

Karelia, Overture, Op. 10. TEL 643241 AZ; TEL 843241 ZK CD.

Karelia, Suite, Op. 11. Philips 412 014-1; Decca 648193 DM, 2 LP; FSM (Fono Schallplatten, Munich) PCD 7434; UR 7038 LP.

Lemminkäinen's Return. EMI 067-107704; EMI 567-747484, 2 CD.

Mignonne, Suite for Orchestra, Op. 98a. FA 354; EMI 567-199995-2T.

Nightride and Sunrise, Op. 55. CHAN 1027/8 C, 2 LP; Decca 643596 AD.

Oceanides, Op. 73. CHAN 8395/6 DC, 1027/8 LP.

Pan and Echo, Op. 53. BIS 500359 CD.

Pelléas et Mélisande, Op. 46. FA 338; UR 7038 LP.

Pohjola's Daughter, Op. 49. CHAN 1027/8, 2 LP; CHAN 8395/6, 2 CD; Decca 643596 AD.

Romance in C for Strings, Op. 42. FA 354; Decca 643596 AD.

Serenades for Violin and Orchestra, Op. 69, 1-2. Starek (Patmos-Schwann) 1604.

Serious Melodies, Op. 77, 1-2, for Violin and Orchestra. Starek (Patmos-Schwann) 1604.
The Swan of Tuonela. Ariola 201 992-250; EMI 555-169017-2; CHAN 8395/6 CD, CHAN 1027/8 LP; Decca 643596 AD; 067-107704, EMI 567-747484, 2 CD.
Swanwhite, incidental music for Strindberg's play, Op. 54. BIS 500 359 CD.
Tapiola, Op. 112. EMI 567-747484, 2 CD; CHAN 8395/6 CD, 1027/8 LP; EMI 555-769017-2.
Valse romantique, Op. 62, 2. FA 354; BIS 311, also CD.
Vårsång (Spring song), Op. 16. CHAN 8395/6 CD.

INSTRUMENTAL:

Complete Piano Music (Erik T. Tawaststjerna). BIS 221, 222, etc. LP.
Five Pieces for Violin and Piano, Op. 81, 1-3, 5. FA 301.
Four Pieces for Violin and Piano, Op. 78. FA 301.
Four Pieces for Violin and Piano, Op. 115. FA 301.
Kyllikki, for piano, Op. 41. MHS 1218, stereo.
Malinconia, for cello and piano, Op. 20. Decca 93710.
Piano Music, recorded in the 1950s by Cyril Szalkievicz (reissue). FA 802, 804.
Romance, for piano, Op. 24. EMI 5E063-34472.
Rondino, for piano, Op. 68. EMI 5E063-34472.
Scaramouche, Op. 71, Balletpantomime, flute solo. BIS 350, also CD.
Sonata in F Major for Piano, Op. 12. MHS 1218.
Sonatas, Op. 78, 116, for Violin and Piano. Da camera 93343.
Sonatina, Op. 80, for Violin and Piano. Da camera 93343.
String Quartet in A Minor (1889). FA 345, also CD.
String Quartet in B-Flat Major, Op. 4 (1890). FA 345, also CD.
String Quartet in D Minor (*Voces intimae*), Op. 56. H71140, stereo.
Three Pieces for Violin and Piano, Op. 116, 1-2. FA 301.
Three Sonatinas, Op. 67, for piano. MHS 1218; EMI 5E063-34472.

VOCAL, CHORAL:

Atenarnes sång (The Song of the Athenians), for boys' and men's voices, saxhorn septet, triangle, bass drum, and cymbals, Op. 31, 3. BIS 313-14 2 LP, also CD.

Har du mod?   (Have you courage?), for male chorus and orchestra, Op. 31, 2. BIS 313-14 2 LP, also CD.

Jääkärimarssi (March of the Finnish Jäger Battalion), for male chorus and orchestra, Op. 91, 1. BIS 313-14 2 LP, also CD.

Sandels, for male chorus and orchestra, Op. 28. BIS 313-14 2 LP, also CD.

Tulen Synty (The Origin of Fire), for baritone, male chorus, and orchestra. EMI 667-747496-8, 2 CD.

VOCAL, SOLO:

Complete vocal works: *Arioso,* Op. 3; Lieder Op. 1, 13, 17, 27, 35, 36, 37, 38, 46, 50, 57, 60, 61, 72, 86, 88, 90 (Elisabeth Söderström, Tom Krause; Vladimir Ashkenazy, Irving Gage; Carlos Bonell, guitar). TIS (Teldec Import Service, Hamburg) 411739-1 SH, 5 LP.

Lieder (Hynninen, Gothóni). FA 202, 2 LP.

Lieder, Op. 13, 4; 17, 7; 36, 1, 4, 6; 37, 1, 4, 5; 88, 3 (Ingrid Björner, Einar Steen-Nökleberg) (+ Wagner: *Wesendonck Lieder*). SST (Sound Star) 0178.

Lieder, Op. 3; 13, 4; 17, 1, 5; 36, 1, 2, 4, 6; 37, 1, 4, 5; 38, 1, 2; 60, 1 (Flagstad, London Sym. Orch.). Decca 648276 DM, 2 LP.

Lieder, Op. 13,4; 17, 1, 6; 36, 1, 4; 37, 1, 4, 5; 38, 2; 50, 3 (Nilsson; Janos Solyom) (+ Strauss: Lieder). BIS 015.

Lieder, Op. 13, 4-6; 17, 3, 7; 36, 1, 4, 6; 46, 4; 50, 3; 60, 1, 2; 61, 4 (Kim Borg, Erik Werba). Decca DL 9983.

Lieder, Op. 3; 13, 4; 17, 1; 27, 4; 36, 6; 37, 3; 38, 1, 2; 60, 1 + *Luonnotar* and *Koskenlaskijan morsiamet* (The Rapids-Shooter's Brides) (Häggander, Hynninen; Gothenburg Sym. Orch., Panula). BIS 500270 DC.

Lieder, Op. 13, 4; 17, 1, 4, 6, 7; 27, 4; 36, 1, 4; 37, 4, 5; 38, 2; 46, 4; 50, 3; 60 (Hynninen, Gothóni; Siirala, guitar). HM (Harmonia Mundi) 5142 C.

Arioso (Runeberg), Op. 3. Decca 648276 DM LP, BIS 500270 DC.

Come away, Death, Op. 60, 1. Decca 648276 DM, BIS 270 (also CD).

Demanten på marssnön (The Diamond on March Snow) (Wecksell), Op. 36, 6. SST 0178; Decca 648276 DM, BIS 270 (also CD); Da camera 90007; Decca 9983.

Den första kyssen (The First Kiss) (Runeberg), Op. 37, 1. SST 0178; Decca 648276 DM; BIS 015.

Der Wanderer und der Bach (Greif), Op. 72, 5.   TIS 411739-1SH.

Flickan kom ifrån sin älsklings möte (The Tryst) (Runeberg), Op. 37, 5.   SST 0178; Decca 648276 DM; FA 202, BIS 015.

Fool's Song of the Spider, Op. 27, 4.   BIS 270 (also CD); HM 5142 C; TIS 411739- 1 SH.

Höstkväll (Autumn Evening) (Runeberg), Op. 38, 1.   Decca 648276 DM; BIS 270 (also CD).

Hundra vägar (A Hundred Ways) (Runeberg), Op. 72, 6.   TIS 411739- 1 SH.

Illalle (To the Evening) (Forsman-Koskimies), Op. 17, 6.   FA 202; HM 5142 C; BIS 015; Da camera 90007; Decca 9983.

Im Feld ein Mädchen singt (Susman), Op. 50, 3.   HM 5142 C; BIS 015; Decca 9983.

Kaiutar (The Echo Nymph) (Larin-Kyösti), Op. 72, 4.   FA 202; TIS 411739- 1 SH.

Kyssen (The Kiss) (Rydberg), Op. 72, 3.   TIS 411739- 1 SH.

Luonnotar, tone poem for soprano and orchestra, Op. 70. CHAN 1027/8 C LP, 2 MC; CHAN 8395/6 CD.

Men min fågel märks dock icke (But my bird is long in homing) (Runeberg), Op. 36, 2.   Decca 648276.

Norden (The North) (Runeberg), Op. 90, 1.   FA 202.

På verandan vid havet (On a balcony by the sea) (Rydberg), Op. 38, 2.   Decca 648276 DM; BIS 270 (also CD); HM 5142 C; BIS 015.

Säv, säv, susa (Sigh, rushes, sigh) (Fröding), Op. 36, 4.   Con B 163, Con B 187; SST 0178; Decca 648276 DM, FA 202; BIS 015; Decca 9983.

Se'n har jag ej frågat mera (Since then I have questioned no further) (Runeberg), Op. 17, 1.   Decca 648276 DM; BIS 270 (also CD); HM 5142 C; BIS 015.

Serenad (Stagnelius), 1939.   TIS 411739- 1 SH; BIS 270, also CD.

Six Songs with Piano, (K. A. Tavaststjerna, Karlfeldt, Snoilsky, Lybeck), Op. 86, 1-6.   TIS 411739- 1 SH.

Six Songs with Piano (Franzén, Runeberg), Op. 88, 1-6.   TIS 411739- 1 SH.

Six Songs with Piano (Runeberg), Op. 90, 1.   TIS 411739- 1 SH.

Soluppgång (Sunrise) (Hedberg), Op. 37, 3.   BIS 270 (also CD).

Svarta rosor (Black Roses) (Josephson), Op. 36, 1.   Con B 187; SST 0178; Decca 648276 DM; FA 202; BIS 015; Da camera 90007; Decca 9983.

The Three Blind Sisters, from *Pelléas et Mélisande*, Op. 46. HM 5142 C, TIS 411739- 1 SH; Decca DL 9983.

Two Songs from Shakespeare's Twelfth Night, with piano or guitar, Op. 60, 1, 2. FA 202; TIS 411739- 1 SH; Decca DL 9983.

Var det en dröm? (Was it a dream?) (Wecksell), Op. 37; 4. Decca 648276 DM; SST 0178; FA 202; BIS 015.

Våren flyktar hastigt (Spring is flying) (Runeberg), Op. 13, 4. Decca 648276 DM; SST 0178; BIS 270 (also CD); HM 5142 C; BIS 015; Decca 9983.

Vitsippan (The star-flower) (Franzén), Op. 88, 3. SST 0178.

Sonninen, Ahti (b. 1914)
Four Suites for String Orchestra. FUGA 3037.

Tiensuu, Jukka (b. 1948)
Aspro, for clarinet, cello, trombone, piano. CAP 3013.
Prélude non-mesuré, for piano. SALP 1.

Wessman, Harri (b. 1949)
Four Episodes, for guitar. PEALP 12.
Duo, for flute and guitar. PEALP 12.
Pan and the Nymph Pitus, for flute and guitar. PEALP 12.
Three Pieces for Flutes and Guitar. PEALP 12.
Suite for Alto Recorder and Guitar. PEALP 12.
Towards the Night, for flute and guitar. PEALP 12.

INDEX

ABOUT THE AUTHORS

LISA DE GOROG was born in Finland several kilometers from Sibelius's birthplace. She studied piano, music theory, Finnish literature, and folklore and received the M.A. from the University of Helsinki. She also studied in England and was the recipient of a Fulbright-Asla grant to study in the United States. She has taught in both Finland and the United States. In addition to several reference works written with her husband, she is the author of folklore studies published in Finland. She has also translated textbooks from Finnish into English, and from English into Finnish.

RALPH DE GOROG is a native of Montreal, Canada and was educated in New York, where he received three degrees including the doctorate, at Columbia University. In addition to preparing music programs for the Latin American Division of the Voice of America, he is the author of five books and some forty articles published in America, Germany, Spain, France, Belgium, and Finland. Dr. de Gorog is Professor Emeritus at the University of Georgia, where he taught for twenty-seven years after several years of teaching in New York.